Interorganisat

Contributions to Management Science

Ulrich M. Löwer

Interorganisational Standards

Managing Web Services Specifications for Flexible Supply Chains

With 45 Figures and 27 Tables

Physica-Verlag

A Springer Company

Series Editors
Werner A. Müller
Martina Bihn

Author
Dr. Ulrich M. Löwer
Bustellistraße 18
63739 Aschaffenburg
Germany
uml@umlo.de

Diss., Univ. München 2005, D 19

ISSN 1431-1941
ISBN-10   3-7908-1653-1 Physica-Verlag Heidelberg New York
ISBN-13   978-3-7908-1653-2 Physica-Verlag Heidelberg New York

Cataloging-in-Publication Data applied for
Library of Congress Control Number: 2005927952

Physica-Verlag is a part of Springer Science+Business Media

springeronline.com

© Physica-Verlag Heidelberg 2006
Printed in Germany

Cover-Design: Erich Kirchner, Heidelberg

SPIN 11550716   88/3153-5 4 3 2 1 0 – Printed on acid-free and non-aging paper

Foreword

Standards play a crucial role in a globally networked economy. This is especially true for supply chains and flexible configurations of specialised firms transgressing the traditional boundaries between industries, countries and continents. Such production and supply networks can only reap the advantages of specialisation if players can cooperate smoothly by interlinking their activities in an uncomplicated and compatible fashion. However, this poses an extraordinary challenge since increasingly complex interorganisational processes are at stake. Therefore, many efforts are under way to create and implement standards that could lower the costs of coordinating and managing interorganisational transactions.

The author of this book addresses such issues in a thorough and creative manner. Little is known about how such interorganisational standards come into existence and in what way their emergence could be managed. Former experiences with EDI-standards may provide some guidance but do not seem to be applicable to the new world of Web Services or electronic business based on XML, which is much more complex. Based on a clear epistemological position and a deep understanding of the nature and functions of interorganisational information systems, the author applies actor-network theory in order to explore the structures and processes that bring about new generations of interorganisational standards such as RosettaNet and ebXML.

Based on a convincing theoretical framework as well as on detailed case study data, this book explores and explains for the first time the development and evolution of interorganisational standards that are of the utmost importance for the formation and functioning of future supply chains. Thus, this exciting book not only offers stimulating explanations of these important phenomena, but also recommendations for the design and management of interorganisational standardisation efforts from the perspectives of the players involved. It can serve as a frame of reference for all those who deal with the creation of interorganisational technical infrastructures as a precondition for efficient production and supply networks of the future.

Munich, July 2005   Arnold Picot

Acknowledgements

A typical feature of standards is their dualistic nature. They enable and constrain at the same time. On the one hand, the existence of a standard eases the exchange of information or goods. On the other hand, an existing standard often constrains the variety of such exchange. Some Internet applications, for example, cannot be implemented with the existing Web standards and thus either require these to be changed or call for the use of new standards. In either case, the development of standards plays a crucial role. Users for whom the original standards are not sufficient and who need them to be extended thus have to get involved in the development of standards.

This is particularly the case for 'interorganisational standards', which are used for the exchange of information between organisations. As their goal is to enable the quick establishment of interorganisational relationships to form efficient supply chains, these standards have to cover many different aspects and are thus very complex. Although the existing Web Services technologies already offer a solid foundation for interorganisational standards, the standardisation of most interorganisational tasks is far from completed. In the face of permanently changing business environments it probably never will.

How such interorganisational standards can jointly be developed and continuously improved is thus the main topic of this work.

If tasks can be standardised, machines are extremely good at executing them much faster and more accurately than humans ever could. When it comes to flexibility and creativity, however, machines are not good at all, as here the opposite of standardised thinking is required. To write a book such as this one is an enormous undertaking that requires both standardised routines and human creativity. While well-known software proved to be valuable for the first, I want to express my great gratitude to all the humans that formed my personal actor-network enabling the second.

First of all, I cordially thank my academic teacher and supervisor Prof. Dr. Dres. h.c. Arnold Picot for employing me as a research assistant and lecturer at his Institute for Information, Organisation and Management. He provided me with a perfect combination of responsibility for the Institute's information technology, the challenge of teaching students, and involvement in research projects. Moreover, the freedom he gave me for pursuing my dissertation project was remarkable. Nevertheless, I could always rely on his inspiring comments and constructive suggestions, without which this study would not have been possible. The supervising committee of the Munich School of Management at the Ludwig-Maximilians-University in Munich accepted this work as a dissertation on 13 July 2005.

Next, I should like to express my thanks to Prof. Dr. Thomas Hess for the co-supervision of my thesis and for smoothing my way for a research visit at the Nanyang Technological University in Singapore. There, Prof. Dr. Christina Soh generously took me on her Ph.D. courses on information systems research. The insights I gained there clearly enriched the research approach of my work. I owe both of them a debt of gratitude for that. I also thank the Haniel Foundation and the German Academic Exchange Service for supporting this research experience on the financial side.

Naturally, I am deeply indebted to all my friends and colleagues who supported and inspired me on the long way to completing this work. Even though I cannot mention them all, they have contributed to my work in many different and decisive ways: Oliver Baumann, Victoria Burns, Dr. Thomas Dorlöchter, Dr. Wolfgang Faisst, Dr. Marina Fiedler, Tim Fischer, Michael Haas, Christine Hartig, Jun.-Prof. Dr. Berthold Hass, Tobias Hauser, Till Kruse, Dr. Martin Lange, Ulrike Lange, Angela Sanganas, Christian Tausend, Dr. Isabell Welpe, and Christian Wernick. I extend my thanks to all the students who assisted my research at the Institute and all others not mentioned here.

Very special thanks go to Stefan Riedel, Dr. Florian Steiner and Dr. Carolin Wolff. In our debate club called 'DissPro', we engaged in relentless discussions of methodological and theoretical research issues. Although we often ended up quite confused, the resulting insights eventually laid solid grounds for our studies.

Above all, I should like to express my deepest gratitude to my sisters Angrit and Beatrix and my parents Christel and Dr. Robert Löwer, and also my grandparents. They were always open to my complaints about the (assumed) hard life of a Ph.D. student. Their endless support in even the most difficult of situations showed me the importance of a stable family in today's turbulent world. I thus dedicate this work to my family.

Munich, July 2005   Ulrich M. Löwer

Contents

1 Introduction

> "It is no longer clear if a computer system is a limited form [of] organisation or if an organisation is an expanded form of computer system. Not because, as in the engineering dreams and the sociologists' nightmares, complete rationalization would have taken place, but because, on the opposite, the two monstrous hybrids are now coextensive."[1]
>
> *Bruno Latour*

The goal of interorganisational standards is easily explained: if interfaces between organisations are standardised, then organisations can be plugged together to form complex value chains just as children assemble Lego blocks to form impressive toys. Moreover, newly plugged-in organisations can give value chains new shapes and can easily come apart again if external forces so dictate.[2] Without standards, the same models might also be possible, but they would be much more expensive and it would take much longer to couple the different modules to form a working whole. Consequently, some authors call the vision of broadly adopted interorganisational standards a 'plug & play economy'.[3]

Indeed, companies are very interested in this idea, as it enables high adaptability to changing market demands, while keeping costs low. One example is Exel, a large logistics provider which globally ships products between tens of thousands of firms. As the customers of Exel have to send products to often changing business partners, Excel also permanently has to deal with new customers. The existence of different procedures in almost every company is the main reason Exel is very much interested in standardising processes with its customers. It would result in much lower costs of coupling with new customers, while greatly improving the accuracy of Exel's logistics services. Exel thus participates in the RosettaNet

---

[1] Latour (1996), p. 302.

[2] See, e.g., Picot/Reichwald/Wigand (2003), pp. 227ff. on modular and dynamic organisational structures.

[3] See Glushko (2000), Veryard (2001), Angeles/Nath (2001), and Alt/Österle (2003).

initiative, which develops interorganisational standards for the electronics industry.[4]

Another example is the world's largest semiconductor firm Intel. In the highly dynamic electronics industry, Intel has to deal constantly with staggering market demands and changing business partners. Moreover, the industry's thin margins and permanently dropping prices demand highly efficient solutions for the coupling of suppliers and customers with Intel's business processes. Intel thus also engages in the RosettaNet initiative. In 2002, Intel already transacted 5 billion US$ with its business partners via RosettaNet standards.[5] It reports savings up to 80% of interorganisational process costs.[6] Moreover, Intel is going to use these standards in all its electronically conducted business relations in 2006.[7]

Interorganisational standards such as the RosettaNet standards, however, are highly complex and very costly to develop. RosettaNet is thus a standards development organisation with many different participants, ranging from large multinational corporations such as Intel to software vendors such as webMethods and governmental organisations such as the Chinese Ministry of Science and Technology. Moreover, many other organisations aim to develop similar standards, which seem to overlap and compete, rendering the field somewhat confusing. RosettaNet itself is a subsidiary of UCC, participates in the ebXML initiative, and uses more than 80 different standards, from CPFR to SWIFT.[8] Many firms are thus often puzzled about how to participate in these initiatives, although they appreciate the fundamental benefits of such interorganisational standards.[9]

In order to facilitate decision-making, this study will illuminate the nature of interorganisational standards and derive strategic options for participating in the different initiatives. Section 1.1 outlines the challenges of developing interorganisational standards in more detail. Then, section 1.2 derives three research questions and discusses the way this study will answer them.

---

[4]   See RosettaNet (2004m) and section 5.2.

[5]   See Intel (2002).

[6]   See RosettaNet (2003c).

[7]   See RosettaNet (2003c).

[8]   See chapter 5.2.

[9]   See Kotinurmi/Nurmilaakso/Laesvuori (2003), p. 144.

1.1   The Challenges of Interorganisational Standards

To analyse the driving forces behind innovations, Nelson/Winter (1977) introduced the notion of market pull and technology push.[10] Both perspectives reveal two major trends fostering the development and use of interorganisational standards.

First, in the face of global competition, firms have to focus on their core competencies.[11] This leads to more specialisation and division of labour, but also to more relationships with other firms that offer complementary goods and services. Firms form supply chain networks that adapt their shape quickly to meet the changing demands of consumers.[12] Virtual organisations are created for just one project and dissolve after completion.[13] Mergers, acquisitions and buyouts permanently change the shape of firms.[14] Therefore, firms have to manage a rising number of dynamic interorganisational relationships, for which efficient and flexible information systems play a crucial role.[15]

Second, as today's Enterprise Resource Planning (ERP) systems demonstrate, information systems can execute many structured business tasks. This automation of work has two major operational advantages humans can never compete with: fewer errors (converging to zero) and higher speed (converging to real-time). Substantial progress in computer science allows the formal description and automated execution of increasingly complex scenarios with lower costs than ever before. Combined with the ubiquitous Internet and Web technologies, this could enable a 'plug & play real-time economy', in which computers can execute business processes within and between firms more and more.[16] Some proponents also talk of

---

[10] See Nelson/Winter (1977), p. 54.

[11] See the seminal paper of Prahalad/Hamel (1990).

[12] See Swaminathan/Smith/Sadeh (1998).

[13] See, e.g., Picot/Reichwald/Wigand (2003), pp. 289ff. and pp. 388ff.

[14] See, e.g., Hagel (2002), pp. 98ff.

[15] See Picot/Ripperger/Wolff (1996), Faisst (1998), Selz (1999), and Picot/Reichwald/ Wigand (2003), pp. 287ff.

[16] See Atkinson/Brooks (2003), p. 2896, Broy/Hegering/Picot, et al. (2003), pp. 296ff, and Picot/Hess (2005).

new kinds of division of labour enabled by the computer-supported coupling of firms.[17]

These trends are not completely new. Indeed, back in the 1960s, logistics firms had to deal with enormous document exchange volumes accompanying their transport services. They thus developed standards to exchange these documents automatically between the business partners involved.[18] These were the first interorganisational standards, today widely used in electronic data interchange (EDI) systems. The success of EDI is somewhat ambivalent. On the one hand, EDI systems are the backbone of today's electronic business, transacting a volume of several trillion US$ each year.[19] On the other hand, EDI systems are mostly limited to large companies. To get closer to the vision of a 'plug & play economy', however, small and medium enterprises (SMEs) also have to broadly adopt interorganisational standards. To achieve this, several major challenges have to be met:

High costs

Coupling information systems across boundaries is costly, as all the systems involved have to be precisely adjusted to the data exchanged. While it is possible to couple systems with proprietary solutions, the use of standards can significantly lower these costs. Still, EDI standards-based installations are expensive because of outdated data formats, highly specific software, and the transport via proprietary communication infrastructures.[20] Thus, the use of EDI systems usually only pays when a high volume of data has to be exchanged over a longer period, which is rarely the case for SMEs. Several initiatives have tried to improve EDI with regard to the requirements of SMEs.[21] However, it needed the emergence of the eXtensible Markup Language (XML) to attract more interest from SMEs. The main advantages of XML are its tag-based tree structure using plain text, the use of common Web standards, its extensibility and modularity, and its broad adoption. XML and several related technologies offer a proven and reliable way of exchanging structured data via the Internet infrastruc-

---

[17] See Hagel/Singer (1999), Beekun/Glick (2001), and Fritz (2003). Weick (1976) introduced the concept of loose coupling.

[18] See Wigand (1994), pp. 376ff.

[19] See Kanakamedala/King/Ramsdell (2003).

[20] See discussion in 5.1.1.

[21] See ISO/IEC (1997).

ture. Today, XML is used in almost any field of information systems, such as media content, Web pages, databases, and, of course, business documents. While this makes XML an inexpensive enabling technology, it is only a first step towards lowering the high costs of interorganisational information systems significantly.

Numerous standards

XML does not specify any application-related content. It is only a standardised meta-language, useful to define other application-specific standards. Thus, it is not possible to use plain XML to couple information systems without previously defining the semantics of the data fields used. Several hundreds of 'standards development organisations' (SDOs) were formed to develop such semantics for very diverse fields of information exchange.[22] Even when focusing only on interorganisational standards, a vast number of standards can be identified. For example, the SDOs ebXML, OASIS, RosettaNet, UCC and UN/CEFACT are all interconnected, while each offers several different interorganisational standards. In this confusing situation, many firms are unsure which of these standards best meet their requirements. Moreover, the adoption of very diverse standards massively lowers their value, as firms cannot couple their systems without major adaptations. An important goal is thus to agree on one set of interorganisational standards at least in sectors in which firms often cooperate, such as specific industries. RosettaNet, for example, is limited to the electronics industry, while still dealing with more than 80 standards.[23]

Complex relationships

A comprehensive set of interorganisational standards has to cover many different aspects, as interorganisational relationships are often complex. While EDI standards only define the semantics of electronic documents, recent interorganisational standards also include, among other things, discovery mechanisms and process descriptions. For example, the CPFR standards describe processes to conduct collaborative forecasting between firms in supply chain networks. Supply chain mechanisms in general are well suited to standardisation, as they are highly structured in most cases. These mechanisms, however, often reveal the technical limits of the exist-

---

[22] OASIS (2004a) gives an overview of 593 XML initiatives (updated November 2004).

[23] See the discussion of RosettaNet in section 5.2.

ing EDI standards, for example, the very limited support of real-time processes. To enable more complex interorganisational systems as well, new
technical architectures have thus been emerging in recent years, such as
Services Oriented Architectures including what is known as Web Services.[24] While these technologies promise major improvements in interorganisational relationships, their implementation also affects more aspects
of business than conventional EDI systems, such as the choice of business
partners.

Diverse interests

Often, interorganisational standards are assumed to be externally given,
for example, set by organisations such as UN/CEFACT. In reality, however, the development of such standards involves many different actors,
including user firms[25], software vendors, and governmental organisations
(see Figure 1.1). The importance of the development process is largely
underestimated, while the diverse and conflicting interests of the different
participants strongly influence the quality and long-term prospects of interorganisational standards.[26] For example, user firms want to shape and
control the standards according to their business requirements, whereas
software vendors need the standards to sell their software systems. When
dozens of participants have to agree on one single standard, this can rarely
be achieved without fierce political discussions. Thus, while the required

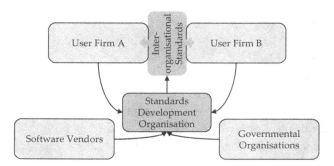

Figure 1.1: Participants in Standards Development Organisations

---

[24] See, e.g., Graham/Pollock/Smart, et al. (2003), p. 1.

[25] User firms are the firms actually using the interorganisational standards for their
business.

[26] See Hanseth/Monteiro (1997), p. 183.

technologies are often available, political manoeuvres often prevent their quick adoption for broad use in day-to-day business.[27]

As interorganisational standards will gain further importance for the many interorganisational relationships of today's firms, it is important to get a better understanding of these challenges and how to approach them. The existing literature, however, largely neglects this topic.[28] This work thus offers a case study- and theory-based analysis of interorganisational standards and derives strategic options for the different actors involved in the development processes.

1.2   Research Questions and Chapter Overview

The main goal of this study is to analyse how the development of interorganisational standards actually occurs and how the actors involved can coordinate this process. To achieve this goal, it looks at three main research questions:

1. *Why and how do information systems support interorganisational relationships?*
2. *Why and how are interorganisational standards developed?*
3. *How should the actors involved coordinate the development of interorganisational standards?*

Before discussing these questions in the main chapters, I clarify my research approach in chapter 2 (see Figure 1.2). This gives an overview of my epistemological assumptions and my research focus. In doing so, it explains the method applied, and introduces the methodological aspects of actor-network theory as an innovative and promising approach to research on standards.

Chapter 3 aims at answering question 1. It briefly discusses the nature of interorganisational relationships in general and of supply chain networks in particular. It also reviews the foundations of interorganisational information systems (IOS) and the existing research on EDI. A positivistic framework of IOS management aggregates the main insights from EDI research. It covers the adoption, use and impact of IOS, while the literature

---

[27] See several experts on the 'Semantic Web Tour', July 2003.

[28] See the overview in King/Lyytinen (2003), p. iii.

largely neglects the development of EDI standards. A review of the work on Web-based IOS gives a similar picture, as the development of the required standards has also attracted little academic attention until recently.

Chapter 4 lays the ground for answering question 2. It gives a general overview of standards and theories to explain their emergence and development. A short introduction to technical approaches is followed by economic theories on standards, including neo-classical and neo-institutional theories. A third theoretical perspective is the social construction of standards. Actor-network theory belongs to these social theories, including technical and economic aspects. As it will guide the further analysis, it is discussed in more detail.

Chapter 5 completes the answer to research question 2 by analyzing the actual development of interorganisational standards. First, the basic concepts are discussed, including recent technologies such as Service Oriented Architectures and Web Services. Then, I propose an interorganisational standards stack for classifying existing standards. This essentially comprises the aspects of messaging, description, discovery, business semantics, business processes and trading partner agreements. As the existing literature does not analyse the organisation of the development in major SDOs, this chapter describes two in-depth case studies on RosettaNet and ebXML. Using these case-study data, actor-network theory guides the deduction of a process model for interorganisational standardisation in the final section.

Chapter 6 answers research question 3. It presents strategic options for different stakeholders in the development of interorganisational standards, which are discussed along the two dimensions 'benefits from participating' and 'diverging interests'. It considers user firms, software vendors, standards development organisations and governmental organisations.

A final chapter gives both a conclusion to the insights gained and recommendations for further research. It also attempts to predict what the development of interorganisational standards will be like in the near future.

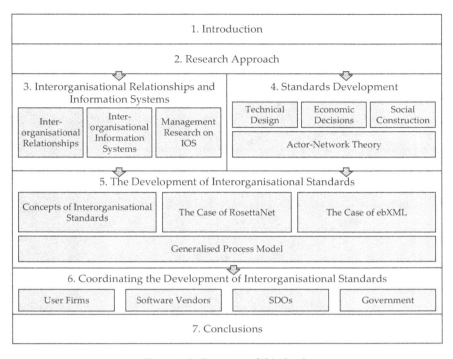

Figure 1.2: Structure of this Study

2 Research Approach

> "The social world is a pattern of symbolic re-
> lationships and meanings sustained through
> a process of human action and interaction.
> Although a certain degree of continuity is
> preserved through the operation of rule-like
> activities that define a particular social mi-
> lieu, the pattern is always open to reaffirma-
> tion or change through the interpretations
> and actions of individual members."[29]
>
> *Gareth Morgan and Linda Smircich*

In increasingly complex research areas such as information systems (IS),
one single approach is not usually sufficient to capture multifaceted real-
world phenomena exhaustively. To study diverse facets, researchers combine different research methods in pluralist methodologies.[30] Moreover,
the variety of topics and methods in IS research results in specialisation
and a division of labour between researchers, as no individual will ever be
competent in all methods and topics. In order to coordinate research efforts efficiently and to judge results fairly, all researchers should clearly
point out their research approach.[31]

The choice of a suitable approach, however, is accompanied by many
methodological problems, especially in qualitative research.[32] Hence, there
is an abundance of discussions on proper approaches for IS research.[33]

---

[29] Morgan/Smircich (1980), p. 494 on the approach to seeing reality as symbolic discourse.

[30] See Mingers (2001), pp. 240ff. He also discusses the differences between the terms
'method' and 'methodology', which are not precisely defined and are used differently in the US and Europe as well. Here, methodology is seen as research on research methods ('meta-research'), while a specific research project uses one or more
research methods.

[31] See Robey (1996), p. 407. "Principles for collaboration in IS research" and
Morgan/Smircich (1980), p. 499: "The development of organisation theory, like other
social science disciplines, would be better served if researchers were more explicit
about the nature of the beliefs they bring to their subject of study."

[32] See Morgan/Smircich (1980), p. 491.

[33] See the comprehensive books by Avison/Myers (2002), Galliers (1992b),
Nissen/Klein/Hirschheim (1991), and Mumford/Hirschheim/Fitzgerald, et al. (1985).

Although I risk omitting some aspects, I classify research approaches along six dimensions (see Table 2.1).

Table 2.1: Dimensions of Research Approaches[34]

Epistemology	Interpretive			Positivist
Focus	Technical			Social
Goal	Describing	Explaining		Recommending
Theorising stage	Explorative	Theory-building	Theory-testing	Theory-extension
Data	Qualitative			Quantitative
Number of researched objects	One	Multiple		Many

The further structure of this chapter distinguishes the first two dimensions from the other four. The former describe the mindsets of researchers, which develop historically and usually evolve slowly (section 2.1). The other dimensions can vary between different research projects undertaken by the same researcher. Moreover, larger projects can combine several or all research approaches (section 2.2).

2.1   Epistemology and Focus

Reviewing the literature in the field of interorganisational information systems (IOS) reveals an obvious difference between the approaches of US and German researchers. Most of their work is based on different philosophical paradigms. As my background is in German IS research, I shall position this background in relation to the US research before continuing this study.[35] To ease the further discussion, I will use 'IS' for the US domi-

---

[34] Note that the first two dimensions are seen as continuous, while the other four are discrete.

[35] I understand that there are other IS research philosophies in other countries as well. However, I believe that the US and German IS philosophies are somewhat extremes on a continuum.

nated IS research and 'WI' for the German IS research, in accordance with the abbreviation of its German term 'Wirtschaftsinformatik'.[36]

Burrell and Morgan's seminal work aims at relating the philosophical background of social researchers to each other.[37] While their central matrix consists of two dimensions, i.e., subjective/objective and regulation/change,[38] the first is of greater importance for my further discussion.[39] The contrast between subjectivist and objectivist research philosophy is widely known in terms of interpretive and positivist epistemology today.[40] It often serves for the classification of research work in overview articles.[41] Moreover, it is the starting point for many discussions of appropriate research approaches.[42] Although many of these works describe interpretive and positivist positions as a dichotomy, Morgan/Smircich (1980) stress the continuum between them and classify different ontological assumptions.[43] On the basis of their work and the taxonomy of Galliers (1992a), I also place the most common research methods along this continuum (see Table 2.2).

Morgan/Smircich (1980) have already noted that such a juxtaposition of ontological assumptions and research methods cannot be very concise.[44] Obviously, some methods can be used with several different ontological assumptions. For example, both interpretive and positivist researchers often use the case study method.[45] Nevertheless, the table gives useful orientation on which methods are typical for which ontological assumptions.

---

[36] Wirtschaftsinformatik means roughly 'computer science for business'; usually it is translated with 'information systems', if WI researchers publish in English.

[37] See Burrell/Morgan (1979).

[38] See Burrell/Morgan (1979), p. 22.

[39] See Morgan/Smircich (1980), pp. 491 and Hirschheim/Klein/Lyytinen (1995), pp. 171.

[40] See, e.g., the overview of Myers (1997). German researchers often use the term constructivist as synonym for interpretivist. See, e.g., Kieser (2002), p. 297.

[41] See Elgarah/Falaleeva/Saunders, et al. (2005) and Orlikowski/Baroudi (1991).

[42] See Jönsson (1991), Lee (1991), Orlikowski/Baroudi (1991), Turner/Bikson/Lyytinen, et al. (1991), Galliers (1992a), Walsham (1995), Myers (1997), and Mingers (2001).

[43] See Morgan/Smircich (1980), pp. 492.

[44] See Morgan/Smircich (1980), p. 498.

[45] See Lee (1989) for a positivist and Klein/Myers (1999) for an interpretive guide to case studies.

Table 2.2: Epistemological Assumptions and Research Methods[46]

Epistemology	Interpretive			Positivist		
Core ontological assumptions	Reality as a projection of human imagination	Reality as a social construction	Reality as a realm of symbolic discourse	Reality as a contextual field of information	Reality as a concrete process	Reality as a concrete structure
Assumptions about human nature	Man as pure spirit, consciousness being	Man as a social constructor, the symbol creator	Man as an actor, the symbol user	Man as an information processor	Man as an adaptor	Man as a responder
Basic epistemological stance	To obtain phenomenological insight, revelation	To understand how social reality is created	To understand patterns of symbolic discourse	To map contexts	To study systems, process, change	To construct a positivist science

Research method	Society	Organization	Individual	Technology	Theory building	Theory testing	Theory extension	Prevailing data
Phenomenology	Yes	**Yes**	Yes	**Possibly**	**Yes**	**Possibly**	**Possibly**	Qualitative
Role playing	Possibly	Yes	Yes	Yes	Yes	Possibly	No	
Futures research	Yes	Yes	Possibly	Yes	Yes	No	No	
Conceptual	Yes	Yes	Yes	Possibly	Yes	No	No	
Action research	Possibly	**Yes**	Possibly	**Yes**	**Yes**	**Yes**	**Possibly**	
Case study	Possibly	**Yes**	Possibly	**Yes**	**Yes**	**Yes**	**Possibly**	
Grounded theory	Yes	Yes	Possibly	Yes	Yes	No	Possibly	
Field experiment	Possibly	Yes	Yes	Yes	No	Yes	Possibly	
Forecasting	Yes	Yes	Possibly	Yes	Possibly	No	No	
Simulation	Possibly	Yes	Yes	Yes	Yes	Possibly	No	
Survey	Yes	**Yes**	Possibly	**Possibly**	Yes	**Possibly**	**Possibly**	Quantitative
Laboratory experiment	No	Possibly	Yes	Yes	No	Yes	Possibly	
Theorem proof	No	No	No	Yes	No	Yes	Possibly	

---

[46] Based on Morgan/Smircich (1980), p. 492 and Galliers (1992a), p. 149.

While the interpretive/positivist continuum aims at research in social sciences, IS/WI research is also concerned with technical aspects of IT. To place IS/WI work in relation to each other more clearly, I propose to use a continuum between technical and social aspects. There are several ways to subdivide this continuum. For instance, the layers 'technical', 'individual', 'organisation', and 'social' are often used.[47] Another possibility is to distinguish technical, process, and strategic aspects.[48] A third one is an extended semiotic framework, based on Stamper (1991).[49] This divides the technical aspects into the physical world, empirics and syntactics. Electrical engineering and computer science mainly cover this. The social aspects are divided into semantics, pragmatics, and the social world. This is where the focus of management research and other social sciences lies. Figure 2.1 depicts this semiotic layer framework. IS/WI research as a bridging discipline is mainly concerned with the upper part of the technical and the lower part of the social layers. Actor-network theory (ANT) is one theoretical approach aiming at a better understanding of the interplay of both layers. Section 2.3 thus introduces ANT, which argues that a researcher might miss important insights if he is too quick in subdividing a research domain into social and technical aspects without linking both together.

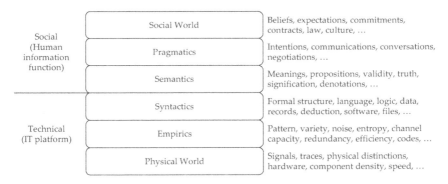

Figure 2.1: Semiotic Framework[50]

---

[47] See, e.g., Vitalari (1985).

[48] See, e.g., Scott Morton (1991) and Österle (1995), p. 16.

[49] Morris (1938) introduced the distinction between syntax, semantics, and pragmatics into the theory of semiotics, which goes back to Locke (1690 [1994]).

[50] Slightly adapted from Stamper (1991), p. 516.

Combining the interpretive/positivist and the technical/social dimension produces a matrix that provides a reasonable framework for placing the philosophies of IS and WI in relation to one another (Figure 2.1).

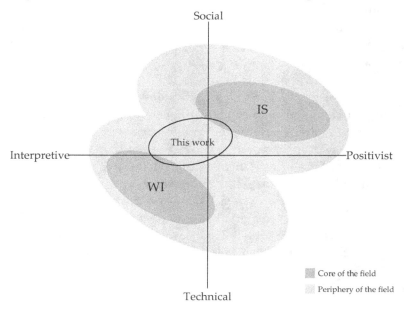

Figure 2.1: IS and WI in the Epistemology/Focus Matrix

To my knowledge, the relevant literature lacks a comprehensive overview of the philosophies in WI research. However, a recent review categorises 164 WI research papers along with the goals describing (35%), explaining (11%), and recommending (27%).[51] The explaining papers represent empirical work, mostly surveys and case studies, but no laboratory experiments. Empirical research thus seems to play a minor role in WI. The philosophy of the recommending papers is seen as mainly constructivist.[52] This speaks for a strong interpretive epistemology, as constructivism is

---

[51] See Heinrich (2001), pp. 294ff. Most of the describing works are reports from practical projects or product descriptions. The missing 27% did not fit into any one of the categories considered.

[52] Moreover, two conferences on the philosophy of science in WI included many contributions concerned with constructivism. See Becker/König/Schütte, et al. (1999) and Schütte/Siedentopf/Zelewski (1999).

closer to the interpretive extreme than to the positivist.[53] Moreover, WI tradition usually demands coverage of technical details and regards developing IS prototypes as a major goal of the discipline.[54] Thus, many WI researchers often have a technical focus, which locates the core of WI in the interpretive/technical field.[55]

A comprehensive overview of philosophies in IS research reveals the domination of positivist epistemology. Orlikowski/Baroudi (1991) checked 155 IS papers and counted 97% as positivist, with 49% surveys, 27% laboratory experiments, and 14% case studies.[56] A similar picture is given by the more recent review of Elgarah et al. (2005) on 68 IOS papers, of which 90% are classified as positivist, 7% as interpretive, and 3% as critical.[57] Given the social research focus of many IS researchers I place the core of IS in the positivist/social field. This is supported by many discussions on the appropriate research philosophy for IS, in which the domination of positivism is stated, reasons are explained, and complementary philosophies are proposed.[58] One major point is the importance of rigorous research methods for the careers of researchers.[59] It is in the nature of interpretive research, however, that its methodical steps are not as strictly defined as for positivist methods. Thus, interpretive research is often seen as less rigorous than positivist. As positivist methods are often quantitative, they need to narrow down real-world phenomena. One consequence is a lack in relevance of many IS research results and only moderate recognition by practitioners.[60]

The opposite seems to apply to WI. During the last decade, many new institutes for WI research have been founded at German-speaking universities. Close relations to companies characterise most WI research projects. To deliver relevant results to practitioners, interpretive methods such as

---

[53] See Morgan/Smircich (1980), p. 494 and Table 2.2, "Reality as a social construction".

[54] See Mertens/Bodendorf/König, et al. (2004), pp. 3ff.

[55] Please note that the boundaries of the ellipses should not be considered as very precise. They are meant to give an estimate of the dominant philosophical position of the respective research traditions.

[56] See Orlikowski/Baroudi (1991), pp. 4ff.

[57] See Elgarah/Falaleeva/Saunders, et al. (2005), p. 16.

[58] See Nissen/Klein/Hirschheim (1991) and the discussion in Turner/Bikson/Lyytinen, et al. (1991).

[59] See Turner/Bikson/Lyytinen, et al. (1991), pp. 724ff.

[60] See Turner/Bikson/Lyytinen, et al. (1991), p. 723.

conceptual work and action research dominate, often combined with the development of reference models and software prototypes. Probably because of the high practical demand for the results of WI researchers, they seldom think about a solid methodological underpinning for their discipline.[61] Some call for more empirical WI research[62] and others for more building of one's own theories.[63]

By analysing an IS researcher's discussion about the relevance of their work, Frank (2003) also states the obvious differences between IS and WI research.[64] However, with the positioning of IS and WI in Figure 2.1, I share his opinion that the strengths and weaknesses of both could complement each other very well.[65] In this study, I am following this idea. By explaining my position on the matrix in the next paragraph, I lay the ground for my research approach.

In the field of EDI, 90% of the IS research in the last ten years can be classified as positivist.[66] Almost none of it paid any attention to the tremendous qualitative changes the Internet has brought EDI systems.[67] As my research goal is to analyse new phenomena and derive insights for the management of interorganisational standardisation, a strong positivist epistemology is not (yet) appropriate. On the other hand, a strictly interpretive approach does not take into account the existing insights from EDI research. In accordance with Lee (1991), I believe that interpretive and positivist approaches should be combined to develop theories in a discipline. Put simply, at the beginning of theory-building, interpretive approaches dominate, while positivist ones take over to test and refine theories. However, this is a cycle, as theories might have to be revised when the underlying assumptions are not valid any more.[68] In this case, more

---

[61] See Mertens/Heinrich (2002), p. 486. Some exceptions can be found in Rolf (1998), Fuchs-Kittowski/Heinrich/Rolf (1999), Becker/König/Schütte, et al. (1999), Eversmann (2002), and Hess/Picot (2003).

[62] See Heinzl (2001).

[63] See Rolf (1998), pp. 3-11.

[64] See Frank (2003).

[65] Several papers from the IS field support the approach of combining of IS and WI research. See, e.g., Olaisen (1991), p. 261 and Benbasat/Zmud (2003), p. 191.

[66] See Elgarah/Falaleeva/Saunders, et al. (2005), p. 17.

[67] See Elgarah/Falaleeva/Saunders, et al. (2005), p. 20.

[68] See Calas/Smircich (1999), p. 651, who talk of theorising as a temporary language game.

interpretive approaches are needed to understand the changed assumptions.[69] In a fast-moving field like IS, these cycles might be quite short. In the terms of Morgan/Smircich (1980) this ontological assumption is close to seeing 'reality as a realm of symbolic discourse' (see the introductory quotation and Table 2.2). Thus, I place my work in a middle-left position within the epistemology/focus matrix, which shows that it is neither a 'typical' work of WI, nor a 'typical' work of IS, but in the overlapping periphery of both (see Figure 2.1).

This discussion about my epistemological background is important for two reasons. It underpins the selection of my research method, described in the next two sections. Moreover, it explains the further steps I will take in my research. First, I sum up the current theoretical knowledge on IOS and standardisation, where positivist research has led to a high maturity of theories (chapters 3 and 4). Then I use an interpretive approach to analyse the development of interorganisational standards (chapter 5). In doing this, I will discover new aspects that positivist theories have not yet covered.

2.2   Case Study Research Method

Galliers (1992a) summarises the likely applicability of IS research methods for particular research objects. He distinguishes between social, organisational, individual, technical and methodological focuses. Moreover, he lists whether a method is useful for theory-building, theory-testing, and/or theory-extension.[70] Classifying all methods with respect to their ontological and epistemological assumptions on the interpretive/positivist continuum yields the taxonomy in Table 2.2.

This study is concerned with technologies and organisations. Moreover, it examines theories in order to extend them or build a new one. According to the research method taxonomy (), only phenomenology, action research, case study research, and survey research meet these criteria. Phenomenology and survey research are not suited to my epistemological background and the maturity of the phenomena under consideration. Moreover, survey research requires a large number of different entities to be studied,

---

[69] See Morgan/Smircich (1980), p. 493.

[70] See Galliers (1992a), p. 159.

which is inherently difficult as standardisation initiatives explicitly aim at as few different standards as possible. Action research requires the researcher to be actively involved in a practitioner's project. Although my research institute is a member of the RosettaNet organisation, its academic status gives it a purely observing function. As I am not participating in a project on developing standards or implementing an IOS, action research is no viable option either.

Case study research remains as the most appropriate research method for my research topic and my epistemological background. Benbasat et al. (1987) sum up the main advantages of case study research:

> "To summarize, there are three reasons why case study research is a viable information systems research strategy. First, the researcher can study information systems in a natural setting, learn about the state of the art, and generate theories from practice. Second, the case method allows the researcher to answer 'how' and 'why' questions, that is, to understand the nature and complexity of the processes taking place. (...) Third, a case approach is an appropriate way to research an area in which few previous studies have been carried out."[71]

These reasons correspond well to the character of my research topic: under-investigated phenomena, unanswered 'why' and 'how' questions, and linking practical problems with existing theory.[72]

Eisenhardt (1989) gives an overview of the typical steps and activities needed in case study research, based on concepts from Glaser/Strauss (1967), Miles/Huberman (1984), and Yin (1984). A condensed and slightly adapted version comprises the steps *a priori understanding*, case selection, *data collection*, data analysis, and *theory building and extension* (Table 2.3). Chapters 3 and 4 and the section 5.1 are concerned with the a priori understanding of the topic and the selection of the cases. I collected data in several iterations. First, I identified interesting initiatives and examined their Web pages in terms of goals, scope and maturity. Second, I collected primary data through conducting interviews and attending conferences and plenary meetings of standards development organisations (SDOs) (see appendix A). Third, I gathered secondary data available from Web resources of the SDOs. While ebXML-related resources are all publicly available, I gained access to RosettaNet resources as an Associate Member.

---

[71]   See Benbasat/Goldstein/Mead (1987), p. 370.

[72]   See the research questions as discussed in section 1.2.

Sections 5.2 and 5.3 present the results of the data analysis, focusing on the organisational structure and development processes of the SDOs. Finally, in section 5.4 I discuss the similarities and differences between the two cases and a theoretical model derived from theory and case insights.

Table 2.3: Performed Case Study Activities[73]

Step	Performed Activities
A priori understanding	- Literature review on IOS and standards - General framework for managing IOS (chapter 3) - Theories on standardisation (chapter 4)
Case selection	Reasons for selecting RosettaNet as case: - Strong industry support - High maturity Reasons for selecting ebXML as case: - Joint effort of UN/CEFACT and OASIS - High practical relevance
Data collection	Primary data: - Interviews - Conference and plenary participation Secondary data: - Web pages (including member access) - Conference proceedings - Presentations - Press releases - Specifications
Data analysis	Within case: - Section 5.2: RosettaNet organisational structure and development process - Section 5.3: ebXML organisational structure and development process Cross-case: - Section 5.4: Similarities and differences
Theory building/extension	- Section 5.4: Theoretical approach towards interorganisational standardisation

---

[73] Adapted from Eisenhardt (1989), p. 533.

These and similar steps are recommended for positivist epistemology in order to find constructs, independent and dependent variables, and to formulate hypotheses that denote causalities between these.[74] This work, however, takes a more interpretive stance. To meet the requirements of interpretive research, it also follows the seven principles of Klein/Myers (1999) for conducting rigorous interpretive research. Table 2.4 explains these principles and their application to my research.

Table 2.4: Application of the Principles of Interpretive Research[75]

Principle of Interpretive Research	Explanation	Application in this Work
1. The fundamental principle of the hermeneutic circle	This principle suggests that all human understanding is achieved by iterating between considering the interdependent meaning of parts and the whole that they form. This principle of human understanding is fundamental to all the other principles.	Iterations between the description of details and putting them into the whole picture of ebXML and RosettaNet.
2. The principle of contextualisation	Requires critical reflection on the social and historical background of the research setting, so that the intended audience can see how the current situation under investigation emerged.	Description of the environment, driving forces and historical background of ebXML and RosettaNet.
3. The principle of interaction between researchers and the subjects	Requires critical reflection on how the research materials (or 'data') were socially constructed through the interaction between the researchers and participants.	Interaction between researcher and SDOs: Associate Partner of the RosettaNet initiative, participation in SDO conferences and plenary sessions, interviews with SDO participants, internal knowledge of some (former) SDO participants on the Web

---

[74]   See Yin (2003), Eisenhardt (1989), Lee (1989), Benbasat/Goldstein/Mead (1987).
[75]   See Klein/Myers (1999), p. 72.

Table 2.4 (continued): Application of the Principles of Interpretive Research[76]

Principle of Interpretive Research	Explanation	Application in this Work
4. The principle of abstraction and generalisation	Requires relating the idiographic details revealed by the data interpretation through the application of principles one and two to theoretical, general concepts that describe the nature of human understanding and social action.	Use of actor-network theory to derive general insights from both cases (section 5.4).
5. The principle of dialogical reasoning	Requires sensitivity to possible contradictions between the theoretical preconceptions guiding the research design and actual findings ('the story which the data tell') with subsequent cycles of revision.	First description of the cases without too much theoretical guidance. Then analysis from a theoretical perspective. Finally shaping of new theoretical constructs.
6. The principle of multiple interpretations	Requires sensitivity to possible differences in interpretations among the participants as are typically expressed in multiple narratives or stories of the same sequence of events under study. Similar to multiple witness accounts even if all tell it as they saw it.	Different stories told by different sources. Interpretation of data with care, second source where possible. E.g., interview statements vs. actual specification content.
7. The principle of suspicion	Requires sensitivity to possible 'biases' and systematic 'distortions' in the narratives collected from the participants.	IOS users are very likely biased towards the specifications they are currently investing in. E.g., RosettaNet users enthusiastically promoted RosettaNet, while EDI users heavily defended EDI as a sufficient approach.

---

[76] See Klein/Myers (1999), p. 72.

2.3   Actor-Network Theory

Actor-network theory (ANT) further complements the case study research method used in this work. Increasingly, IS researchers are using ANT for case studies on information systems.[77] One reason for the success of ANT is the combination of an empirical case study approach with a new theoretical language of network dynamics.[78] This makes ANT especially "...useful for studies of information systems in situations where interactions of the social, technological and political are regarded as particularly important."[79] As the development of interorganisational standards is very much such a situation, I have chosen ANT for conducting the case studies.[80] Before further discussing ANT, the most important point to be noted is that it combines both theory and methodology.[81] This section is concerned with the methodological aspects of ANT, while section 4.5 presents the theoretical concepts and their use in the further case study research.

The roots of ANT can be traced back to the École des Mines in Paris. In the mid 1980s, the two social researchers Bruno Latour and Michel Callon were working on social studies of science and technology. The main question of this strand of research is: What social processes are behind scientific research and how do they influence the scientific results? Two books are regarded as the first major works on ANT. Callon (1986b) investigates a scientific field experiment and the social reasons for its failure, while Latour (1987) gives general instructions on "how to follow scientists and engineers through society."[82] John Law, the third researcher associated with the roots of ANT, summarises the insights of Callon and Latour:

"So this is the actor-network diagnosis of science: that it is a process of 'heterogeneous engineering' in which bits and pieces from the social, the techni-

---

[77] See the overview in Walsham (1997). Very recent works using ANT for IS research are Olla/Atkinson/Gandceha (2003), Purao/Truex/Cao (2003), Virili (2003), Fomin/Lyytinen/Keil (2004), and Pouloudi/Gandecha/Papazafeiropoulou, et al. (2004).

[78] See Braun (2000), p. 7.

[79] Tatnall/Gilding (1999), p. 963.

[80] See also the arguments of Hanseth/Monteiro (1997) to show that ANT is a very useful approach for capturing the complexity of interorganisational standards.

[81] See Walsham (1997), p. 469 and Latour (1999a), p. 20.

[82] Latour (1987), from the title of the book.

cal, the conceptual and the textual are fitted together, and so converted (or 'translated') into a set of equally heterogeneous scientific products."[83]

Like Glaser/Strauss (1967) and Eisenhardt (1989), ANT also proposes not to theorise before analysing an empirical setting, but rather to let theoretical insights emerge through learning "… from the actors without imposing on them an a priori definition of their world-building capacities."[84] There are two main reasons for this stance. First, by simplifying too early in the research process, one might miss crucial links that would explain a certain behaviour.[85] Second, ANT assumes that actors usually have very good reasons for acting as they do. The most important task of ANT researchers thus has to be not only to learn what actors do, but rather to understand the motivations determining how and why they do it.[86]

One main contribution of ANT is the insight that social concepts are not sufficient for understanding how and why actors act as they do. In their social studies on scientific research, Callon and Latour revealed the eminent influence of 'artefacts' – such as laboratory equipment and research papers – on the behaviour of scientists.[87] Their main claim is to open the black box of artefacts and analyse the interactions between human and non-human actors.[88] This helps one to understand the behaviour of actors better, especially in a world where humans and technology are increasingly interweaved.

As IS research has always been concerned with humans on the one hand and technology on the other, discussion of their relationships is not new in this field. For instance, Markus/Robey (1988) discuss the causal agency of organisational change.[89] The technological imperative regards technology as the main cause for change. An opposing position is the organisational imperative: people in an organisation shape technology exactly according

---

[83] Law (1992).

[84] Latour (1999a), p. 20.

[85] See Law (1999), p. 8.

[86] See Latour (1999a), p. 19.

[87] See Callon (1986a) and Latour (1987).

[88] Latour (1999b) prefers the terms human/non-human to the notion of a subject/object-dichotomy in order to avoid the many discussions of the latter.

[89] See Markus/Robey (1988), p. 584.

to their needs. Most researchers tend to take one of these stances.[90] Markus/Robey (1988) advocate a third causal agency, the emergent perspective. Their main point is the mutual influence of people and technology, which is more realistic but also more difficult to capture with rigorous theories.[91] Similarly,

> „ANT considers both social and technical determinism to be flawed and proposes instead a socio-technical account (…) in which neither social nor technical positions are privileged. Thus an actor may be human, non-human or a networked hybrid combination of both."[92]

While other research often only states the need for an integrated analysis of social and technical aspects,[93] ANT also offers an apparatus for a symmetrical treatment of humans and non-humans.[94] This principle of generalised symmetry, i.e., analysing humans and non-humans with the same conceptual framework, triggered many discussions on ANT.[95] Law (1992) admits that ANT "… is analytically radical in part because it treads on a set of ethical, epistemological and ontological toes." Underlying ANT is the assumption that social networks not only consist of interactions between humans, but also of interactions between humans and many heterogeneous non-human entities.[96] To understand behaviour in social networks, non-humans must not be banished to a different level.

Mapping the emergence and disappearance of ordered structures in such 'ontologically flat' actor-networks is the central goal of ANT.

> "The object is to explore and describe local processes of patterning, social orchestration, ordering and resistance. In short, it is to explore the process that is often called translation which generates ordering effects such as devices, agents, institutions, or organisations."[97]

---

[90] See the short overview in Stalder (1997). In a comprehensive review of EDI research literature Elgarah/Falaleeva/Saunders, et al. (2005) show, that 73% of the papers adopt the technological imperative and 26% an organisational imperative.

[91] See Markus/Robey (1988), p. 588.

[92] Olla/Atkinson/Gandceha (2003), p. 106.

[93] See the discussion in Monteiro/Hanseth (1996).

[94] See Walsham (1997), p. 467.

[95] See the assessment of ANT later in this section.

[96] See Law (1992), p. 2.

[97] Law (1992), p. 1.

Translation, which is the central concept of ANT,[98] allows the formation, growth, stabilisation, destabilisation and disappearance of networks to be described, be they made of mainly human or mainly non-human actors. During translation, the diverse interests of heterogeneous actors are 'translated' in such a way that every actor 'understands' its purpose in the actor-network. Depending on the stage of translation, an actor-network can be very loosely coupled or highly stabilised. An actor-network in the latter stage acts as a single block and in a predictable way. Thus, it can be 'black boxed', i.e., considered as one single actor.

With the notion of translation as a process of network stabilisation, it is important to understand that ANT researchers do not take a purely interpretive or purely positivist stance. It just depends on how stabilised the actor-network under consideration is. The formation and disappearance of actor-networks calls for interpretive research, while positivist research should focus on stabilised actor-networks. Taking the overview of Morgan/Smircich (1980), ANT is located in the middle, but open to both sides. Humans (and non-humans) are actors using symbols to act. The main goal is to discover and understand patterns in symbolic discourses, called 'translations' in ANT.[99]

How can a researcher use all these insights from ANT to approach an actual research project? First, he accepts the three principles of ANT:[100]

– Agnosticism: analytical neutrality is demanded towards all the actors involved in the project under consideration, be they human or non-human.
– Generalised symmetry: explains the conflicting viewpoints of different actors in the same terms by using of an abstract and neutral vocabulary that works the same way for human and non-human actors.
– Free association: requires the elimination and abandonment of all a priori distinctions between the technological and the social.

Second, he gains access to the sources for his analysis, which can be both interviews with participants ('follow the actors') and technological artefacts ('follow the traces').

---

[98] 'Sociology of Translation' is sometimes used as a synonym for ANT. See Law (1992), p. 1.

[99] See section 4.5 for a detailed discussion of the concepts of ANT.

[100] See Tatnall/Gilding (1999), p. 958.

Finally, the analysis consists of three major steps:[101]

- Identification of a socio-technical network and the actors involved
- Describing the actor-network dynamics
- Variation of the perspectives

I follow this method of ANT for my case studies in chapter 5.

As the dualism of humans and non-humans is at the heart of information systems, ANT is a natural choice for IS research.[102] Walsham's overview of ANT-based IS research reveals its value especially for cases of IS development.[103] One often-cited example is the process of defining an EDI message standard analysed by Hanseth/Monteiro (1997).

Walsham (1997) also discusses the four major critical appraisals of ANT.[104] The first one concerns the limited analysis of social structures, as ANT focuses only on action. Walsham (1997) proposes adding Giddens' duality of action and structure, in which structure enables action and action changes structure.[105] Stabilised actor-networks can be regarded as structure, in which (constrained) action is possible. On the basis of this idea, Atkinson/Brooks (2003) combine Giddens' structuration theory and ANT to from the "StructurANTion Framework".[106]

The second criticism targets the amoral stance of ANT. A simple reaction from Latour (1991) is to use ANT for 'first describing the network'. Moral issues have to be debated later using other theoretical approaches.

The third criticism concerns the generalised symmetry between humans and non-humans, which might be considered the most 'revolutionary' element of ANT. In ANT, an actor is not an actor because he is human, but rather because he acts in a certain way. Action constitutes an actor. If a machine executes the same task as a human, why not treat the machine as an actor too? Pels (1995) not only doubts that non-humans can really act, but also fears that humans will be treated like non-humans, 'like pawns on a chessboard'.[107] While this is again a moral issue, even the critics see the

---

[101] Based on Degele (2002), p. 134.

[102] See Atkinson/Brooks (2003), p. 2896.

[103] See Walsham (1997), pp. 470ff.

[104] See Walsham (1997), pp. 472ff.

[105] See Giddens (1984).

[106] See Atkinson/Brooks (2003), Brooks/Atkinson (2004).

[107] See Mowshowitz (1994) using the example of virtual organisations.

idea of generalised symmetry as an important impetus for rethinking the difference between humans and non-humans. Collins/Yearley (1992) propose a compromise in using the word 'actant' to distinguish non-human actors from human ones. Overall, if not accepting non-humans as actors, the ANT researcher can regard 'acting' non-humans as 'hybrids', as 'spokespersons' that stand in for the interests of their human masters.[108]

Finally, the length of ANT works is criticised. Although this relates to any in-depth case study, it concerns ANT in particular as ANT emphasises the importance of detail.[109] Thus, Walsham (1997) calls for acceptance of longer case descriptions and for new ways of reporting on case studies in a short manner.[110]

For established communities in general management and IS research it has always been difficult to accept postmodern research such as ANT.[111] As Weik (1996) puts it, postmodern approaches are less useful for consulting projects, but very fruitful for basic organisational research.[112] Moreover, Calas/Smircich (1999) conclude their assessment of ANT:

> "If nothing else, ANT, with its focus on irreductionism and relationality, rather than facts and essences, may become a very useful exercise to counter conventional 'theoretical tales' in organisation studies. More immediately, as organisational studies face contemporary technologies in a reconfiguration of the time/space of organisations, as 'the Web' and 'virtuality' become part of our everyday mode of existence, and as our interactions with machines incrementally define our life experiences, ANT provides ways to navigate and represent these (dis)locations while displacing more conventional 'organisational' thinking."[113]

While this section has only discussed the methodological aspects of ANT, I will introduce its theoretical concepts in section 4.5 and apply them to two cases of interorganisational standards in section 5.4.

---

[108] For further discussion see Braun (2000).

[109] See Walsham (1997), p. 476.

[110] See Walsham (1997), p. 476.

[111] For a comprehensive discussion of postmodern research in general see Calas/Smircich (1999), for organisational research see Weik (1996).

[112] See Weik (1996), p. 394.

[113] Calas/Smircich (1999), p. 664.

2.4   Summary and Conclusions

In the face of increasingly specialised research projects, an explicit discussion of one's research approach is crucial to facilitate the positioning of one's research results in relation to others. On the epistemology dimension, this study is located in the middle-left of the interpretive/positivist continuum. It analyses technical and social aspects to the same extent (see Table 2.5).

Table 2.5: Characteristics of the Research Approach Used

Epistemology	Interpretive			Positivist
Focus	Technical			Social
Goal	Describing	Explaining		Recommending
Theorising stage	Explorative	Theory-building	Theory-testing	Theory-extension
Data	Qualitative			Quantitative
Number of researched objects	One	Multiple		Many

Its main goal is to describe and explain the phenomenon of interorganisational standards and derive recommendations for practice. Therefore, case study research is chosen as a research method aiming at exploration and theory-building, on the basis of qualitative data from multiple cases. Actor-network theory extends the general case study approach with the concept of tracing the dynamics of heterogeneous networks consisting of human and non-human actors.

3 Interorganisational Relationships and Information Systems

> "In short, if our predictions are correct, we should not expect the electronically interconnected world of tomorrow to be simply a faster and more efficient version of the world we know today. Instead, we should expect fundamental changes in how firms and markets organize the flow of goods and services in our economy."[114]
>
> *Thomas W. Malone, Joanne Yates and Robert I. Benjamin*

This chapter will answer the first research question:

Why and how do information systems support interorganisational relationships?

In doing so, it summarises the main aspects of interorganisational information systems on the basis of the existing literature. As interorganisational information systems are embedded in the context of interorganisational relationships, section 3.1 gives an overview of their nature, focusing on supply chain networks. Section 3.2 briefly introduces the nature of information systems, the general features of interorganisational information systems, and the characteristics of EDI-based systems. To summarise the current state of research on interorganisational information systems, section 3.3 sketches a management framework, and reviews recent literature on Web-based interorganisational information systems.

3.1 The Nature of Interorganisational Relationships

Smith (1776) already noted that the division of labour and specialisation increases the welfare within and between nations. To this day, the tendency to further specialise organisations has not stopped.[115] As a result, organisations have to establish and maintain many relations to other organisations if they want to offer complex goods and services. Effective and

---

[114] Malone/Yates/Benjamin (1987), p. 497.
[115] See Brown/Durchslag/Hagel (2002).

efficient management of such interorganisational (IO) relationships is a critical task for today's firms.

Considerable research results on the management of relationships between organisations have been available since the 1950s.[116] Referring to the quest for a theory on IO relationships, Evan (1965) stated:

> "Describing and measuring networks of inter-organisational relations presents a substantial methodological challenge."[117]

As in most management research fields, no single theory can explain IO relationships exhaustively. Rather, the research literature on IO relationships is growing fast and has resulted in a long list of applied theories: actor-network-theory, behavioural theories, contract theory, exchange theory, game theory, institutional theory, learning theory, political economy theory, principal agent theory, property rights theory, resource dependence theory, social exchange theory, stakeholder theory, strategic choice theory, systems theory, and transaction cost theory. [118] This is probably not all of them. While they use different perspectives, they can also lead to comparable insights.[119]

Although the term 'interorganisational relationship' has a broad meaning, authors seldom give a precise definition. Simply stated, IO relationships are linkages across the boundaries of two or more firms. According to the transaction cost theory initiated by Coase (1937) and further developed by Williamson (1975), firms are an alternative to markets for the organisation of input resources. Whether tasks are organised via markets or within firms depends on where the costs of organisation are lower.[120] Such a dichotomy between markets and hierarchies implicitly assumes clear boundaries where a firm ends and a market begins. In reality, however, it is often difficult to determine where the organisational boundaries of a firm are:

---

[116] See Levine/White (1951), Macaulay (1963), and Evan (1965).

[117] Evan (1965), p. 10.

[118] See the overviews in Rößl (1993), Barringer/Harrison (2000), Humphreys/Lai/Sculli (2001), and Picot/Reichwald/Wigand (2003).

[119] See, e.g., Rößl (1993), pp. 378ff., who used game theory, systems theory, behavioural theory and institutional theory and found corresponding results.

[120] Coase (1960) later calls these costs transaction costs.

"One can sometimes say 'Now I am inside' or 'Now I am outside' but he can never confidently say 'This is the boundary'."[121]

More often than not, organisational arrangements have a hybrid form, as they are neither strict hierarchies nor pure markets.[122] Here I understand IO relationships as such forms of hybrid coordination. However, this is still very broad as many different kinds of hybrid arrangements can be observed. The literature differentiates between several types of IO relationships. The most frequently discussed are buyer-supplier relations, consortia, firm networks, joint ventures, licensing, shared capital, strategic alliances, supply chain networks and trade associations.[123] Several characteristics serve for a further differentiation of IO relationships (see Table 3.1).

Table 3.1: Characteristics of Interorganisational Relationships

Dimensions	Characteristics			Sources
Goal	Market power		Efficiency	Picot et al. (2002), pp. 186
Direction	Horizontal	Vertical	Diagonal	Kraege (1997), p. 66
Resources	Coordinated		Joint	Kraege (1997), p. 67
Contract	Classical	Neo-classical	Relational	Williamson (1985), pp. 69.
Activities	Primary		Supporting	Porter (2001), pp. 74
Typology	Dyadic (1:1)	Set (1:n)	Network (n:m)	Hall (1999), p. 340
Specificity	Low		High	Klein et al. (1978)
Time horizon	Limited		Unlimited	Wurche (1994), pp. 135
Coupling	Loose		Tight	Barringer/Harrison (2000), p. 383
Formalisation	Low		High	Vlaar (2003), p. 10

---

121 Starbuck (1976), p. 1071.

122 See Picot/Reichwald/Wigand (2003) and Williamson (1991).

123 See the overviews in Gulati (1998), Barringer/Harrison (2000), Hess (2002), Elgarah/Falaleeva/Saunders, et al. (2005), and Picot/Reichwald/Wigand (2003).

The main topic of this study is interorganisational standards. These are especially important for supply chain networks (SCNs), as here the quick and efficient coupling of trading partners is crucial.[124] The study thus focuses on the role of interorganisational standards in SCNs, without neglecting the transferability of its insights to other fields. Christopher (1998) gives a practical definition of SCNs:

> "The supply chain is the network of organisations that are involved, through upstream and downstream linkages, in the different processes and activities that produce value in the form of products and services in the hands of the ultimate consumer."[125]

Concepts for managing SCNs are subsumed under the term supply chain management (SCM).[126] The main goal is higher efficiency through intense coordination of resources and primary activities between several vertical partners, mainly secured through neo-classical contracts. Together they either form sets with one focal firm or distributed networks without one. The exchanged goods and services can be of low or high specificity. The time horizon can be unlimited or limited, with focus on the latter. Coupling can be loose or tight, often depending on the specificity. Finally, SCNs typically have a high degree of formalisation (see Table 3.1).

Although a relatively new approach, management science has accepted SCM as an important research stream.[127] One prominent research result is the discovery of what is called the 'bullwhip effect'. Small demand changes at one location in the supply chain can lead to high demand changes at another location.[128] The main reason is a slow and limited exchange of information between firms, resulting in isolated planning and safety stocks. In today's SCNs the bullwhip effect is of high practical relevance as

---

[124] See Handfield/Nichols (2002), pp. 271ff.

[125] Christopher (1998), p. 15.

[126] See Kortmann/Lessing (2000), pp. 19ff. and pp. 117ff. for an overview of different definitions of SCM. Some authors call for use of the term 'demand chain management' (DCM) (e.g., Selen/Soliman (2002)). I follow the majority of researchers and see SCM and DCM as synonyms; see Vakharia (2002), pp. 495ff.

[127] See Mabert/Venkataramanan (1998) and Müller/Seuring/Goldbach (2003). See Otto (2002) for a comprehensive discussion of supply chain management concepts.

[128] See Lee/Padmanabhan/Whang (1997) and Lee (2000), p 33. At many business schools, logistics students experience this effect by playing the 'beer-game', based on systems dynamics models. See Forrester (1958) and Milling (1999).

- demand changes are getting stronger because of faster innovation rates and consumer behaviour that is harder to forecast, and
- an increasing number of firms participate in SCNs.

The latter point is a result of further specialisation of firms. Several researchers have assumed that interorganisational information systems (IOS) lower the transaction cost of market-like coordination forms, causing a shift from hierarchical to more hybrid organisational arrangements and leading to smaller firms.[130] However, many mergers and acquisitions in recent years seem to tell a different story of ever-larger hierarchies. Nevertheless, a more differentiated view reveals the tendency of firms to shrink vertically and grow horizontally, which is the specialisation of firms mentioned above.[131] Modularity in the design of products intensifies this phenomenon, as firms do not have to develop all the parts of a product themselves, but can focus their competencies on certain modules. Thus, modular product architectures lead to increasingly modular SCNs, which

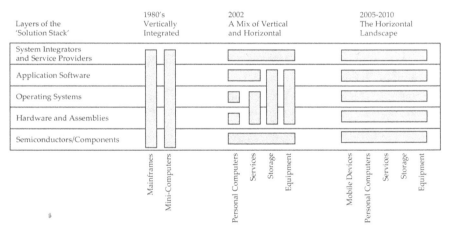

Figure 3.1: From a Vertical to a Horizontal Computer Industry[129]

---

[129] Based on e2open (2003). Note that the figure depicts who is actually producing the components. Although Microsoft, for example, offers hardware products, independent electronics manufacturing service companies always produce them.

[130] See Malone/Yates/Benjamin (1987) and Clemons/Reddi/Row (1993). This topic is also discussed under the terms 'move-to-the-middle'- and 'move-to-the market'-hypotheses.

[131] See Bieberbach (2001) and Afuah (2003).

can offer very complex products.[132] One example is the structure of the computer industry, which changed from few vertically integrated firms to a horizontally specialised industry (see Figure 3.1).[133] As a result, there are more firms involved in the creation of a product, and these have to manage an increasing number of interorganisational relationships. Moreover, these are often not limited to straight buyer-supplier relationships, but comprise complex scenarios such as joint product development, collaborative forecasting or contract manufacturing. Frictions and interruptions in these complex interorganisational relationships can significantly affect the overall efficiency of SCNs, leading, for example, to the bullwhip effect.

To avoid such distortions, a good fit of all organisational domains involved is crucial, as shown in Figure 3.2. This is based on the MIT 90s model of Scott Morton (1991) and its extension to interorganisational relationships by Chatfield/Yetton (2000).[135] At the core of this model are business processes, which are embedded in the organisational structure, executed by people, and supported by information technology, while strategy sets the long-term goals. The model comprises three layers of interorganisational relationships. First, decisions of establishing and ending interorganisational relationships are made on the strategic level. Second, interpersonal relationships link organisations through direct contact between employees. Third, interorganisational information systems (IOS) couple business processes across boundaries via information technology.

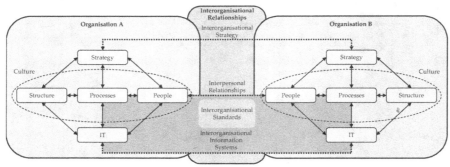

Figure 3.2: Levels of Interorganisational Relationships[134]

---

[132] See Göpfert (1998) and Steiner (2005), pp. 45ff.
[133] See Grove (1996), p. 44.
[134] Based on Scott Morton (1991), Chatfield/Yetton (2000), Stegwee/Rukanova (2003).
[135] See Chatfield/Yetton (2000), pp. 200ff.

The information exchanged in SCNs often has high volumes and requires accuracy and speed, making it difficult to process manually. It thus became almost impossible to manage SCNs without the use of IOS. For instance, carmakers connect their production lines to suppliers via IOS to enable the just-in-time delivery of parts.[136] The rest of this study focuses on such IOS including information technology, people and processes (see darkest rectangle in Figure 3.2) and the role of standards in such systems.

3.2   The Nature of Interorganisational Information Systems

This section first introduces general concepts of interorganisational information systems (subsection 3.2.1). Then it discusses EDI systems as the most common type of interorganisational information systems (subsection 3.2.2).

3.2.1   Concepts of Interorganisational Information Systems

Interorganisational information systems are a specific form of general information systems. Davis (1999) gives a comprehensive definition of IS:

> „The information system or management information system of an organisation consists of the information technology infrastructure, application systems, and personnel that employ information technology to deliver information and communications services for transaction processing, operations, administration, and management of an organisation. The system utilizes computer and communications hardware and software, manual procedures, and internal and external repositories of data. The systems apply a combination of automation, human actions, and user-machine interaction."[137]

The automation of information processing is a fundamental aspect of IS.[138] On his quest to understand human rationality, Simon (1965) describes three fields of decision-making in firms, each with different levels of potential automation. In top management, unprogrammed decision-making prevails, which has almost no automation potential. Programmed deci-

---

[136] See Pfeiffer (1992), pp. 106ff.
[137] Davis (1999), p. 196.
[138] See Denning/Comer/Gries, et al. (1989), p. 12.

sion-making dominates middle management and has medium automation potential. The highest automation potential is offered by clerical work with repeated work processes.[139] This can be explained in terms of the potential formalisation of knowledge in the three fields. If the environmental conditions are stable, as for clerical work, formal rules for the execution of tasks can be explicated. A constantly changing environment, however, requires a lot of expertise to make successful decisions. Formalisation of such expertise is possible only to a very limited extent.[140] Even if formalisation succeeds, the permanent semantic change requires frequent 'repairs' of the formal system to be consistent with the underlying real world.[141]

It is very unlikely that formal systems based on artificial intelligence will match the capabilities of the human mind within the next few decades.[142] Instead, human skills and computer potentials can be combined in a reasonable manner. Taking Simon's work as his starting point, Langlois (2003) analyses the comparative advantages of humans and computers for certain tasks. Humans have advantages in accomplishing tasks requiring problem-solving activities or perceptual-motor activities. Computers are better suited for tasks that are predictable, repetitive sequences of activities, or potentially complex and well-structured calculations.[143] Placing these comparative advantages in relation to the three primary businesses of a firm yields Table 3.2.[144]

---

[139] See Simon (1965), pp. 98 & 110.

[140] See the discussion of explicit versus tacit knowledge. For an overview, see Fiedler (2004), pp. 44ff.

[141] See Franck (1991), p. 51.

[142] See Franck (1991), p. 230. In his general discussion of artificial intelligence, Franck (1991) concludes that no formal systems will ever completely substitute human experts.

[143] See Langlois (2003), p. 183.

[144] The three businesses were first described by Treacy/Wiersma (1993) and later by Hagel/Singer (1999).

Table 3.2: Activities in the Three Primary Businesses

	Product innovation	*Customer relations*	*Infrastructure*
Human			
Problem-solving activities	↑	→	↓
Perceptual-motor activities	↑	→	→
Computer			
Predictable, repetitive sequences of activities	→	→	↑
Complex, well-structured calculations	→	↓	↑

Activity is of low (↓), medium (→), or high (↑) importance for this business

This shows a clear comparative advantage for computers in the infrastructure business, which comprises, for instance, order-processing, logistics, storage, manufacturing and communications.[145] These are typical supply chain activities.[146] Indeed, Simon (1965) already predicted that the use of computers would lead to large savings through inventory reductions and the smoothing of production operations across organisational boundaries.[147]

Such an interorganisational information system (IOS) can be defined briefly as "… an automated information system shared by two or more companies."[148] Johnston/Vitale (1988) add:

"An IOS is built around information technology, i.e., around computer and communication technology, that facilitates the creation, storage, transformation and transmission of information. An IOS differs from an internal distributed information system by allowing information to be sent across organisational boundaries. Access to stored data and applications programs is shared, sometimes to varying degrees, by the participants in an IOS."[149]

---

[145] See Hagel/Singer (1999), p. 134.
[146] See Schary/Skjøtt-Larsen (2001), p. 23.
[147] See Simon (1965), p. 105.
[148] Cash/Konsynski (1985), p. 134.
[149] Johnston/Vitale (1988), p. 154.

As discussed above, organisational boundaries can often not be clearly drawn. For instance, an IS linking subsidiaries in a large multinational company has many of the properties of an IOS, as it also crosses organisational (e.g., business unit) boundaries. I propose to speak of an IOS whenever an IS supports an IO relationship as defined in section 3.1.

Although IOS have been attracting a lot of attention since the rise of the Internet, research on IOS is rooted in the 1960s. For instance, Mertens (1966) conducted comprehensive research on automated data-processing in IO relationships.[150] In the same year, Kaufman (1966) discussed the impacts of IOS on organisations, competition, and policymaking:

> "We are now witnessing the prospective development of systems broad enough to cut across company boundaries. Obviously, such systems can have a profound impact on the way business and commerce are conducted."[151]

The rapid improvement of computer hardware and software in the following decades led to a wide use of very diverse types of IS used in IO relationships: computer-supported cooperative work (CSCW) systems, customer-relationship management (CRM) systems, electronic data interchange (EDI), electronic mail, electronic markets, instant messaging, supply chain management (SCM) systems, Web Services, and Web sites.[152] Table 3.3 gives an overview of dimensions useful for classifying different IOS types.

This study focuses on IOS for SCM. These support vertical role linkage on an operational and strategic level, frequently execute structured tasks, use standard specifications, are based on asynchronous or synchronous machine-to-machine communication, enable at least application-to-application coupling, and automate communication up to a pragmatic level.[153] This excludes CSCW systems (unstructured content, human-to-human, and syntactic layer), CRM (human-to-machine, mostly syntactic layer), electronic mail (unstructured content, human-to-human, and syntactic layer), instant messaging (unstructured content, human-to-human, and syntactic layer), and Web sites (mostly singular, human-to-machine, and syntactic layer).

---

[150] See Mertens (1966).

[151] Kaufman (1966), p. 141.

[152] See, e.g., Hagel (2002), Paulen/Yoong (2001), and Bakos (1991).

[153] In the following work, the term IOS is only used for systems with these characteristics.

Table 3.3: Characteristics of Interorganisational Information System Types

Dimension	Characteristic			Source
Role linkage	Horizontal	Vertical		Hong (2002)
System support level	Operational support	Strategic support		Hong (2002)
Frequency	Singular	Repeated		Zollo et al. (2002)
Task type	Unstructured	Structured		Gorry/Scott Morton (1971)
Specification	Proprietary	Standard		Hart/Saunders (1998)
Human/machine involvement	Human-to-human	Human-to-machine	Machine-to-machine	Reimers (2001)
Interaction mode	Asynchronous	Synchronous		Paulen/Yoong (2001)
Coupling depth	File-to-file	Application-to-Application	Coupled work environment	Massetti/Zmud (1996)
Semiotic layer	Syntactic	Semantic	Pragmatic	Killian et al. (1994), pp. 42.

Typical SCM mechanisms are:

– Available-to-Promise: Offering precise information to customers about price and availability of products.[154]
– Collaborative Forecasting: Customer and supplier jointly forecast the demand for supplied parts.[155]
– Efficient Consumer Response: Suppliers replenish products at the point of sale as soon as a certain amount is sold.[156]
– Mass Customisation: A product is produced only after a customer has configured and ordered it.[157]

---

[154] See Bowersox/Closs/Cooper (2002), p. 257.
[155] See Schary/Skjøtt-Larsen (2001), pp. 339ff.
[156] See Schary/Skjøtt-Larsen (2001), pp. 335ff.

Especially for large companies with many suppliers it is almost impossible to use such mechanisms based on manual work alone. They have to rely on highly automated IOS, which are still in most cases electronic data interchange (EDI) systems.

3.2.2   Electronic Data Interchange Systems

Four features classify an IOS as an EDI system:

"1. It must have *at least two organisations* in a business relationship as users;

2. Data processing tasks pertaining to a transaction at both (all) organisations must be supported by *independent application systems*; (This property is unique to EDI; other IOSs are based on a single application system that is used by multiple users.)

3. The integrity of the data exchange between application systems of trading partners must be guaranteed by *agreements concerning data coding and formatting rules*; and

4. Data exchange between the application systems must be accomplished via *telecommunication links.*"[158]

Agreements on data coding and formatting play a crucial role, as they determine the compatibility and implementation time of an IOS. If these agreements are not specific to one particular EDI implementation, but are developed and maintained by a standards development organisation (SDO) and have a broad adoption, one usually speaks of EDI standards.[159] The most important EDI standard is the Electronic Data Interchange for Administration, Commerce and Transport (EDIFACT) standard, coordinated by the United Nations Economic Commission for Europe (UNECE). This is an international standard focusing on transactional documents independent of any industry.[160] 'Subsets' are adaptations of EDIFACT for certain industries, such as EDIFICE for the electronics industry and

---

[157] See Schary/Skjøtt-Larsen (2001), pp. 326ff. For a comprehensive discussion, see Piller (2000).

[158] Iacovou/Benbasat/Dexter (1995), p. 466, including original emphasis and based on Pfeiffer (1992), p. 18.

[159] See chapter 4 for the discussion of standards.

[160] See Neuburger (1994), p. 22.

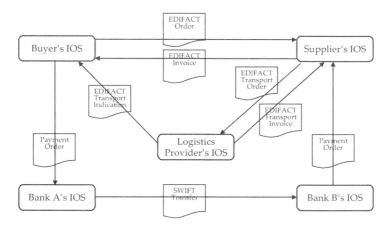

Figure 3.3: Order Processing with EDI[162]

ODETTE for the car industry. Some industries also use independent standards, such as SWIFT in the financial industry.[161]

Figure 3.3 illustrates how EDI enables the complete electronic processing of an order between a buyer and a supplier, a logistics provider and two banks. As a result, no manual tasks or physical document exchange are needed, except for the actual transport of the ordered products.

The roots of EDI go back to the 1960s. As the US transportation industry suffered from vast amounts of unstructured paper documents, it developed the first solutions for transferring documents electronically. Later in 1975, the Transportation Data Coordination Committee (TDCC) published the first EDI standard.[163] Although many different EDI standards emerged, ANSI and the Data Interchange Standards Association (DISA) managed to establish ASC X12 as the preferred, industry-independent EDI standard in the US. In Europe, EDIFACT and several industry-specific subsets dominate. While ANSI and UNECE jointly aimed to push through EDIFACT as the only global EDI standard, many different EDI specifications are still in use.[164]

---

[161] See Niggl (1994) for a further discussion of EDI standards.

[162] Slightly adapted from Killian/Picot/Neuburger, et al. (1994), p. 49.

[163] See Wigand (1994), p. 376.

[164] See Killian/Picot/Neuburger, et al. (1994), p. 263.

Besides the fragmentation of EDI standards, the cautious adoption of them by small and medium-sized enterprise (SMEs) is also an unresolved drawback of EDI. For example, in a survey of German firms, 36% of the respondents had no knowledge of EDI, of which 88% were SMEs, even though SMEs only represented 60% of all companies responding.[165] A more recent study reveals that the three main obstacles to SMEs using EDI are high personnel costs (few experts available), high operations costs (use of 'value added networks' (VANs) often required), and high setup costs (specific software and converters needed).[166] Several initiatives have tried to counter these problems, such as the Open-edi specification of the International Organisation for Standardisation (ISO).[167] Moreover, the broad adoption of Internet and Web technologies promises to foster EDI adoption by SMEs. Indeed, approaches such as AS2, ebXML, RosettaNet and Web Services aim at the migration of the concept of EDI to the Internet. Experts expect these Web-based successors to EDI to drive out the 'classic' EDI based on EDIFACT and similar standards within the next decade.[168]

Nevertheless, EDI has a large installed base, which is still growing in traditional standards and VANs too.[169] For example, even Amazon, an enterprise 'born' on the Web, relies on EDIFACT to exchange business data with partners.[170] Thus, EDI can still be seen as the backbone of today's interorganisational electronic business. Kanakamedala et al. (2003) assessed the volume of EDI-based business transactions to be more than two trillion US$ for the year 2001.[171] Moreover, case studies show the economic significance of EDI. For instance, Teo et al. (1997) analyse the huge impacts of EDI use on Singapore's TradeNet platform. Some also stress the important role EDI has played in the strong economic growth of Singapore in the recent decades.[172] As this work is focused on interorganisational standards

---

[165] See Killian/Picot/Neuburger, et al. (1994), p. 235.

[166] See Weitzel (2004), p. 177.

[167] See ISO/IEC (1997).

[168] See Broy/Hegering/Picot, et al. (2003), pp. 207 and 297.

[169] See Threlkel/Kavan (1999) and Sliwa (2004) and recent interviews with EDI consultants and users.

[170] E.g., book purchases at Amazon Germany reveal the text EDIFACT on bank statements.

[171] See Kanakamedala/King/Ramsdell (2003), p. 9.

[172] See Neo (1994) and Brenner/Neo (1997).

used in interorganisational relationships, it cannot ignore the importance of EDI. Therefore, the next section first reviews the results of existing EDI research, followed by recent research on the currently emerging Web-based IOS.

3.3   Research on Interorganisational Information Systems

Many IS researchers "… believe that EDI systems (or IOS in general) affect the very nature of competition between suppliers."[173] A great deal of IS management research on EDI is thus available. Elgarah et al. (2005) give an overview of 68 research articles published from 1993 to 2002. The next paragraphs will briefly summarise the main aspects of their review. As an analytical framework they use four conceptual lenses: causal agency, transaction cost economics, interorganisational (IO) relationship motives, and IO relationship typology.[174] Furthermore, they classify the papers by underlying epistemology, research approach, and the time span of data collection.[175]

Classified by transaction arrangements, 49% of the reviewed papers analyse EDI in market-like IO relationships, 44% in hybrids, and 7% in hierarchies. Efficiency dominates as a main motive for EDI use in 97% of all articles. While 47% deal with dyadic IO relationships, 31% are concerned with sets, and 22% with networks. The main research topic areas are the impacts of EDI (57%), its use (38%), and its adoption (21%). Further topics such as power, risk, strategy or trust are special aspects of these three. Similar to other IS research fields, 90% of the articles are based on positivist, 7% on interpretive, and 3% on critical epistemology.[176] The applied research methods are surveys (50%), case studies (26%), conceptual work (18%), and phenomenology (5%). Finally, Elgarah et al. (2005) also checked for the underlying theories. While 20% use diffusion of innovation, 16% transaction cost economics, and 7% organisation theory, almost half of the papers do not rely on any well-established theories. One reason

---

[173] See Barua/Lee (1997), p. 401.

[174] See Elgarah/Falaleeva/Saunders, et al. (2005), p. 10.

[175] See Elgarah/Falaleeva/Saunders, et al. (2005), p. 6.

[176] See the discussion in section 2.1. Very technical papers are excluded from the review (Elgarah/Falaleeva/Saunders, et al. (2005), p. 20.)

might be the lack of genuine theories on IS-based innovations such as EDI. Overall, Elgarah et al. (2005) identify a stable and consistent body of EDI literature. They also note, however, that IS research largely neglected the shift towards Web-based IOS and the development of the standards needed.[177] Thus, subsection 3.3.1 first derives an IOS management framework, which summarises the core insights of existing EDI research. Then it reviews recent contributions that extend these insights to Web-based IOS. Based on the few works already available, subsection 3.3.2 discusses the existing insights into the development of interorganisational standards and refines the gap in research that the rest of this study is targeting.

3.3.1 Review of the Literature on the Management of IOS

This subsection gives a review of the existing literature on the management of interorganisational information systems and the standards required. The first part is focused on the large body of EDI-based research, while the second adds insights from the recent work on Web-based IOS.

IOS Management Framework Based on EDI Research

To summarise the main insights of the existing body of research, I have derived a general framework for the management of IOS using concepts and causal links as described in the relevant literature. As the review by Elgarah et al. (2005) is primarily concerned with the approaches and main topics of EDI research, it does not analyse the concepts of the papers in greater detail. Most of the research contributions cover the benefits, followed by the use, and the adoption of EDI systems.[178] These topics represent the main phases of IOS deployment in organisations:

– In the adoption phase, participants have to decide whether and how to use an IOS.
– In the use phase, organisational changes are made, the IOS is set up and is used for day-to-day business.
– In the impact phase, participants receive the benefits and shortcomings of IOS use.

---

[177] See Elgarah/Falaleeva/Saunders, et al. (2005), p. 20. See also Gebauer/Shaw (2002).
[178] See Elgarah/Falaleeva/Saunders, et al. (2005), pp. 14.

These three phases form the core of the framework, which is similar to those of several other authors.[179] So far, it is very generic, as it could be applied to management research on almost any new technology. I thus further refine it on the basis of 43 research works on EDI. In order to synthesise the causal relations and statements of the works considered, I classify their main concepts in terms of three phases. Clustering related concepts and consolidating their descriptions yields the three tables shown in appendix B. Figure 3.4 depicts the whole framework based on these tables. In the following subsections, I will describe each phase and the respective concepts.

The implementation and use of IOS usually requires considerable organisational change. To justify the efforts, a firm needs convincing reasons for the decision to *adopt* a new IOS. The adoption phase comprises all aspects influencing the top management decision whether and how to implement and use an IOS.[180] Iacovou et al. (1995) posit a parsimonious adoption model comprising the main concepts 'external pressure', 'organisational readiness', and 'perceived benefits'.[181] Several authors apply this adoption model to their research on IOS.[182] As 'external pressure' often comprises many factors, I propose to split it up into 'environmental conditions' and 'interorganisational relations'. *Environmental conditions* refer to competitive pressure and uncertainty, while *interorganisational relationships* are characterised by the specificity of employed assets, power influence and trust between the participants. The *organisational readiness* for IOS adoption can best be explained by the size of an organisation, the top management support, the flexibility of an organisation, the formalisation of routine tasks, and the compatibility of existing IS infrastructure. The *Perceived advantages* result from comparing the perceived costs and the perceived benefits of the IOS being considered (see Figure 3.4).

---

[179] See Iacovou/Benbasat/Dexter (1995), p. 467, Bergeron/Raymond (1997), p. 321, Peffers/Dos Santos/Thurner (1998), Maingot/Quon (2001), p. 319, and Lim/Palvia (2001), p. 197.

[180] See Cooper/Zmud (1990), p. 124.

[181] See Iacovou/Benbasat/Dexter (1995), p. 480.

[182] See Chwelos/Benbasat/Dexter (2001), Premkumar/Ramamurthy (1995), Crook/Kumar (1998), Ramamurthy/Premkumar/Crum (1999).

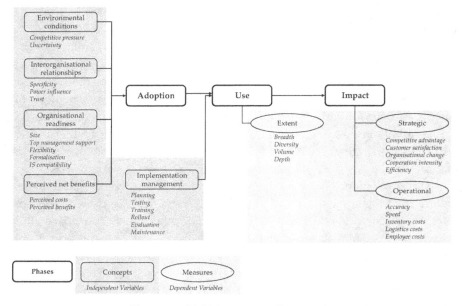

Figure 3.4: IOS Management Framework

All these factors influence the decision to adopt an IOS. The empirical significance varies according to the survey in question. The repeated use of these factors during a decade of EDI surveys indicates a robust explanatory power. Remarkably, in these surveys the installed base of EDI systems seems to have no critical role in the decision to adopt.[183] A possible explanation is that the frequent need for specific adaptations of EDI systems lowers their network externalities more than in the case of typical network products, which can be used without modifications. The direct value of connecting one partner via EDI might be much higher than the potential of connecting further partners. Subsection 4.3.1 further discusses the network externalities of standard-based products.

After a positive top management decision to adopt an EDI-based IOS, middle management has to execute its implementation and its *use* by employees. The use phase comprises all aspects concerning the necessary organisational change, the selection and set-up of the IOS, and its use on a daily basis. In a longitudinal study, Bergeron/Raymond (1997) examine the importance of planning, testing and evaluation for successful implementa-

---

[183] See also Killian/Picot/Neuburger, et al. (1994), p. 262.

tion management.[184] As with other projects, convincing and training employees plays an especially crucial role in implementation success.[185] Adding rollout and maintenance, the process of *implementation management* comprises planning, testing, training, rollout, evaluation and maintenance. Though these seem to be identical to other IS implementation projects, the involvement of employees from at least two companies adds further complexity, which is typical of IOS projects.[186]

On the basis of seven case studies, Massetti/Zmud (1996) posit four concepts for measuring the *extent* of IOS use: breadth, diversity, volume and depth.[187] Breadth represents the number of external partners linked via IOS in relation to all external partners. Diversity is the number of different document types exchanged via IOS in relation to all document types exchanged with external partners. Volume is the number of all documents of a certain document type exchanged via IOS in relation to all documents of a certain document type exchanged with external partners. Depth is the degree of coupling of IOS with internal systems. Massetti/Zmud (1996) propose the grades 'file-to-file', 'application-to-application', and 'coupled work environment'.[188] Several further EDI researchers use some or all of these concepts, though sometimes termed differently.[189]

Naturally, the use of an IOS has *impacts* on the participating firms. Most of the available EDI research considers the aspects of the benefits and shortcomings it has for the organisations using it.[190] On a firm level, researchers use many different measures for IOS impact.[191] A distinction between strategic and operational impacts is often drawn.[192] The main *strategic impacts* of an IOS affect competitive advantage, customer satisfac-

---

[184] See Bergeron/Raymond (1997).

[185] See Maingot/Quon (2001).

[186] See the definition of EDI in section 3.2 that stresses the existence of two IS in different organisations.

[187] See Massetti/Zmud (1996).

[188] See Massetti/Zmud (1996), p. 340.

[189] See Truman (2000), Son/Narasimhan/Riggins (1999), Hart/Saunders (1998); different terms have been used by Williams/Magee/Suzuki (1998).

[190] See Elgarah/Falaleeva/Saunders, et al. (2005), p. 16. Thirty-nine (57%) of the reviewed papers fall into this category.

[191] See appendix B for a comprehensive overview of 22 research works.

[192] See, e.g., Fearon/Philip (1999), p. 7, Iacovou/Benbasat/Dexter (1995), p. 469, and Niggl (1994), p. 60.

tion, cooperation intensity, organisational change and efficiency. The concept of the efficiency of the strategic perspective can be refined on an operational level. The most important *operational impacts* are accuracy, speed, inventory costs, logistics costs and employee costs. Once more, these measures emphasise the importance of IOS for supply chain management.

IS Research on Web-Based Interorganisational Information Systems

The literature considered for the IOS management framework only analysed EDI-based IOS. Since the mid-1990s, however, the Internet and accompanying Web technologies have emerged offering new approaches for the coupling of IOS. There are two main differences with respect to EDI. First, a Web-based IOS uses the public Internet infrastructure to transfer data between organisations, instead of proprietary VANs. Second, the Web-based architecture permits a modular approach not limited to document exchange as with EDI, but also including other automated mechanisms such as discovery, agreements and process integration.[193] XML and Web Services standards in particular have been attracting significant attention from practitioners, which is resulting in many technically oriented publications,[194] while there has been a certain delay in IS research regarding these developments.[195] Although there has been some progress made recently, the many different names used for the same standardisation efforts even within the same conference proceedings reflect the early stage of this research field (see Table 3.4).

---

[193] For a more detailed discussion see section 5.1.

[194] A search on Amazon.com in January 2004 retrieved about 300 English books with the term 'Web Services' in the title.

[195] See Gebauer/Shaw (2002).

Table 3.4: Different Names for Interorganisational Standards[196]

Name	Examples	Source
"Interorganisational System Standards and Process Innovations"	HR-XML, PIDX, RosettaNet	Nelson/Shaw (2003)
"Open E-Business Standards"	ebXML, Rosetta-Net	Xia et al. (2003)
"Standards for Domain-Specific Interoperability"	ebXML, HL7	Stegwee/Rukanova (2003)
"Vertical Industry Languages"	ACORD, ebXML, HL7, HR-XML	Jain/Zhao (2003)
"Vertical IS Standards"	RosettaNet, CIDX, MISMO	Markus et al. (2003)
"XML-Based E-Business Frameworks"	ebXML, Rosetta-Net, xCBL	Kotinurmi et al. (2003)
"XML-Based E-Business Standards"	ebXML, Rosetta-Net, UBL, xCBL	Graham et al. (2003)

In this study, I will use the term 'interorganisational standard' (abbreviated as IO standard), as this is not limited to XML/Web technologies or vertical industries, but also includes organisational aspects such as process and agreement standards. When adding 'Web-based', I am explicitly excluding EDI standards, which otherwise also belong to interorganisational standards (see Figure 3.5). The same holds for the use of the term interorganisational information systems (IOS).

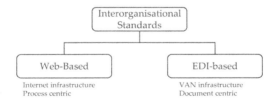

Figure 3.5: Relation of Web-Based and EDI-Based Interorganisational Standards

---

[196] All from King/Lyytinen (2003).

Table 3.5 lists IS research contributions on Web-based IOS including the main topics and the IOS phases covered, as described in the IOS management framework . Without discussing all the sources in detail, it can be noted that very different aspects of Web-based IOS and IO standards have recently attracted increasing attention from IS researchers. However, this is still at an early stage, as most of the sources are taken from conference proceedings, because only a few works have already been published in scholarly IS journals or as books.[197] Without devaluing other sources, I will discuss two exemplary works.

Table 3.5: Research on Web-Based Interorganisational Standards

Source	Main Topic	Phases
Albrecht et al. (2003)	Comparison of EDI, Web sites, B2B hubs, e-procurement, Web Services	Adoption, Use
Beimborn et al. (2002)	Comparison of ebXML and Web Services	Adoption, Use
Chen (2003)	Three groups of adoption factors: stakeholders, organisation, standards characteristics	Adoption
Downing (2002)	Comparison of EDI- and Web-based IOS performance	Impact
Frank (2001)	Comparison of BMEcat, CPFR, cXML, ebXML, OAGIS, OBI, RosettaNet, and xCBL	Adoption, Use
Gosain (2003)	Three strategies for dealing with imperfect IO standards: bridge dependencies, minimise dependencies, or maximise adaptation	Use
Hagel (2002)	Strategies for using Web Services for loosely coupled firm networks	Use, Impact
Haines (2003)	Four types of Web Services adoption levels: external technical solution, internal IS solution, internal business solution, external business solution	Adoption
Iyer et al. (2003)	Web Services permit quick finding, use and combination of resources, but with little guaranteed performance	Use, Impact

---

[197] The large amount of practitioner books focusing on the technical use of IO standards are excluded. Two examples are Glass (2002) and Hauser/Löwer (2004)

Table 3.5 (continued): Research on Web-Based Interorganisational Standards

Source	Main Topic	Phases
Jain/Zhao (2003)	Concepts for comparing IO standards: competition, customer pressure, need for cooperation, need for automation, dominant players, history of standardisation, governmental regulation, standardisation practice	Adoption, Use
Kotinurmi et al. (2003)	The 'classic' economics of standards mechanisms 'free-rider', 'network externalities', and 'standards control' work differently for IO standards	Adoption
Kotok/Webber (2002)	Use of ebXML from business perspective	Adoption, Use
Lim/Wen (2003)	Threat of incompatibility of semantics and process IO standards	Use, Impact
Löwer/Picot (2002)	Web Services analysis from transaction cost and resource-based perspective	Use
Nelson/Shaw (2003)	Hypothesis testing via a comprehensive IO standards adoption and diffusion model	Adoption, Use, Impact
Patankar (2003)	Need for further Web Services specifications for complex interorganisational processes	Use
Ratnasin-gam/Pavlou (2002)	Trust in Web Services specifications	Use, Impact
Singh et al. (2003)	Knowledge exchange using domain ontologies, Web Services and software agents	Use
Steg-wee/Rukanova (2003)	Typology of IO standards	Adoption, Use
Stiemerling (2002)	Web Services for component-based, evolvable IS	Use

The first notable contribution is Frank (2001), as it is one of the first journal publications on Web-based IO standards. Although most of them were not very mature at the time, he assesses the initiatives BMEcat, Collaborative Planning, Forecasting, and Replenishment (CPFR), cXML, ebXML, Open Application Integration Specification (OAGIS), Open Buying on the Internet (OBI), RosettaNet and xCBL. Today OBI no longer exists, while cXML is losing significance because it is a proprietary specification of Ariba. Analysing the technical architecture of the specifications, Frank (2001) notes that most have challenging visions, but often use outdated architectures to achieve them. This is where IS/WI research should engage, as it already offers superior methods, such as first modelling the business processes, then deriving information models, and finally defining the interface specifications. Moreover, Frank (2001) expects the increasing interest in ontology modelling to strengthen such advanced architectures and methods in the future. Although the different initiatives were difficult to compare because of their different goals, Frank (2001) juxtaposes them in terms of several criteria. He concludes that xCBL was the most advanced approach at that time, but with the disadvantage of having been controlled by the software vendor Commerce One. Today, the xCBL approach is continued in UBL at OASIS, while Commerce One went bankrupt in November 2004 and shut down the Web resources on xCBL.[198]

Nelson/Shaw (2003) offer a comprehensive research contribution that deserves a more detailed analysis. It aims at "the need for bridging the research gap between prior studies in IOS adoption and diffusion (based predominantly on EDI technology) versus modern-day IOS solutions."[199] On the basis of the large stream of EDI research literature and an exploratory analysis of RosettaNet,[200] they develop a conceptual model to test eight hypotheses on the adoption and diffusion of interorganisational standards. The empirical sample consists of questionnaires from 102 firms in 10 industries, including 15 industry-based standards development organisations (SDOs) such as papiNET, PIDX and RosettaNet. The model comprises four groups of independent variables:

- Organisation Readiness: Top Management Support, Feasibility, Technology Conversion
- External Environment: Competitive Pressure, Participation Level in SDO
- Innovation Attributes: Relative Advantage, Compatibility, Shared Business Process
- Standards Development Organisation: Management Practices, Architecture, Governance

---

[198] See subsection 5.3.2. This case already illustrates the importance of an SDO's reliability.

[199] Nelson/Shaw (2003), p. 259.

[200] See Nelson (2002).

Dependent variables are *adoption* (using/not using standards) and *use* (volume, diversity, breadth).[201] Moreover, direct (financial, operational) and indirect (loyalty, entry barriers) *impacts* are also measured. Although developed independently, the model has many similarities to the IOS management framework I sketched above. Especially noteworthy is the addition of the SDO variables, which indicates that SDOs were neglected before, but are gaining importance. Table 3.6 gives an overview of the tested hypotheses and the results.

Table 3.6: Nelson/Shaw's Hypotheses Results[202]

Organisational Readiness attributes will have a positive (and significant) relationship with Adoption.	Supported
Organisational Readiness attributes will have a positive (and significant) relationship with Use.	Partial support (w.r.t. Feasibility)
External Environment attributes will have a positive (and significant) relationship with Adoption.	Supported
External Environment attributes will have a positive relationship with the external Use. Participation Levels in an SDO will have significant relationship towards Use.	Supported (and Competitive Pressure is significant)
SDO attributes will have a positive relationship with Adoption. Governance and Architecture will also have a significant relationship towards Adoption.	Partial support (w.r.t. Architecture)
Innovation attributes will have a positive relationship with Adoption. Relative Advantage and/or Shared Business Process attributes will also have a significant relationship towards Adoption.	Not supported
SDO attributes will have a positive (and significant) relationship with Use.	Partial support (w.r.t. Architecture). Governance was significant, but negative
Innovation attributes will have a positive (and significant) relationship with Use.	Partial support (w.r.t. Compatibility and Shared Business Process).

---

[201] See Massetti/Zmud (1996), pp. 335ff.

[202] See Nelson/Nelson (2003), p. 281. Some expressions adapted (e.g., deployment→use), variables with first letter capitalised.

Without discussing these results in detail, two counterintuitive findings should be noted here. First, it is surprising that the innovation attributes (including items such as direct benefits and compatibility with existing IS) have no positive relationship with adoption. Nelson/Shaw (2003) try to explain this result in terms of other factors such as competitive pressure inducing top management to decide on adoption. Second, SDO governance is negatively related with use. The fact that firms using the standards very intensively disagree with the SDO governance more often than others might account for this.

They also stress the finding that most standards-based IOS result in significant benefits for the user firms. Moreover, the SDOs clearly play a pivotal role in the development and adoption of such specifications. Nelson/Shaw (2003) conclude their work with recommendations for further research. First, they propose the inclusion of the new variables 'SDO Governance', 'Architecture', 'SDO Management Practices' and 'Technology Conversion' in future IOS diffusion studies. Second, further understanding of SDOs and their specifications is needed. Finally, they identify two major management challenges for SDOs: horizontal convergence and the versioning of specifications. In short, they propose further research on the coordination of interorganisational standards development. As this is the main topic of this study, the next subsection reviews the already existing IS research on it.

3.3.2   Lacking Research on the Development of Interorganisational Standards

This subsection briefly reviews the few available works on the development of EDI-based IO standards, before discussing recent contributions to the development of Web-based IO standards and sketching the existing research gaps.

Research on the Development of EDI-based IO Standards

Most IS researchers assume EDI standards to be exogenously given facts that cannot be influenced by adopters.[203] While consumers, for example,

---

[203] See the discussion in Hanseth/Monteiro (1997). One example is Buxmann (1996), p. 8, who develops an economic model for decisions on standard adoption including EDI,

usually cannot directly change the standards used for Internet access or mobile phones, this is not necessarily the case with IO standards. On the contrary, many standards used in IOS were originally developed by the user firms and then submitted to SDOs such as ANSI or UN/CEFACT. Killian et al. (1994) thus propose a distinction between the two phases 'development' and 'adoption', as both have very different characteristics and implications for management.[204] Although development also comes directly within the focus of IS research, it was largely neglected until recently.[205] One reason for this might be the difficulties in grasping standards development with positivist research methods, which dominate in the IS field.[206]

To my knowledge, only a few scholarly works have investigated the development of EDI standards from a managerial perspective. One is Niggl (1994), who analyses factors influencing different approaches to the development of EDI standards. He also describes the UN/EDIFACT structure and development process at that time.[207] Another contribution of note is Reimers (1995). Using transaction cost theory, Reimers (1995) argues that IOS standards are institutions that lower transaction costs in economic markets.[208] Graham et al. (1995) use actor-network theory to explore the development of EDI specifications within ANSI and UNECE. They reveal a significant difference between the two organisations, as ANSI's ASC X12 involved mainly user companies, while official representatives from different nations dominate EDIFACT. Despite both organisations' desire to cooperate, Graham et al. (1995) predict that there will always be a different mentality in both, in turn reflected in the different results of ASC X12 and EDIFACT. Hanseth/Monteiro (1997) analyse the development of an IO standard for the health care sector in Norway based on EDIFACT. They state that most participants have high expectations regarding the benefits, while largely underestimating the complexity of developing such an IO

---

assuming a given set of standards from which the actors have to chose the best alternative.

[204] Killian/Picot/Neuburger, et al. (1994), pp. 64ff.

[205] See King/Lyytinen (2003), p. iii.

[206] See the discussion in section 2.1.

[207] See Niggl (1994), pp. 83ff.

[208] See the discussion in subsection 4.3.2.

standard. Hanseth/Monteiro (1997) also use actor-network theory to describe and get a better understanding of this complexity.[209]

Although most EDI standards were originally developed by user firms, quasi-governmental organisations such as ANSI and UNECE have aimed at unifying the dispersed standards. EDIFACT is an EDI standard that covers requirements from many industries. Still, many domains use specialised EDIFACT subsets (e.g., ODETTE for the car industry) or even independent EDI standards (e.g., VDA, also for the car industry).[210] At the beginning of this chapter, I describe the phenomenon of modular products causing the modularisation of supply chain networks. In a similar way, Web-based technologies for modular standards also change the shape of the standards producing 'industry', resulting in even more specialised, but highly interwoven SDOs. Only recently have IS researchers started to pay more attention to these important changes.

Increasing Interest in the Development of Web-based IO Standards

The first major research effort on this topic was a workshop at the International Conference on Information Systems in December 2003, titled "Standard Making: A Critical Research Frontier for Information Systems".[211] The editors King and Lyytinen state in their call for papers:

> "As important as this topic is, there have been relatively few scholarly papers on standardisation informing the scholarly discussion in the IS field. Slightly more than 2% of the published journal articles in the IS field have dealt with standards over the past 10 years, and most of this work has reported on newly established ICT standards rather than examining the processes and importance of standard setting processes. Notably absent are studies that analyse different standardisation concepts, standardisation processes, industrial coordination and strategy, and economics of standards."[212]

While several contributions to this workshop analyse other standards, 12 papers are concerned with IO standards, of which five focus fully on development (see Table 3.7).[213]

---

[209] See the discussion of their contribution in subsection 4.5.3

[210] See Killian/Picot/Neuburger, et al. (1994), p. 267.

[211] See King/Lyytinen (2003).

[212] King/Lyytinen (2003).

[213] The other seven papers are concerned with adoption, use and/or impact and thus listed in Table 3.5 of the previous subsection.

Table 3.7: Research on Development of Web-Based IO Standards

Source	Theories/Method	Standards (Mentioned) [214]	Main Insights
Graham et al. (2003)	Social construction, new institutional theory/ Case study	UBL, (cXML, ebXML, EDI-FACT, HL7, OAGIS, Rosetta-Net, SOAP, UDDI, WSDL, xCBL)	Contributions of participants are critical; development is complex and dynamic. SDOs have to improve their organisation. Standards force isomorphism of firm boundaries
Markus et al. (2003)	Case study	MISMO, (CIDX, RosettaNet)	Standards development and setting is a highly complex process. Still much work to be done to integrate theoretical and empirical literature with the case phenomena
Nickerson/zur Muehlen (2003)	Actor-network theory, economic decision theory/ Case study	(BPEL, ebXML, SOAP, Wf-XML, WSDL, REST, …)	Model of standards processes, which are complex and have to be explored from multiple perspectives. Technical principles play an important role, similar to open source communities
Reimers (2001)	Case study	ebXML, Rosetta-Net, (ASC X12, EDIFACT)	SDOs with new institutional arrangements required
Virili (2003)	Design theory, sense-making theory, actor-network theory/ Case study	SOAP, WSDL	D-S-N model consisting of Design, Sense-making, and Negotiation seems to be useful for explaining complex IO standards development
Xia et al. (2003)	Economics of standards/ Game-theoretic model	RosettaNet, (ebXML)	Strong interaction between development and adoption makes previous research frameworks inapplicable. Three types of firms: active developers, following adopters, non-adopters.

---

[214] Standards in parentheses were mentioned, but not researched in more detail.

Besides these and Reimers (2001) (also in Table 3.7), I am not aware of any other IS research concerned with the development of Web-based IO standards.

The main insight of these works is that:

The development of IO standards is highly complex, as the adopting firms are often also participants in development, which renders existing economics of standard setting largely inapplicable.

Some authors thus propose new ways to approach this topic. I will discuss two such contributions in more detail. The first is Xia et al. (2003), who offer an attempt to extend the economics of standards to the characteristics of IO standards. Second, Nickerson/zur Muehlen (2003) analyse the important role of technical and social aspects in the development of IO standards.

Xia et al. (2003): "Open E-Business Standard Development and Adoption"

The authors see three special characteristics of IO standards compared to 'traditional' standards:

– The developing firms are mainly also the adopters of the specifications. In traditional economics of standards, creators and users of standards are separate actors.
– The development is extremely interactive, with many iterative development cycles. In traditional economics of standards, standards are usually assumed to be exogenously developed.
– The development cannot be done by a single firm, as developing costs are very high due to the enormous scope of such standards while the certainty of adoption is relatively low. The traditional economics of standards usually considers the case of separate firms trying to establish their standards.

The existing economics of standards cannot simply be transferred to IO standards, therefore, and Xia et al. (2003) aim to provide the modifications required. In IO standardisation, firms have three basic options:

– Joining the development of specifications
– Only adopting the specifications
– Not joining or adopting at all

A short overview of RosettaNet reveals that a consortium can further differentiate the first option by providing different levels of development participation. Next, Xia et al. (2003) pursue three research questions:

- What kind of companies are likely candidates to be leading developers and which ones are expected to be following adopters in an IO standards-setting process?
- For firms that choose to be developers, how much effort will each firm invest in the process of standards development?
- How to induce the incentive for firms to participate in the standardisation process of IO standards so as to maximise the total value of the standards?

As in economics of standards, they assume positive network externalities of IO standard adoption. Further, these are linked to development:

> "The size of the adopter network will determine the developers' payoff, which serves as a determining factor for firms' decision to join the developer network. On the other hand, the developer network also has impacts on the adopter network formed later. The quality of the standards is an increasing function of the overall effort level in the developer network. It will influence firms' adoption decisions, which in turn determines the size of the adopter network."[215]

Based on these and several other assumptions, Xia et al. (2003) form a three-stage, game-theoretical model, for which they compute the equilibria using backward induction. For example, they assume that

Net benefit for developer =
Insider factor * direct benefit + network externalities + quality
– development costs – adoption costs.

'Direct benefit' is the benefit of using an IO standard without considering the benefits from 'network externalities'.[216] The 'insider factor' indicates the benefit of participating in the development of an IO standard, while 'development costs' are the costs of participating. 'Quality' is the quality of the IO standard itself and 'adoption costs' the costs of adopting the standard. As a first step, the size of the adopter network is determined. The resulting equation leads to

---

[215] Xia/Zhao/Shaw (2003), p. 225.

[216] For a detailed discussion of network externalities see section 4.3.

> "Proposition 1: The size of the adopter network is positively related with the network effect and the quality of the standards; however, it is negatively related with the adoption cost."[217]

Second, the optimal investment level in the developer network is induced, which leads to the following propositions:

> "Proposition 2.a: The optimal individual effort level of a developer firm is positively related with the network effect and the total number of firms interested in the forthcoming [interorganisational standard]. (...)
> Proposition 2.b: The individual valuation of the standards will not influence the optimal individual effort level."[218]

The latter proposition seems counterintuitive, but it is a result of the assumption of symmetric value for the developers. Finally, calculating the size of the developer network results in

> "Proposition 3.a: The size of the developer network is positively related with the insider effect and the network effect. (...)
> Proposition 3.b: If the firms in the developer network are myopic, the optimal effort level will be lower."[219]

With their model, Xia et al. (2003) can also "conceptually show the difference between the individual optimal investment level and the consortium optimal investment level."[220] Moreover, using propositions 3.a and 3.b they deduce two ways for a consortium to close the gap between these two levels. First, it can raise the 'insider effect' through clarifying the potential benefits and granting the developers more rights. Second, it can try to lower the 'myopia' of developers by clearly communicating the benefits of a future adopter network.

Xia et al. (2003) have built a formal economics model for interorganisational standards development. As with all formal models, they have to make some assumptions that can be seen as too strict, such as the assumption of symmetric value. Still, the insights and recommendations derived are of great value for further research on IO standards development. However, this formal analysis is unable to reveal, where the 'insider factor' comes from, as it does not explain the mechanisms of the actual standard

---

development processes. This is the goal of the next work under consideration.

Nickerson/zur Muehlen (2003): "Defending the Spirit of the Web"

The authors investigate in detail the standardisation process of Web Services choreography specifications.[221] These specifications add to the basic Web Services standards[222] the ability to conduct long-running business transactions. Their standardisation is an interesting case for studying competition among IO standards, as twelve specifications have already emerged and there is still no clear winner.[223]

To better explain the phenomenon of standardisation, Nickerson/zur Muehlen (2003) analyse the factors influencing the decision to participate in standards development. On the one hand, the individual beliefs and norms of the technical community and corporations have an effect on the actions. On the other hand, competing standards and standards bodies with their bylaws have an influence. Nickerson/zur Muehlen (2003) argue that these mechanisms can be studied from three perspectives: actor-networks, economic decisions and technical culture. While all three can serve for studying the development and adoption of interorganisational standards, economic game theories in particular "are more suited to the adoption than the development process."[224]

The main insight from the actor-network perspective on Web Services choreography standardisation is the frequent migration of actors between the different standards committees. Thus, many specification proposals that are backed, discussed and completed are never implemented and adopted. The movement patterns themselves, however, cannot be explained from this perspective.

Nickerson/zur Muehlen (2003) discover the main reason for this migration behaviour from the technical perspective: "The participants in technical standards committees often consider themselves architects."[225] Their designing expertise thus determines their aesthetic feelings as to when a

---

[221] One example of a Web Services choreography specification is BPEL.

[222] These are SOAP and WSDL; see subsection 5.1.1 for further discussion.

[223] E.g., some of the more importan initiatives resulted in the standards BPEL, BPSS, PIPs, and WS-CDL. See also the discussion in Hauser/Löwer (2004), pp. 162ff.

[224] Nickerson/zur Muehlen (2003), based on Fomin/Keil (2000).

[225] Nickerson/zur Muehlen (2003), p. 333.

specification design is appropriate for certain objectives or not. Nickerson/zur Muehlen (2003) argue that in several cases too many stakeholders contribute to Web Services choreography specifications, making them too complex. Hence, some contributors switch to other committees promising a more 'elegant' specification. The authors also compare the development of standards specifications to the development of open source software: "It may be the case that standards participants are similar – that their allegiance to a community of like-minded architects is greater than their allegiance to their sponsoring institution."[226]

The economic discussion by Nickerson/zur Muehlen (2003) is mainly from the developers perspective. First, there are the opinions and motivations of individual developers. Like open source software developers, many individual specification developers show a general aversion to large software companies. These are suspected of unnecessarily complicating specifications, as this increases the chance of selling more software and services. Further, the motivation for individuals to contribute to specifications development is very similar to that for the development of open source software. Not only monetary incentives have to be considered, but also ego satisfaction and reputation.

Second, Nickerson/zur Muehlen (2003) analyse strategies of corporate contributors. The entrance and switching barriers seem to play an important role. If conflicts of interest between the participants occur, it is relatively easy to leave a committee and form another. This leads to some competition between standards consortia, particularly W3C and OASIS.[227] Further, the low barriers allow vendors to diversify the risk of missing a successful standard by participating in several committees. For example, SAP contributes to five Web Services choreography committees: BPMI/BPML, OASIS/BPEL, RosettaNet/PIPs, WfMC/Wf-XML and W3C/WSCI.

Finally, Nickerson/zur Muehlen (2003) discuss the main drivers of standards consortia and distinguish between vendor-driven, user-driven, and research-driven. In Web Services choreography standardisation, they identify a clear dominance of software vendors, and ask whether a greater balance towards users and research institutions might result in more successful specifications. Though Nickerson/zur Muehlen (2003) do not inte-

---

[226] Nickerson/zur Muehlen (2003), p. 336.
[227] For a further discussion of OASIS see section 5.3.

grate their findings within a concise model, they illuminate several important social, technical and economic aspects of IO standards development processes.   .

Research Gaps

All the recent works on the development of IO standards underpin the importance of this topic, but also stress that the research is still at an early stage. While considerable progress has been made with these contributions, they also leave several research gaps:

- ebXML and RosettaNet are recognised as the most important initiatives in developing IO standards, but none of the works offers a comprehensive description and analysis of their activities.[228]
- Most works stress the importance of standards development organisations (SDOs) and their functions, while none gives a consistent picture of how these SDOs coordinate the contributions of their different participants.
- Thus, they derive only a few dispersed recommendations as to how different actors should ideally participate in IO standards development.
- Finally, several works cite actor-network theory (ANT) as a fruitful approach to analysing standardisation processes without giving a concise overview of this theory.[229]

This study is a major attempt to fill these gaps. After a thorough discussion of ANT, two comprehensive case studies on ebXML and RosettaNet are conducted. Both are analysed using ANT in order to derive a general model of IO standards development, which results in recommendations for different actors on how to participate in such initiatives.

---

[228] For instance, the papers in King/Lyytinen (2003) mention 26 specifications. The technical specifications SOAP and WSDL are both mentioned in ten of them and each is further analysed in 2 papers. The universal specifications of ebXML follow with 8 mentions and 1 analysis. Next are the sectoral specifications of RosettaNet (7/2), followed by UDDI (4/0), BPEL (3/1), UBL (3/1), CIDX (3/0), xCBL (2/1), and ANSI X12 (2/0).

[229] One exception is Hanseth/Monteiro (1997), which is discussed in subsection 4.5.3.

3.4 Summary and Conclusions

This chapter answered the first research question:

Why and how do information systems support interorganisational relationships?

Although interorganisational relationships are difficult to grasp, they are playing an increasing role especially in industries with modular products. Several dimensions help to characterise them, for example, their goals, directions, time horizon and formalisation. Various theories aim to explain interorganisational relationships, for instance, transaction cost theory and resource-dependence theory. This study focuses on supply chain networks, which are a certain type of interorganisational relationships relying heavily on information systems to coordinate resources across organisational boundaries.

These interorganisational information systems automate tasks to permit mechanisms that are manually not executable on a large scale, such as quickly gathering available-to-promise information from several supply chain participants. Until today, most interorganisational information systems have used EDI standards to transfer electronic business documents between independent information systems. Rooted in the 1960s, EDI has a long history and plays a critical role in today's global commerce, supporting the trade of goods and services worth several trillion US$ each year. Therefore, a large body of research is available on the adoption, use and impact of EDI.

An extensive review of this research literature results in a causal framework for the management of interorganisational information systems. It comprises independent variables categorised as environmental conditions, interorganisational relations, organisational readiness, perceived net benefits and implementation management. The dependent variables describe the use extent, and operational and strategic impacts. As Web-based technologies have been gaining in significance for interorganisational information systems in recent years, this chapter gives an overview of the available work on the subject and reviews two contributions in more detail. One uses a similar framework to the one derived above to test several hypotheses on the adoption and impact of Web-based interorganisational information systems. It also reveals the growing importance of standards development organisations, which has been largely neglected by researchers until recently.

Some works can be identified that analyse such standards development organisations, for both EDI- and Web-based standards. These mainly describe the development efforts through case studies, while one offers a formal model. Although there is some consensus that ebXML and RosettaNet are the most important initiatives, no work contributes either an in-depth case study on their development practice or a generalised model for standards development organisations. Below, I will focus on this research gap.

4 Standards Development

> "Standards and classifications, however dry
> and formal on the surface are suffused with
> traces of political and social work."[230]
>
> *Geoffrey C. Bowker and Susan Leigh Star*

This chapter lays the theoretical ground to answer the second research question:

Why and how are interorganisational standards developed?

It will discuss general theories on standards without being limited to interorganisational standards. The term 'standard' is often used with an only intuitively attributed meaning. Its precise meaning, however, is not itself standardised, and calls for a more detailed discussion before further using it in the context of interorganisational relationships and information systems. Thus, section 4.1 discusses the nature of standards. Further, this chapter presents theoretical approaches towards standards. Section 4.2 briefly introduces technical considerations, section 4.3 neo-classical and neo-institutional economic theories, and section 4.4 a social approach. Because of its increasing use and its unique approach towards standards, section 4.5 discusses actor-network theory in detail.

4.1 The Nature of Standards

The roots of the term 'standard' can be traced back to the Germanic words 'standan' (~to stand) and 'ord' (~point). In medieval times, the old French noun 'estandard' denoted a place marked with a conspicuous object where scattered troops in a battle were supposed to rally.[231] In situations of confusion, it served to call to order and prevent further chaos. To this day, flags have functioned as standards for this purpose. Though keeping order is still the main purpose of standards, their precise meaning depends on the context in question. A universally applicable definition of the term 'standard' is thus impossible. Nevertheless, the International Organisation

---

[230] See Bowker/Star (1996).

[231] See Merriam-Webster (2004).

for Standardisation,[232] which is the worlds largest organisation concerned with standards, gives one of the most general definitions:

> A standard is a "document, established by consensus and approved by a recognized body, that provides, for common and repeated use, rules, guidelines or characteristics for activities or their results, aimed at the achievement of the optimum degree of order in a given context."[233]

I will briefly discuss the elements of this definition. Almost any kind of standard is somehow codified in a document to facilitate its adoption and lower its ambiguity.[234] Not every standard, however, has to be established by a 'recognised body'. Clearly, as ISO is probably the most broadly recognised standards body, it mentions this to differentiate its de jure standardisation from de facto standardisation through market mechanisms. Moreover, standards do not necessarily need consensus for their establishment, but rather a broad adoption by the target group, which is not the same.[235] Common and repeated use is one of the core elements, as a standard only makes sense if it describes something that is of interest for many actors and has to be repeated often. Further, a standard provides "rules, guidelines or characteristics for activities or their results".[236] As ISO offers standards in almost any field possible, this part of the definition is very unspecific. All it stipulates is that a standard describes what certain activities and results should be like. Finally, the definition stresses the goal of achieving order in the context in question, just like the standards in ancient battles.

---

[232] Often 'abbreviated' to ISO, which does *not* stand for 'International Standards Organisation' (which would discriminate against languages other than English), but is derived from 'isos' meaning 'equal' in classical Greek.

[233] ISO/IEC (1996), Clause 3.2.

[234] If this aspect of codification is dropped, the scope of the term 'standard' becomes very broad and much resembles the general character of an 'institution'. For a further discussion of the relation between standards and institutions, see Antonelli (1994). In this work, I regard codification as an essential feature of a standard. This codification, however, does not have to be in a physical document, but can also be an electronic document or another technical artefact such as a software programme.

[235] Prominent examples are several Microsoft products and formats, which are clearly standards, but not established by consensus and a recognised standards body. For details, see later this chapter.

[236] ISO/IEC (1996), Clause 3.2.

Types of Standards

The literature provides many ways of categorising different types of standards.[237] Frequent reference is made to the dimension of coercion, usually distinguishing between the two characteristics 'de jure' and 'de facto' standards. De jure standards are defined and sometimes also enforced by governmental organisations, while de facto standards emerge through voluntary development and adoption.[238] A second dimension concerns the openness of standards, which gained special importance through the broad adoption of the open Internet and open source software. An open standard is available at no or very low cost and is free to use. In contrast, a proprietary standard is controlled by a firm, which aims to make a profit with the standard and charges fees for the use of it.[239]

The dimensions 'coercion' and 'openness' give a rough classification of standards. For a different, more detailed view, I propose to use the two dimensions 'standards object' and 'standards coordinator'. The latter can be seen as a refinement of the dimension of coercion. Many works, however, do not discuss the object of standardisation explicitly. Drawing on Timmermans/Berg (1997), I shall distinguish between product, semantics, process and performance, which can all be the object of standardisation.

A *product standard* defines the properties and functions of physical or digital products. Such standards play a crucial role in system products, where products are built out of modules and can be enhanced by adding or exchanging modules. Moreover, product standards can also enable the coupling of products, which results in product networks. One example is the European GSM standard, which specifies mobile phones and associated infrastructure networks and is the most successful standard for mobile phone networks today. Understanding such product networks is critical for business strategies in what are known as network industries.[240]

A *semantic standard* describes the meaning of terms unambiguously. In many fields, this is a prerequisite for the cooperation of different actors, which would otherwise be distorted by frequent misunderstandings. One example is EDIFACT, in which all the terms and data fields used are pre-

---

[237] See Stegwee/Rukanova (2003), David/Greenstein (1990), Antonelli (1994), Fomin/Keil/Lyytinen (2003), Hemenway (1975), Besen/Saloner (1989), Sivan (2000).

[238] See Antonelli (1994), pp. 196ff.

[239] See West (2003), p. 318.

[240] For a detailed discussion see Shy (2001) and Steiner (2005), pp. 23ff.

cisely defined. While human actors can cope with making suppositions about meanings (although this can cause a lot of friction), unambiguous definitions are required for machine-to-machine communication.

A *process standard* proposes how to coordinate and execute certain tasks. It describes the steps needed, their order of execution, and the respective results. Process standards are especially important where different actors, departments or firms have to work together. ISO 9000 is the best known example of such an organisational standard. ISO calls it a 'generic management system standard',[241] as it provides a generic model to follow in setting up a quality management system. Hence, it helps organisations to run their processes more reliably and serve their customers better.

A *performance standard* defines the outcome level of a product or process. It contains a set of quantitative criteria to measure the outcomes against a certain standard outcome. One example is the Supply Chain Council's SCOR model, which defines many performances indicators to measure the performance of supply chains. Moreover, it provides benchmarks to compare the performances of different supply chains.[242] In the context of performance, the term 'standard' has an additional meaning. 'Standard performance' indicates a performance that is average, neither poor nor excellent.

This categorisation of standards is not without its overlaps. For instance, standardised semantics are required in product, process and performance standards. Similarly, a performance standard requires that a product or process to be measured is standardised. Even the line between product and process standards is not always clear. First, the product of one firm can involve a process for another firm. EDI standards, for example, are product standards for software vendors, while they are a kind of process standard for EDI software users. Second, in the case of services, the product sold is mainly a process and not a physical product. For instance, an electronic service offered via Web Services standards would fit into both categories. Nevertheless, I believe that the distinction between product and process standards can benefit the analysis of standards.

The main coordinator of standardisation efforts represents another dimension to the classification of standards. Many works use a classification similar to the one used by David/Greenstein (1990): free market, dominant

---

[241] See ISO (2004).

[242] See Supply Chain Council (2004).

firm, consortium and government. However, the distinction between a free market and a dominating firm can be misleading. If there is no government or consortium involved in the standardisation process, then there is usually a free market at the beginning, in which firms with their specifications compete with one another. When the specification of one firm drives out the others, this firm gains market share and becomes the dominating firm. It is thus a question of the time when there is a free market and when there is a dominant firm.[243] In the face of the many open source initiatives, I propose to add open communities as another way of coordinating standardisation.

In the *community* case, no organisation explicitly leads the development and diffusion of a standard. Some actors voluntarily contribute to the development, and even more actors adopt the open standard without any external coercion. The success of the open source development approach offers many examples to show that the community mechanism can lead to excellent standard semantics and products, such as Wikipedia and Linux.[244]

In the *market* case, firms compete in the development and adoption of standards. Depending on their position, they rely on the voluntary cooperation of other firms or can force them to contribute to one standard in certain ways. The most prominent example is Microsoft, whose products Windows and Office are obvious de facto and proprietary standards in the software market. These give the firm a strong position from which it can dominate related technologies, such as the development of media technologies.

In the *consortium* case, a separate organisation is formed to develop standards. Different individuals and firms contribute to the development, while the consortium mainly coordinates these efforts and decides on the final specifications. Compared to the dominant firm case, consortium standards are usually open standards, as most consortia are non-profit organisations and provide their standard free of charge. One example is the World Wide Web Consortium (W3C), which coordinates many different specifications concerning the Web.

---

[243] See the economics of standards as discussed in subsection 4.3.1.

[244] For a further general discussion of open source software see Brügge/Harhoff/Picot, et al. (2004). For a discussion from the standards perspective see Dedrick/West (2003).

In the *government* case, a governmental department or a separate organisation with governmental authority sets standards and supports or even enforces their adoption. Governmentally enforced standards are the typical case of de jure standardisation. However, even with governmental standards individuals and firms can contribute to their development, as they do in EDIFACT standardisation.

Combining the two dimensions 'standards object' and 'standards coordinator' results in the matrix depicted in Figure 4.1. I have also added examples to illustrate the different categories of standards. I believe that this matrix is of great value for categorising most standards. Hence, it helps to clarify what kind of standard a certain research work is considering. While this chapter discusses standards in general, chapters 5 and 6 focus on semantics and process standards developed by consortia (see the ellipse in Figure 4.1). As already mentioned, this does not completely exclude other types of standards, especially the bordering ones.

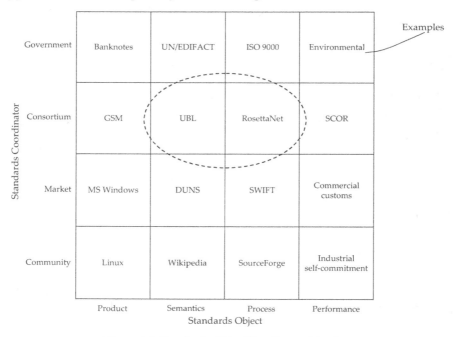

Figure 4.1: Standards Object/Coordinator Matrix

Organisations engaged in developing and promoting standards are called standards development organisations (SDOs), be they a governmental organisation, a consortium or a formalised user community. In many cases, the differences are not obvious if both firms and governmental departments are participating in the SDO, as with UN/CEFACT (see section 5.3). The influence of such SDOs varies from national to international in its reach. For instance, the Deutsches Institut für Normung (DIN), the American National Standards Institute (ANSI), and the National Institute for Standards and Technology (NIST) are national SDOs, while the Comité Européen de Normalisation (CEN) and the European Telecommunications Standards Institute (ETSI) cover Europe. In the face of globalisation, international standardisation is playing an increasing role. The most important international SDO is ISO, which covers many different topics from screws to management practices. For information systems, the Institute of Electrical and Electronics Engineers (IEEE), the Internet Engineering Task Force (IETF), the International Telecommunication Union (ITU), the Organisation for the Advancement of Structured Information Standards (OASIS), and the World Wide Web Consortium (W3C) are the most important SDOs.

The Standardisation Process

Farrell/Saloner (1986) give the main reason why one should use standards. A standard creates "demand-side economies of scale: there are benefits to doing what others do. These benefits make standardisation a central issue in many important industries."[245] The term standardisation, however, bears some ambiguity. Roughly, a standard has to go through two phases: first, the process in which the standard documents are developed, and second, the process in which they are adopted by the users. Often, the first phase is already called standardisation. Indeed, the alignment of the diverse opinions and requirements of all the participants can be seen as standardisation. For example, ISO calls approved proposals submitted by external organisations 'specifications', while it defines only intensively reviewed specifications as standards, regardless of their adoption by users. In a more rigorous sense, however, an important property of a standard is its adoption by many users. Thus, when a distinction is appropriate, I will call the resulting standard proposal of the first phase a 'specification' and only a broadly adopted specification a 'standard'.[246]

---

[245] Farrell/Saloner (1986), p. 940.

[246] This distinction between specifications and standards is more usual in German than in English literature. See Niggl (1994), p. 34. Also used is the term *norm*, which de-

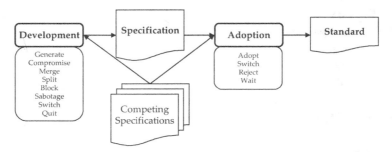

Figure 4.2: Generic Standardisation Process[247]

Figure 4.2 represents a generic model of a standardisation process. It consists of the two main decision phases: development and adoption. In the *development* phase, the participants create and agree on a specification that they want to establish as a standard. First, they generate a proposal and reach a compromise on it. However, as there are mostly competing specifications, merging with them or splitting one's own are also alternatives. If a participant is not content with a compromise, he can try to block or even sabotage the specifications, or he can switch to a competing specification, if it seems superior. Lastly, he can leave the process completely. A completed specification is published and the target actors can decide on its *adoption*. However, they can also reject the specification, switch to a competing one, or just wait.

Although some authors such as Gaillard (1934) contributed theoretical insights on standards very early, it was not until the 1980s that standards research became established as a separate research field.[248] Standards and standardisation are highly complex phenomena, whose many facets can hardly be captured by any single theory. Most theories rely on strict assumptions and cover only some aspects of standards.[249] Nickerson/zur Muehlen (2003) thus call for multi-method approaches to standardisation

---

notes a de jure specification, and the term *type* for a user specification, both regardless of their adoption; see Kleinaltenkamp (1993), pp. 20ff. Another issue is the definition of when a specification can be called 'broadly adopted'. As this depends on the topic to be standardised, no single percentage value can clearly distinguish between specifications and standards.

[247] Adapted and simplified from Nickerson/zur Muehlen (2003), p. 329.

[248] See Weitzel (2004), p. 15.

[249] See Weitzel (2004), p. 14.

research.[250] Very much like Fomin et al. (2003), they distinguish between three main theoretical perspectives on standardisation:[251]

- Theories of technical design cover the creation of technical specifications.
- Economic theories are concerned with the questions of why actors choose a specific standard and which outcomes are economically most efficient.
- Theories of social construction examine why and how a standard is created and what social and technical influences are involved.

It is sometimes difficult to classify a research work exactly according to these three perspectives, as researchers increasingly try to integrate some or all of them. One example is the work of Fomin et al. (2003), who aim to create a comprehensive standardisation process theory, including design, sense-making and negotiating activities (hence called the D-S-N model). Their model also inspired this work, though I do not adopt all their ideas. I also expect that it will be difficult to integrate all aspects of standardisation into a unified theory of standardisation. Still, it is important to keep the different perspectives in mind or – even better – to apply and combine them in standardisation research whenever this makes sense.[252]

The following sections review the three perspectives. As the social constructivist approach of actor-network theory will play an important role in what follows, I discuss it in greater detail (section 4.5).

4.2   Technical Development of Standards

Theoretical approaches to technical design aim at the creation of functioning standards specifications. They can be divided into two perspectives. One is concerned with the required activities for managing the actual development projects, while the other develops and discuses technological alternatives.

---

[250] See Nickerson/zur Muehlen (2003), p. 328.

[251] See Fomin/Keil/Lyytinen (2003), pp. 4ff. and Nickerson/zur Muehlen (2003), p. 328.

[252] See also Weitzel (2004), pp. 236ff.

Management of Specification Development

As little literature is available on the management of standards development activities,[253] Fomin et al. (2003) suggest transferring the insights of Cooper/Kleinschmidt (1996) from general product development.[254] In an empirical study, they identify the main factors influencing the success of product development. In this subsection, I summarise their insights with respect to standards development. Three areas are most critical for successful product development: the development process, the product strategy, and the invested resources.[255]

First, a well-organised development process very much increases the probability of a successful product.[256] Such a process comprises all activities and decisions from the first idea to the launch of a new product and beyond. This also applies to an SDO, especially if it has to develop and maintain dozens or hundreds of specifications, as ISO or W3C do. Cooper/Kleinschmidt (1996) suggest an appropriate formalisation and give six criteria for a good development process.

– Up-front assessments: Although many ideas for a specification seem to be a clear success, detailed up-front market and technology assessments have to support a reasonable success probability. While such assessments are already difficult for products, they are even more difficult for standards, as many different stakeholders are usually involved in standardisation.[257] Standards scenarios are no easy ground for quantitative and financial analyses in particular.[258]
– Sharp and early standard definition: Before starting the actual development of a specification, the requirements have to be defined: for example, the target user group, the benefits, the positioning regarding other standards, the basic concept, and the main features. This is of par-

---

[253] One of the few examples is Jakobs (2002).

[254] See Fomin/Keil/Lyytinen (2003), p. 4.

[255] See Cooper/Kleinschmidt (1996). Also relevant, but less important are the overall R&D spending, the product team, management commitment, climate and culture, cross-functional teams, and senior management accountability.

[256] For a more detailed overview on innovation management see, e.g., Hauschildt (2004).

[257] For the chaotic and unpredictable nature of standards see subsection 4.3.

[258] Nevertheless, there are approaches to calculating measures such as a network ROI, as briefly mentioned in subsection 4.3.

ticular importance for distributed development as is often the case with Web specifications coordinated by W3C.

– Tough go/kill decision points: Regular scrutiny of development processes and tough criteria for continuing or aborting them are critical in order not to waste resources on specifications that are likely to fail. Although it is difficult to predict a successful standard, one might imagine a funnelling model for sorting out suspect specifications as early as possible.

– Quality of process: The actual development of specifications has to be executed on a high quality level. Key aspects are good work planning and tight control of deliverables. Again, this represents a challenge in specifications development with many diverse actors and interests involved.

– Completeness of process: The development process has to be completely executed without omitting any steps because of time restrictions. This is especially important for standards specifications. If they get published and are adopted, in most cases it is difficult to make later changes to the specifications.

– Flexibility of process: Despite the rigour discussed so far, a certain flexibility has to be built into the development process. Especially in areas of highly dynamic technology, it is important not to miss the latest inventions, which could quickly render a specification obsolete.

Even if the result of such a specification development process is excellent, a clear standards strategy has to put it into a larger perspective.

– Clear goals: The goals a standards specification is aiming at have to be defined.

– Communication of goals: These goals have to be well communicated.

– Sharp focus: The standards strategy has to focus on defined target groups.

– Long term focus: The standards strategy has to follow long-term goals.

To pursue a standards strategy and development process, the adequate resources have to be provided.

– Resources provided by senior management: The resources needed for the development of the specification have to be devoted by senior management to emphasise its importance.

– Adequate budgets: The financial budgets have to be adequate for the goals and technical challenges of the specification.

– Right people with time available: The right people have to be staffed and have to be freed from too many other tasks.

Technical Details

Besides such management activities, the second perspective is concerned with the technical details of standards specifications. Of course, these depend on the field for which a particular specification should be developed. In the field of information systems, the discipline of software engineering offers many concepts for how to develop software, for example, defining requirements, modelling in UML, and programming software.[259] Here again, the many diverse stakeholders involved in standards specifications often complicate the development by comparison with usual software development projects. Section 5.1 discusses some important technical details of interorganisational specifications.

4.3   Economic Decisions on Standards

Economic theories of standards aim to understand why actors choose a certain standard and what the welfare implications are.[260] They can be divided into neo-classical and neo-institutional theories. The following subsections summarise the main contributions to standardisation of the two types of theory in turn.

4.3.1   Neo-Classical Economics

The neo-classical model of an idealised market makes several strict assumptions,[261] of which three are directly related to standards. First, goods and services are homogeneous, i.e., they are fully standardised and unambiguously described (standardised products and semantics). Second, market processes are frictionless, i.e., they are timeless and do not cause any transaction costs (standardised processes). Third, market exchange hap-

---

[259] See, e.g., Bruegge/Dutoit (2003).
[260] See Fomin/Keil (2000), p. 207.
[261] See, e.g., Shepherd (1990), p. 31.

pens without externalities, i.e., all decisions are made independently and all outcomes of an exchange are included in market prices.

The networked character of standards-based technologies, however, links the decisions of all actors together.[263] No actor makes his decisions isolated. Katz/Shapiro (1985) and Farrell/Saloner (1985) thus dropped the neo-classical assumption of no externalities and described the phenomenon of network externalities. Usually, it is a positive network effect, as there is a positive correlation between the number of users and the value of a network.[264] Figure 4.3 depicts this positive feedback mechanism. A larger installed base leads to more complementary products and to the higher credibility of the standard. This reinforces the value of the standard for the users and encourages further adoption, which expands the installed base again. Katz/Shapiro (1985) differentiate between two kinds of network externalities. Direct network effects raise the value of a product by directly connecting users. Indirect network effects add value through learnt skills connected to the product and the increase in complementary products available. As neo-classical standards theories focus on network effects, they are mainly concerned with product standards.

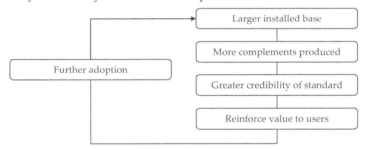

Figure 4.3: Positive Feedback Loop of Standards[262]

The basic principle of network effects leads to several further phenomena, which make the economics of network products different from 'classic industrial' products with diminishing returns. The different phenomena are now discussed in more detail.[265]

---

[262] Grindley (1995), p. 27.

[263] See Weitzel (2004), p. 2.

[264] Weitzel (2004), p. 14.

[265] Based on Weitzel (2004), pp. 19ff. For a more detailed overview see Economides (1996) and Hanseth (2000).

The first phenomenon is *path dependency*, i.e., "the dependence of diffusion results on early random historic events".[266] Arthur (1989) constructs a game theoretic model in which several adopters have to choose between two technologies. He analyses the three different regimes 'constant returns', 'diminishing returns' and 'increasing returns' with respect to four properties of network effects: predictability (actors can predict results), flexibility (no lock-in), ergodicity (small events are averaged away), and path-efficiency (inferior technology is adopted). If increasing returns exist, as is the case with standards and positive network effects, the outcomes are neither predictable, flexible, ergodic, nor path-efficient. Early insignificant events can give one standard a critical advantage over others in later phases. Although a second standard might become superior, the users are locked-in to the first standard, as this was superior at the beginning. This leads to *multiple equilibria* and eventually to a *monopoly* of one standard. One important insight is the unpredictability as to which standard will win this race, as the underlying reinforcement mechanisms lead to chaotic behaviour, similar to chaos theory in mathematics.[267]

Instability characterises the multiple equilibria. Thus, network markets are usually very *tippy*, i.e., they suddenly switch to a single leading standard while driving out competing standards. The 'chicken/egg paradox' is closely related. If the installed base is too small, the value of a technology is low. If the value is low, users do not adopt the technology (see also Figure 4.3). As soon as a critical mass is reached, however, users adopt the technology quite quickly due to the reinforced network effect of standards. Shapiro/Varian (1999) present several strategies for reaching such a critical mass more quickly and to establishing one's own technology as standard.

Excess inertia describes the phenomenon of the *start-up problem*. Even if a new technology is functionally superior, potential adopters wait for others to adopt it first. They do not want to bear the risk of being the first adopter of a technology that will not eventually be established as a standard. Farrell/Saloner (1986) examine this phenomenon on the model of a battle between an existing and a new technology. They describe what is termed a *bandwagon process*. Even if the new technology is superior to the existing one, not all users switch to the new technology at once because of excess

---

[266] Weitzel (2004), p. 20.
[267] See Weitzel (2004), p. 22.

inertia. However, the users with the highest benefit from the new technology start to switch and thus motivate other users to switch, too.

Excess momentum occurs when an incentive is given to switch to a new technology even if the old one is preferred individually. This is often the case when a sponsoring firm tries to establish its technology as standard. Two important strategies are low prices to reach a high penetration and predatory pre-announcements to prevent a competing bandwagon from gaining momentum.[268]

If a technology is sponsored by a firm or a standards organisation, the sponsor can try to *internalise the network effects* to achieve a better standard penetration. Such sponsored technologies are in a strong position if competing with unsponsored technologies, because the sponsor can price the technology strategically.[269] In this way, the problem of excess inertia can be overcome.

From an overall economic perspective, it is important to analyse whether network effects prevent *pareto-efficient market results*. Because of the positive feedback loop of network effects, there is always a tendency for one technology to gain a monopoly position even if it is functionally inferior to alternatives. There is also a timing problem, as an early standard encourages the development of complementary products, but hinders the exploration of superior alternatives.[270]

This raises the question of which of the governmental alternatives *laissez-faire* or *dirigisme* leads to superior welfare results. Despite the market failures described above, in recent years researchers in the economics of standards have reached a consensus

> "(…) that the government suffers from significant informational deficits compared to industry groups. (…) the government is most likely to be incapable of meaningfully determining 'the best' technology among different alternatives, especially as compared to the technology providers."[271]

As Weitzel (2004) remarks, most of the economic models discussed up to now have focused mainly on the decision-making problems of technology vendors and governments.[272] On the basis of these theoretical insights and

---

[268] See Farrell/Saloner (1986).

[269] See Weitzel (2004), p. 27.

[270] See David/Greenstein (1990), p. 12.

[271] Weitzel (2004), p. 28.

[272] See Weitzel (2004), p. 26 and 31.

the work of Buxmann (1996), he builds models to better analyse the decision-making problems of the technology users. As the models are highly complex, he cannot derive analytical solutions, but has to rely on computer simulations.[273] One of the main results is the proof and quantification of a standardisation gap, i.e., inefficient standardisation because of two factors. First, an actor might not see the benefit of a standard from a local perspective, though it would benefit him from a centralised perspective including other actors. Second, even if the actor accepts the benefits of a standard, he is likely to behave unfavourably if he has insufficient information on the standard-adoption behaviour of other actors.[274]

Weitzel (2004) proposes three solutions to the standardisation gap: a network ROI to better capture the value of a standard-based network, a Groves mechanism for lowering information asymmetry, and a bidding mechanism to better distribute the benefits from a standard between the different actors.[275] He also stresses that it is very difficult to compare the economic effects of standardisation according to the different studies, as their definitions and assumptions are just as different as the character of standards in the diverse fields.[276] Finally, Weitzel (2004) concludes his work with the insight that the mainly neo-classical approaches he has used have too many shortcomings to get closer to a general theory of networks and suggests including insights from other currents of theory such as neo-institutional economics.

4.3.2   Neo-Institutional Economics

Neo-institutional economics comprises transaction costs, property rights and principal agent theory as its main elements and aims to loosen several of the tight assumptions of neo-classical economics.[277] In particular, actors do not act fully rationally, but are limited in their ability to make rational choices.[278] Further, they show opportunistic behaviour as they try to

---

[273] See Weitzel (2004), p. 80.

[274] See Weitzel (2004), p. 184.

[275] See Weitzel (2004), pp. 184-235.

[276] See Weitzel (2004), p. 165.

[277] For a detailed introduction see Picot/Dietl/Franck (2002), pp. 37.

[278] See Simon (1978).

maximise their benefits, even by means of guile.[279] Exchange between actors is thus not frictionless, but causes transaction costs. As rationality surrogates, institutions help to lower the negative effects of bounded rationality and opportunistic behaviour.[280] They are "socially sanctionable expectations, related to actions and behaviours of one or more individuals."[281] Examples of institutions are languages, laws, organisations or standards.[282]

Standards have a strong impact on transaction costs.[283] Assuming no standards, the bounded rationality of actors would make economic exchange nearly impossible. Gathering sufficient information on goods, services and appropriate suppliers would be prohibitively costly. Opportunistic behaviour would prosper, as there would be almost no competition because of the difficulty of comparing transaction relations. One of the earliest standards, apart from language, was money.[284] This drastically lowers transaction costs, as at least one part of economic exchange is largely simplified. Exchanging cash represents the most standardised economic transaction as it is perfectly specified and leaves no room for opportunistic behaviour. Similarly, the better a good is standardised (i.e., can be specified along certain dimensions), the lower the transaction costs are. Goods such as oil can thus be traded just like money. The properties of a barrel of oil are fully standardised, which makes an offer easy to assess and opportunistic behaviour almost impossible.[285]

Such standards, as well as other institutional arrangements, are not naturally given, but have to be set up and maintained. North (1990) thus introduces the notion of two different market types: the economic market and the political market.[286] On the political market, the institutions regulat-

---

[279] See Williamson (1975), p. 258.

[280] See Picot/Dietl/Franck (2002), p. 40.

[281] See Wigand/Picot/Reichwald (1997), p. 31.

[282] See Picot/Dietl/Franck (2002), p. 11.

[283] See Kleinaltenkamp (1993), pp. 83ff.

[284] See Reimers (1995), p. 84.

[285] This concerns only the transaction of a barrel of oil and not the long-term behaviour of actors such as OPEC.

[286] North (1990), pp. 48ff.

Figure 4.4: Political Markets and Standard Development

ing the economic market are negotiated. These costs of negotiating and agreeing on economic institutions are also transaction costs.[287]

Transferred to a standard, the development of a standard can be seen as the political market and the use of the standard as the economic market (see Figure 4.4). The actors thus establish a standard if the transaction costs of standardisation are lower than the transaction costs saved through the standard:[288]

Transaction costs of development < Transaction costs saved through use
→ Positive expected net benefits → Actors establish standard

As it is very difficult, if not impossible, to quantify these transaction costs, Reimers (1995) lays the ground for a model for qualitative decisions in the context of this problem. One of the main results is to recommend limiting the maximum number of participants in the development, as otherwise the transaction costs in this political market become too high and surpass the benefits from adopting the standard in the economic markets.[289]

Drawing on the work by Besen/Saloner (1989), Picot/Fiedler (2002) add the concept of diverse interests in a standard. The interests are aligned if all the participants favour the same specification. If they have conflicting interests, they will prefer different specifications. Combining the distinction between low/high expected benefits with that between conflicting/aligned interests results in a 2x2 matrix, as depicted in Figure 4.5.

If the actors have divergent interests and the expected benefits of a standard are low, they use separate specifications as private goods. No broadly adopted specification will become a standard. High benefits from a common specification and non-aligned interests lead to conflict, with actors trying to dominate the shaping of the specification. Only if the participants can eventually agree on common interests, can a universal standard

---

emerge. If the interests are aligned, but the benefits are low, a publicly available specification is adopted as a standard. Finally, if the expected benefits are high and the interests are aligned, the participants cooperate in the development of a new standard, for example, in a consortium.

Although this approach gives some insights into the political market of standardisation, it does not consider the different interests and the resulting negotiations in more detail. However, as current economic approaches to standardisation are still far from complete, a better understanding of the political aspects of standardisation seems to be needed.[290] This is also of high practical relevance as users of standards get increasingly involved in standards development.[291] In the next subsection, therefore, I will introduce the 'Social Construction of Technology' approach as another theoretical perspective on standardisation, which helps to shed more light on the political market of standards.

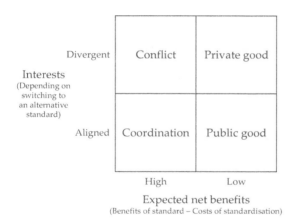

Figure 4.5: Interests and Benefits in Standardisation Processes[292]

---

[290] See Fomin/Keil/Lyytinen (2003), p. 5.

[291] See, e.g., Weitzel (2004), p. 26, who assumes a given standards specification, like most research models on standards, and does not consider the case of participation in the development of the specification.

[292] Based on Besen/Saloner (1989), p. 184 and Picot/Fiedler (2002), p. 249.

4.4   Social Construction of Standards

This subsection first introduces the 'Social Construction of Technology' approach and second shows its use in standardisation research.

4.4.1   Social Construction of Technology

Pinch/Bijker (1987) developed the theoretical approach known as the Social Construction of Technology (SCOT), which is rooted in constructivism[293] and the sociology of knowledge[294]. Egyedi (1996) summarises the central assumption of both:

> "Beliefs and knowledge of individuals compose relative realities. Nevertheless, if shared by a number of people, a body of knowledge becomes 'real'. The sense of objectivity is based on a shared perception of reality. Objectivity is in essence intersubjectivity."[295]

Thus, SCOT assumes that the shape and success of a technology is mainly the result of social processes reaching intersubjective agreements. This interpretive or constructivist approach is a clear antithesis to technical determinism, in which technology shapes the social.[296] In order to analyse the social construction of technology, SCOT "opens the black box" of technology by "following the actors" creating the technology.[297] A SCOT analysis comprises four major concepts:[298]

– Relevant social groups: A group is relevant for a technology if the technology has any meaning for the group. All individuals and groups attributing the same meaning to the technology form one social group.

---

[293] Knorr-Cetina (1998) distinguishes three types of constructivism: social order, cognition, and the Empirical Programme of Relativism (EPOR). See there for a further discussion of constructivism and the relevant literature.

[294] See Bloor (1976) for the 'Strong Programme' and Collins (1981) for EPOR. Pinch/Bijker (1987), p. 17 argue that science and technology are not easy to distinguish and that approaches to science studies such as EPOR are thus also useful for the study of technology creation.

[295] Egyedi (1996), p. 42.

[296] See Egyedi (1996), p. 46.

[297] See Degele (2002), p. 102.

[298] See Pinch/Bijker (1987) and Bijker (1995), pp. 45ff.

Winner (1993), however, emphasises the difficulties in identifying the relevant social groups without missing important ones out.[299]

- Interpretive flexibility: The meanings attributed to the same technological artefact can vary radically between different social groups. Bijker (1995) even states that one artefact to which different meanings are attached has to be treated as several distinct artefacts. He calls this pluralism of artefacts.[300] Further, "[e]ach meaning embeds a potential direction in which an artefact may develop"[301], which is also called multi-directionality. In terms of evolutionary theory, the different meanings lead to variations in the technology. Conflicts, new problems, new knowledge, paradigm shifts, and the unpredicted use of artefacts increase this variation.[302]

- Closure and stabilisation: During the debate concerning a technological artefact, inferior variations are sorted out and eventually one alternative is selected as the superior one. It does not have to be superior in the sense of its technical features, but rather in the interpretation of the relevant social groups. Such closure of a debate can be reached in two ways. First, via rhetorical closure, i.e., the social groups accept the problem as being solved, regardless of whether a 'real' solution has been found. Often, a dominant group imposes the acceptance of a solution on weaker groups. Second, closure can be reached by redefining the original problem, i.e., the meaning attached by some groups is translated into another meaning which no longer poses a problem. The closure of a debate stabilises the technology.

- Wider context: The wider context represents the sociocultural and political situation in which the relevant social groups have to act. For example, political, cultural and religious influences thus also have to be considered in a SCOT study.

These main concepts offer "a heuristic device, a set of sensitising concepts that will allow us to scope out relevant points, but one that will require adaptation and reformulation for use in new instances."[303] SCOT is not a

---

[299] See Winner (1993), p. 369.
[300] See Bijker (1995), p. 77.
[301] Egyedi (1996), p. 44.
[302] See Egyedi (1996), pp. 50.
[303] Bijker (1995), p. 17.

strict theory, therefore, but rather a way of conducting empirical research on the creation of technology.

A classic example of SCOT is the development of the bicycle in the late 19th century.[304] John Boyd Dunlop developed the air tyre as an anti-vibration device, which worked technically well, but not socially. The dominant groups of cyclists did not accept it, as it did not fit their meaning of cycling as a 'tough sport for real men'. Only the later success of air tyres in bicycle races meant that the meaning they attributed to air tyres was translated from 'comfort device' into 'high-speed device'. Eventually, the 'tough guys' too accepted the advantages of air tyres. This case shows how interpretive flexibility changes the meaning attributed to an artefact and how this leads to closure and stabilisation. Since then, air tyres have been state of the art not only for bicycles, but also for almost any rolling techni-cal artefact, from wheelbarrows to aeroplanes.

4.4.2 Social Construction of Standards

The application of SCOT to standardisation aims to answer the question: Why and how was a specific standard created and what social and techni-cal issues influenced its creation?[305] Before applying it to standardisation research, Egyedi (1996) extends the basic SCOT model. She adds the ele-ments 'social setting' (e.g., R&D or politics), 'social locus' (e.g., R&D labo-ratories or government departments) and 'social attributes of actors' (e.g., interests or expectations).[306] Drawing on several theories she also refines the evolutionary process of social construction and stresses the phases 'variation', 'selection', and 'stabilisation'.[307]

In her study of computer network standards, Egyedi (1996) uses SCOT to identify three relevant social groups: the standards development or-ganisation, the standards committees, and the actor-network of standardi-sation. The standards development organisation (SDO) is an established organisation providing an institutional environment based on a certain standards ideology. Its main goal is the social construction of standards processes, which structure the negotiations on standards. The actual nego-

---

[304] See Pinch/Bijker (1987), pp. 28ff.

[305] See Fomin/Keil/Lyytinen (2003), p. 5.

[306] See Egyedi (1996), pp. 46ff.

[307] See Egyedi (1996), p. 53.

tiations of standards problems and possible solutions are done in standards committees as parts of the SDO. These mainly consist of interest groups trying to secure their political or economical interests in the standards and practitioner communities following certain technical paradigms in designing standards. Externally, the different actors of the actor-network on standardisation try to impose their interests on the ideology of the SDO. They socially construct the role of the standardisation through negotiating the meanings and problems of standardisation.

Figure 4.6 depicts the relations between the relevant social actors in standardisation and their object of social construction. On the basis of this framework, Egyedi (1996) analyses the development on standards for computer networks, focusing on ISO/OSI vs. Internet standardisation. Regarding standardisation ideology and processes, the formal ISO/OSI development was very much consensus-oriented, while the 'grey' development of TCP/IP was very pragmatic and output-oriented.[309] If in Internet standardisation no consensus can be reached through reasonable efforts, parallel processes and competing standards are started and the final users have to choose their preferred standard. In formal SDOs, negotia-

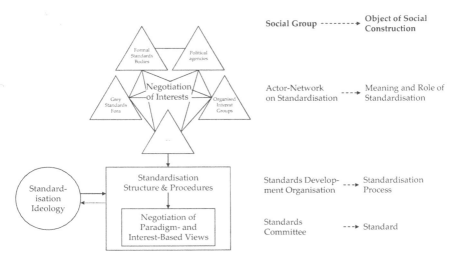

Figure 4.6: Social Groups and Their Objects in Social Standards Construction[308]

---

[308] Slightly adapted from Egyedi (1996), p. 80.

[309] See Egyedi (1996), p. 250.

tions have to run until closure is reached with all interest groups. This makes the formal SDOs slower and less efficient in many cases.[310] While several actors in the actor-network of OSI standardisation urged the formal SDOs to adopt successful 'grey' standards, these tried to remain 'obligatory passage points' arguing that their formal standardisation processes alone are democratic.[311] However, they had to accept 'grey' standards as the importance of implementing standards surpassed the need for formal processes of developing standards.[312] Finally, the technical paradigms also played an important role in standardisation.[313]

Egyedi (1996) stresses the importance of negotiation and uses the two concepts 'actor-network' and 'obligatory passage point'. However, with the chosen theoretical background of SCOT, she was unable to elucidate the process of negotiation in more detail. This is one focus of the actor-network theory (ANT), which has some roots in SCOT and promises to shed even more light on the development of technology in general and standards in particular. As ANT serves as the main guiding theory of this study, the next section will introduce the main concepts in more detail.

4.5   Actor-Network Theory and Standards

Study of the causal agency of information systems is concerned with which factors primarily drive organisational change.[314] The technological imperative regards technology as the main cause for change. An opposing position is the organisational imperative: people in an organisation shape technology exactly according to their needs. As both seem not to fully capture actual situations, Markus/Robey (1988) advocate a third causal agency, the emergent perspective. The main point is the interplay of people and technology, which makes outcomes almost completely unpredictable.[315] This has two implications for research on information systems and

---

[310] A counterexample is the standardisation of GSM, which also took a very long time and required many compromises to be made, but was eventually a huge success.

[311] See Egyedi (1996), p. 253.

[312] See Egyedi (1996), p. 254.

[313] See discussion in subsection 5.1.1.

[314] See Markus/Robey (1988), p. 584 and the discussion in section 2.3.

[315] See Markus/Robey (1988), p. 588.

organisations. First, a researcher should not separate the two elements, but analyse IS and organisations at the same time. Second, process-oriented theories can better capture the evolving interplay between IS and organisations than variable-oriented theories.[316] Mohr (1982) proposes this distinction between variance and process theories,[317] which differ mainly in the formulation of the theoretical arguments made (see Table 4.1).[318]

Table 4.1: Variance vs. Process Theories[319]

	Variance Theory	*Process Theory*
Outcome	A variable	A discrete event
Logical form	If V (independent variable, necessary and sufficient conditions), then O (dependent variable); for example, if more V, then more O	If not E (necessary conditions), then not O (outcome); cannot be extended to 'more E' or 'more O'
Assumptions	Outcome will invariably occur when necessary and sufficient conditions are present	Outcomes may not occur even when conditions are present unless a particular 'recipe', involving external directional forces and probabilistic processes, unfolds
Role of time	Irrelevant; necessary and sufficient conditions can occur in any order	Crucial; the time ordering in which necessary conditions combine is consequential
How to 'read' the theory	The cause is necessary and sufficient to produce the effect	Causation consists of necessary conditions occurring in a particular sequence in which change and random events play a role

While a variance theory looks at which independent variables V_i are necessary and sufficient to influence a dependent variable O_v according to a function $f(V_i)$, a process theory analyses which sequence of events E_i is necessary for a certain output O_E. Moreover, time has a critical role in process theories, while it is irrelevant for variance theories. Figure 4.7 depicts the differences again.

---

[316] See Markus/Robey (1988), pp. 595.

[317] See Mohr (1982).

[318] See Markus/Robey (1988), p. 589.

[319] See Soh/Markus (1995), p. 31.

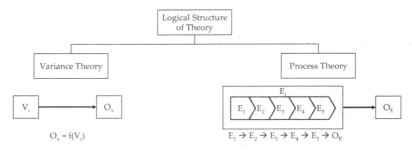

Figure 4.7: Logical Structure of Variance and Process Theories[320]

The main advantage of process theories is that they accept the complexity of causal relationships, while still aiming at generalisability and prediction.[321] Within one research approach, however, the two logical structures should not be mixed.[322] As standardisation processes are highly complex and run over a long time span, process theories seem to be a better choice for analysing them than variance theories.[323] Aiming at an understanding of the dynamics of actor-networks, the actor-network theory (ANT) is an approach to such a process theory which offers several important concepts for analysing standardisation processes.

Holmström/Truex (2003) propose four points to consider when adapting a social theory like ANT for IS research. First, the historical context of the selected theory has to be considered. Second, the theory has an impact on the choice of the appropriate research method. Section 2.3 has already discussed both these points in sketching the roots of ANT and its methodological concepts. Third, the theory chosen should be sensitive towards the details of the phenomenon studied. ANT offers many useful concepts that capture the interwoven political and technical nature of standardisation processes.[324] Finally, the potential contribution of the chosen theory to knowledge creation should be considered. ANT helps to uncover the com-

---

[320] Based on Markus/Robey (1988), p. 590 and Fomin/Keil/Lyytinen (2003), p. 19.

[321] See Markus/Robey (1988), p. 593.

[322] See Mohr (1982), pp. 43ff.

[323] See Fomin/Keil/Lyytinen (2003), p. 19.

[324] See the use of ANT in standardisation research by Hanseth/Monteiro (1997), Fomin/Lyytinen (2000) and Fomin/Keil/Lyytinen (2003).

plex standardisation mechanisms and to reveal critical points where different participants can better defend their interests.

Several researchers have used ANT in their work on standards development. However, they have done so in very different ways. For example, although Egyedi (1996) uses the term 'actor-network' and cites several original sources of ANT, her analysis is based on SCOT instead of the ANT concepts.[325] In contrast, Bowker/Star (1996) discuss ANT from a social perspective as a general theory of classification and standardisation, illustrating it with research on the development of a nursery classification system. Focusing more on the IS perspective, Graham et al. (1995) and Hanseth/Monteiro (1997) use ANT for the analysis of EDIFACT standards development. While ANT is limited to a relatively short section in Graham et al. (1995), Hanseth/Monteiro (1997) provide the most consistent application of ANT concepts to a standards development case.[326] Moreover, in recent years several researchers have been working on a comprehensive theory of standardisation, which blends several theories including ANT. While the work is still in progress, Fomin et al. (2003) is the most important publication on what they call the D-S-N model.[327] ANT mainly plays a role in describing negotiation activities between the participating actors.

As standardisation researchers use ANT in quite different ways, I will give an overview of the ANT based on the original sources. Summarising the concepts and statements of ANT, however, is no easy task, for three main reasons:

– ANT is rooted in post-modern sociology with its rich literature and heavy ideological discussions. Rarely do the authors use figures and tables to make their points. Sometimes the reader is puzzled as to how all the diverse ideas and concepts are supposed to fit together consistently.
– The developers of ANT were (and still are) very open to critics and accordingly improve the ANT concepts where appropriate.[328] To this day,

---

[325] See the previous section. The same goes for the later work Egyedi (2003).

[326] See the illustrative example later in this section and also the related works Monteiro/Hanseth (1996) and Hanseth/Monteiro (1998).

[327] D stands for design, S for sense-making, N for negotiation. See also the related works Fomin/Keil (2000), Fomin/Lyytinen (2000), Virili (2003), and Fomin/Lyytinen/Keil (2004).

[328] See Thompson (2003), p. 84 and Walsham/Sahay (1999), p. 41.

ANT is a living theory that is being further developed by an active research community.[329]

–   Researchers use ANT in very diverse fields such as gender studies or EDIFACT standardisation.[330] In each field, different contributions are made to improve ANT, which are sometimes incommensurable.[331]

Despite the heterogeneity of ANT, this section presents the stable core and additional concepts useful for the further research of this work.

Rooted in the study of relations between politics and science,[332] ANT developed into a general approach to analysing situations in which social and technical aspects are blended into complex settings. The main point of ANT is to avoid the a priori separation of such situations into social and technical components, but rather analyse the interplay between the two with ANT concepts. Simply put, ANT assumes that every actor needs a network of other actors to reach his goals. These networks can comprise very heterogeneous actors, both human and non-human.

A particular feature of ANT is that it provides a general vocabulary for describing the dynamics of almost any kind of actor-network.[333] The most important concepts are translation, inscription and stabilisation. I will present these in more detail. First, however, some basic concepts of ANT are discussed.

4.5.1 Basic Concepts

The term 'actor' has no generally accepted definition and is still being discussed and further refined.[334] Usually, it refers to individual humans, but also collectives of humans.[335] Actor-network theory, however, does not define actors by their substance or characteristics.[336] Actors are simply

---

[329] See Law (1999), p. 10.

[330] See Law/Moser (1999) and Hanseth/Monteiro (1997). Law (2004) provides a comprehensive bibliography of ANT publications.

[331] See Law (1999), p. 10.

[332] See Latour (2002b).

[333] See Stalder (2001), pp. 45ff.

[334] See, e.g., Vollmer (1997), Lamb (2003).

[335] See Braun (2000), p. 6.

[336] See Stalder (2001), p. 31.

"entities that *do* things".[337] Action is what constitutes an actor, regardless of what sort of action it is. With this fundamental assumption, ANT also treats non-human entities as actors, as long as they act in some way.[338] Each actor has certain goals, which it tries to reach by following pro-grammes of action, sometimes also called scripts.[339] The term 'function' is commonly used for the goals and programmes of non-human actors.[340] Although it may have goals and programmes of actions, an entity is not an actor if it is isolated. Action always implies acting upon something, some-where.

> "Acting – that which turns an entity into an actor – is a relational quality. The ability to act does not reside in the entity, but is located in the relationship be-tween entities."[341]

A set of such relationships between entities acting upon each other consti-tutes an actor-network.[342] Latour (1991) stresses that the originality of ANT lies in analysing not only networks of humans (H) such as H-H-H or non-humans (N) such as N-N-N, but rather heterogeneous networks such as H-N-H-N-N-N-H-H-N-H-H.[343] Although it tries to keep its conception as generic as possible, ANT uses three actor types with special properties: intermediaries, delegates and black boxes. Intermediaries are actors pass-ing between other actors and thus defining the relationship between them.[344] Callon (1991) identifies four main types of intermediaries: texts, technical artefacts, human skills and money.[345] Delegates are actors who

---

[337] Latour (1992), p. 241.

[338] Collins/Yearley (1992) propose using the term 'actant' for a non-human actor to keep the fundamental distinction between humans and non-humans. This proposal, how-ever, is often cited but rarely followed.

[339] See Akrich (1992).

[340] See Latour (2002a), p. 219.

[341] Stalder (2001), p. 31.

[342] Stalder (2001), p. 34. As the term actor-network is often misleading, Latour (1999a) thought of recalling ANT, at least its name.

[343] See Latour (1991), p. 110.

[344] See Callon (1991), p. 134.

[345] See Callon (1991), pp. 135ff.

act on behalf of other actors.[346] Black boxes are stable actor-networks that act like a single actor from the perspective of other actors.[347]

With these concepts, ANT also attempts to dissolve the 'micro-/macro' distinction in social theory. It assumes that "macro-actors are micro-actors sitting on top of many (leaky) black boxes".[348] Moreover, ANT has several similarities to the concepts of object-oriented programming: objects (~actors) have encapsulated properties (~properties of actors do not matter) and offer methods (~actions) to other objects. Each object itself consists of several other objects down to basic objects such as numbers and strings.[349]

4.5.2   Dynamics of Actor-Networks

With the concepts presented so far, anything in an actor-network is possible, and no concrete theoretical contribution is made. ANT, however, focuses on the dynamics of actor-networks: how they form, grow and stabilise.[350] Moreover, having described a stable actor-network it is possible to explain and predict the behaviour of the actors. To accomplish this, ANT distinguishes three phases of actor-network dynamics: translation, inscription and stabilisation.[351] In translation, diverse goals and interests are aligned. The programmes achieved are fixed during inscription. The stabilisation phase reveals, whether the programmes stabilise the actor-network or if anti-programmes destabilise it. As depicted in Figure 4.8, ANT offers several more concepts to refine these phases further. The next paragraphs discuss these concepts in more detail, while also explaining the figure.

---

[346] See Walsham (1997), p. 468.

[347] See Callon/Latour (1981), p. 285.

[348] Callon/Latour (1981), p. 286.

[349] See Tatnall/Gilding (1999), p. 958 and Brooks/Atkinson (2004) for an application using the UML. For a general discussion of the object-orientated paradigm and its application to organisational issues, see Lutz (1997).

[350] See Law (1999), p. 4.

[351] Although these phases are rarely explicated, they are implicit in most introductions to ANT. In my opinion, following these phases facilitates the understanding of ANT.

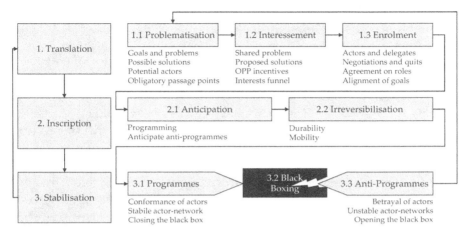

Figure 4.8: Dynamics of Actor-Networks

Translation

Translation is the first phase of a new actor-network. It establishes a new set of relationships between actors. As the diverse interests and goals of different actors are rarely compatible, some goals have to be adapted in order to join an actor-network. The term 'translation' expresses this adaptation and alignment of the actors' goals.[352] With the relational concept of actors being defined by their acting upon other actors, translations also modify the actors themselves.

Since translations can happen very differently in different situations and actor-networks, Law (1992) stresses the importance of empirical investigation into translation processes.[353] Despite the contingency of translations, they always comprise three general stages: problematisation, interessement and enrolment.[354]

While following his goals, an actor may encounter obstacles to reaching them. He can either abandon the goal or search for possible ways to reach the goal by a detour. Usually, the actor cannot solve his problems on his own. Rather, he has to find other actors to help him to achieve his goals.[355]

---

[352] See Latour (1999a).

[353] See Law (1992), p. 6.

[354] See Callon (1986b).

[355] See Latour (2002a), p. 106.

Thus, the *problematisation* phase comprises the development of possible solutions to a problem and the identification of potential actors that might support such solutions. To improve his position before negotiating with other actors on their roles in a new actor-network, an actor often tries to establish himself as an obligatory passage point (OPP).[356] This is a gate-keeping position, as the actor controls crucial resources and claims respon-sibility for the success of the emerging actor-network.[357] It is important to note that actors do not communicate on their problems in this stage. How-ever, they might experience related problems, independently search for solutions, and try to establish themselves as OPPs simultaneously.

After this preparation, an actor articulates the problem to other actors during *interessement*. He tries to convince other actors that it is a shared problem and that they should be interested in jointly solving it.[358] Further, he indicates that he has preliminary plans for setting up an appropriate actor-network. If he sees himself as an OPP, he presents incentives for the other actors to accept him as an OPP.[359] As the other actors are already part of other actor-networks, directing their attention away from these towards a new actor-network is a critical task.[360] It resembles a funnel, as many actors may be interested at first, but these are sorted out as further details of the planed actor-network are presented.[361]

Enrolment is the last and most critical stage of translation. While some actors are directly involved in enrolment, others send delegates, who 'stand in and speak for' the actor that has sent them.[362] All actors and dele-gates then negotiate on the collective goals of the emerging actor-network. During this process of coercion, seduction and/or consent,[363] some actors do not agree with the majority and abandon the negotiations. New efforts of interessement might bring them back. The remaining actors agree on collective goals and their respective roles. To achieve the alignment of all

---

[356] See Callon/Law/Rip (1986), p. 26.

[357] See Martin (2000), p. 719.

[358] See Callon (1986b).

[359] See Sidorova/Sarker (2000), p. 1663.

[360] See Law (1986), p. 71.

[361] See Law (1986), p. 79.

[362] See Walsham (1997), p. 468. Delegates are sometimes also called representatives or spokespersons.

[363] See Underwood (1998).

individual goals with the collective goals, the individual goals often have to be adapted.[364] This is thus also called translation of goals.[365] In the resulting actor-network, one actor can present an OPP. However, as several actors usually try to become an OPP during negotiations, responsibilities can also be distributed more evenly. Before proceeding to action, the programmes agreed upon are inscribed to prevent actors betraying their roles.

Inscription

The activity of inscription is the creation of an artefact that carries the programmes of action needed to achieve the goals of the actor-network that have previously been translated. Therefore, translations are "embodied in texts, machines, bodily skills [that] become their support, their more or less faithful executive."[366] Inscriptions can result in many forms. In ANT studies, inscripts[367] are mostly technical artefacts or texts, but they can also take the form of contracts, institutions, practices, routines or skills.[368] Literally, an inscription is the process of putting a programme into an inscript (see Figure 4.9). The inscript then prescribes to the associated actors how they should act (prescription = resulting effect of a programme).[369] The third scripting activity, description, has important implications for researchers and other analysts: describing the inscripts reveals the goals and programmes of the actors in the actor-network in question. Thus, describing inscripts can explain and predict the behaviour of actors. This, again,

Figure 4.9: Scripting Activities, Scripts and Inscripts

---

[364] See Latour (2002a), pp. 217ff., who calls this 'drift'.

[365] See Callon (1986b).

[366] See Callon (1991), p. 143.

[367] Like the term 'organisation', 'inscription' has two meanings: the activity of inscription and the result of this activity. To avoid confusion, I propose the term 'inscript' to refer to the results of inscriptions.

[368] See Monteiro/Hanseth (1996). To extend the concepts of ANT to institutions and skills, however, might be too great a claim.

[369] See Akrich/Latour (1992).

stresses one of the main propositions of ANT: to explain the behaviour of human actors one has to describe more than just only the associated human actors. Many non-human actors, especially artefacts of different kinds, also influence the behaviour of humans and are often much more accessible to research activities than the influences between humans. For the analysis of inscriptions and inscripts, two aspects are particularly important: anticipation and irreversibilisation.[370]

The success of a programme of action designed according to current requirements relies heavily on environmental conditions not changing. Thus, in an *anticipation* step, one has to consider future scenarios, especially as some actors will often not follow the programme.

> "By inscribing programs of actions into a piece of technology, the technology becomes an actor by imposing its inscribed program of action on its users. The inscribed patterns of use may not succeed because the actual use deviates from it."[371]

Such use not in conformance with or explicitly against the inscribed programme is called anti-programme.[372] Before inscribing programmes into an inscript, the programming actors thus have to identify explicit future scenarios of responses and reactions in order to anticipate potential deviations from the intended programmes.[373] Successful anticipation is crucial for the enduring existence of an actor-network. Otherwise, the inscripts are not able to defend the original goals intended at their creation.[374]

During anticipation, the inscribing actors have many degrees of freedom in designing the inscripts. After deploying them, however, inscripts become difficult to change. The concept of *irreversibility* captures this along two dimensions: durability and mobility. In anticipation, explicit mechanisms are built into the programmes to react to anti-programmes. Durability, however, indicates how long an inscript can exist without its programme being changed by unanticipated anti-programmes. It is a continuum between weak/flexible and strong/inflexible inscripts.[375]

---

[370] Based on Law (1992), p. 6 and Hanseth/Monteiro (1997), p. 187

[371] Hanseth/Monteiro (1997), p. 186.

[372] See Latour (1991).

[373] See Hanseth/Monteiro (1997), p. 187.

[374] See Law (1992), p. 7.

[375] See Hanseth/Monteiro (1997), p. 186.

While durability refers to the irreversibility of inscripts over time, mobility denotes the reach of inscripts through space. Mobile inscripts extend the reach of an actor and thus make acting at a distance possible.[376] Once mobile inscripts are deployed to act, it gets difficult to call them back in order to change them. Taking both durability and mobility together results in Figure 4.10. The more durable and the more mobile an inscript is, the higher is its irreversibility. For highly durable and mobile inscripts, ANT often uses the term "immutable mobiles".[377]

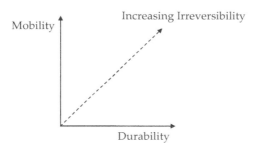

Figure 4.10: Mobility, Durability and Irreversibility

The strength of inscripts, i.e., "the effort it takes to oppose or work around them"[378] depends heavily on their irreversibility. While in general the inscribing actors prefer stronger inscripts, there are many cases where more flexibility is needed to react to new situations not anticipated before. ANT does not give clear statements on how to choose the appropriate degree of durability. Rather, most ANT studies reveal that this is a result of processes of trial and error.[379] The irreversibility of inscripts, however, directly affects the stability of the actor-network in question, which is the topic of the third actor-network phase.

Stabilisation

Law (1992) summarises

"(…) the core of the actor-network approach: a concern with how actors and organisations mobilise, juxtapose and hold together the bits and pieces out of

---

[376] See Law (1992), p. 6.
[377] See Law (1992), p. 6.
[378] Hanseth/Monteiro (1997), p. 187.
[379] See, e.g., Hanseth/Monteiro (1997), p. 186.

which they are composed; how they are sometimes able to prevent those bits and pieces from following their own inclinations and making off; and how they manage, as a result, to conceal for a time the process of translation itself and so turn a network from a heterogeneous set of bits and pieces each with its own inclinations, into something that passes as a punctualised actor."[380]

Thus, a punctualised actor is a stabilised actor-network, which actors regard as a black box. No details of the internal mechanisms of such a black box need to be known.[381] A certain input results in an expected output. A stabilised actor-network is replaced by the performed action itself. From the perspective of the participating actors, an actor-network stabilises when the inscripts work as programmed and all the actors follow the programmes. In socio-technical systems, however, some actors always betray the network goals and contest its stability by running anti-programmes to achieve their own goals.[382] If the inscribed programmes are strong enough, they resist the anti-programmes without endangering the stability of the actor-network.[383] If the anti-programmes are stronger, the actor-network becomes unstable and no longer behaves as a black box. Actors have to open the black box and try to stabilise the actor-network by another sequence of translation and inscription (see Figure 4.8 again).

4.5.3 Illustrating Examples

The Key Weight

Latour (1991) uses a simple example to illustrate the key concepts of actor-network theory.[384] The main actors are a hotel manager, the hotel guests and the hotel keys of the guests. While Latour (1991) did not clearly distinguish the different ANT phases, I will re-interpret this situation using the ANT framework as introduced above.

– Translation 1: The hotel manager has the problem that the guests keep their hotel keys when leaving the hotel. Often the keys are lost, which is

---

[380] Law (1992), p. 6.

[381] For a discussion of such black boxing from the perspective of institutional economics see Dietl (1993) and Scheuble (1998).

[382] See Law (1992), p. 5.

[383] See Hanseth/Monteiro (1997), p. 186.

[384] See Latour (1991), pp. 104ff.

very costly for the hotel. The manager searches for a solution to keep the keys in the hotel. He presents himself as an obligatory passage point by standing at the entrance and courteously asking the guests to drop their keys off at the reception. As the goals of the guests, however, do not usually involve returning the keys, the goals of manager and guest are not aligned.

- Inscription 1: While the manager could not fully anticipate the behaviour of the guests, the inscript of oral notes at the entrance is of low durability and mobility.
- Stabilisation 1: This results in an unstable actor-network, as most of the guests still follow their own goals with their anti-programme of taking the keys outside the hotel.
- Translation 2: The manager wants to improve the situation and thinks of a new solution. He enrols a written sign at the entrance as a new actor to which he delegates the task of reminding guests to leave their keys.
- Inscription 2: The manager anticipates that more guests will follow permanent signs instead of his occasional oral notices. He inscribes the programme "please return your keys" on a sign, which is much more durable than oral notes, but still immobile.
- Stabilisation 2: As a result, more guests bring back the keys and the actor-network becomes more stable.
- Translation 3: The manager is still not happy with the result and thinks of a new solution. Again, he enrols a new actor. This time a metal weight attached to the key should align the goals of the guests with his goals. It acts as a delegate on behalf of the manager.
- Inscription 3: The manager anticipates that more guests might leave their keys if they are heavy and uncomfortable to carry around in one's pockets. This inscript has a high durability, but also a high mobility, as it executes its programme even if the guests leave the hotel with the keys.
- Stabilisation 3: By attaching a metal weight, the manager was able to align his goal (keys stay in hotel) with the goals of the guests (feeling comfortable when leaving the hotel). Now most of the guests act in conformance with the goals of the actor-network under consideration. The manager has thus managed to stabilise the actor-network by the inscription of a programme into a new actor, the metal weight. As he is satisfied with the resulting behaviour of the guests, he closes the black box of the 'key problem' and turns to other tasks. A change in the guest be-

haviour, however, would force the hotel manager to re-open it again and think of new solutions.[385]

This simple example shows that the relation between hotel manager and guests is not a purely social one, but also comprises technical artefacts such as the sign and the metal key weights. The concepts of translation and inscription help us to understand the role of inscripts for the programmes of the different actors. In a sense, this programming can be seen as a kind of standardisation.[386] The hotel manager aims to establish a standard behaviour in the guests and the key weights are a way of enforcing this behaviour.

While this example stresses the importance of inscripts, other ANT studies focus on other aspects of actor-network dynamics. For instance, to demonstrate the translation of interests and goals, Latour (2002a) analyses the relationship between humans and guns. While opponents of private firearms in the US say that 'guns kill people', the National Rifle Association claims that 'the gunner kills people, not the gun.' ANT, however, sees the translation of both the human's and the gun's goals. While the human, for instance, only wants to for instance, rob a bank and the gun was built for shooting bullets, together they become an actor-network capable of killing innocent people.[387] This example reveals the role of non-humans in translating human goals during interessement and enrolment. To stress it again, the analysis of non-humans in actor-networks is essential for ANT.

The 'EDIFACT Mafia'

An important research field for the application of ANT is standardisation.[388] In the following paragraphs, a summary of Hanseth/Monteiro (1997) demonstrates the use of ANT for standardisation. Their starting point is the common goal of creating standards for information exchange in the health care sector of Norway (problematisation and interessement). However, the question of how to standardise and which standards to use

---

[385] Moreover, new technologies such as chip-card-based key locks could also cause an opening of the black box.

[386] In this case, the standards are not codified in a document, but in the technical artefact 'key'.

[387] See Latour (2002a), p. 218.

[388] See the discussion of different standardisation research using ANT at the beginning of this section.

was a long debate lasting from the late 1980s to the mid 1990s (enrolment). It was reflected in many iterative sequences of translations and inscriptions, testing inscripts, then translating again, until a stabilised actor-network was reached.

The main original actors in the health sector were general practitioners, hospitals, laboratories, pharmacies and social insurance offices. In the race to become an obligatory passage point for electronic health care standards, several new actors appeared on the scene: telecommunication companies, consulting companies, governmental agencies and the EDIFACT organisations. Hanseth/Monteiro (1997) describe in detail how these different actors enrol diverse standards and technologies to rule out competing proposals. Often technological arguments hide the real goals of the actors in question and serve as delegates to defend these goals. EDIFACT is the most powerful actor, which is itself is an actor-network mainly comprising several standardisation bodies, the EDIFACT industry of vendors and consultants, the conception and practices relating to how to define and implement messages, the syntax for message structures, tools such as converters and data bases, and artefacts such manuals and documentations.

While several technologically superior proposals failed,[389] EDIFACT succeeded in translating almost all relevant health care actors into its network. The success of EDIFACT, however, also translated many health care problems into software engineering problems. As the so-called 'EDIFACT mafia' insisted on their established procedures and standard concepts,[390] it was very difficult for many health care experts to push through ideas of more practical relevance. As a result, several scenarios with real-time interaction between health care participants were not possible using the EDIFACT standards, although they had been established before on the basis of other available technologies.

After accepting the EDIFACT approach, a further translation was needed to get the general practitioners into the network. The plan involved inscribing their behaviour into the EDIFACT messages through the definition of the semantics of one single data element in which the general

---

[389] Based on standards like IEEE Medix or Health Level 7 and on technologies like bar codes or central data bases.

[390] Especially the reuse of existing elements wherever possible, which made it almost impossible for health care experts without strong EDIFACT knowledge to contribute to the standards.

practitioners were to insert a code for the prescribed drugs. This could only be achieved by granting the general practitioners access to the previously secret drug list of the pharmacies. After all these translations into the EDIFACT network, the actor-network of electronic health care information exchange stabilised. Only one anti-programme succeeded, which was concentrated on a small group of actors without strong competition.

The main conclusion of this example is that a standard cannot be adopted as easily as a purely technical solution. Rather, the whole actor-network attached to it has to be taken into consideration, in this case the 'EDIFACT mafia'. Not only the inscripts themselves stabilise the actor-networks, but also all the actors defending the inscripts. Since many strong programmes of action are inscribed in standards, they have a huge influence on the action of the standards users. Changing these programmes is a difficult task, though the sometimes chaotic nature of such huge standardisation networks enables even small actors to influence the final outcome significantly.

4.5.4 Evaluation

As section 2.3 has already discussed methodological issues relating to ANT, this section is concerned with the theoretical contribution of ANT. Some authors fear that ANT has no theoretical contribution to make at all.[391] "Something that seemingly tries to explain everything about the social ends up explaining nothing about it."[392] Although originally arguing otherwise, today even Latour admits that

> "ANT is a powerful tool to destroy spheres and domains, to regain the sense of heterogeneity and to bring interobjectivity back into the centre of attention. Yet, it is an extremely bad tool for differentiating associations."[393]

Today most ANT researchers see ANT as an 'empty frame' which they can 'fill in' with refined, empirically based theories.[394] In my opinion, ANT is a good starting point for developing more specific process theories along the

---

[391] See, e.g., Stalder (2001), p. 54.

[392] Thompson (2003), p. 79.

[393] Latour (1997).

[394] See Latour (1997).

lines of Markus/Robey (1988).[395] Even if we accept that ANT is no fully-fledged theory but has to be enriched with further theoretical concepts, there are still several critical issues to be considered.

One point is the vagueness about actors. ANT is not based on a stable theory of the actor, but rather on the 'radical indeterminancy' of the actor.[396] Thus in ANT an actor can do anything, as long as he acts somehow. A related point is the difficulty of identifying the goals of an actor and the scripts he is running in order to reach them.[397] Moreover, several authors criticise the 'managerialism' of ANT, i.e., the tendency to consider actor-networks from a centred, privileged view of a leading actor. In many real cases, especially in standardisation, there is no single centred actor, but many actors driving the network.[398] Another of the most difficult parts of an ANT study is to decide where to draw the boundaries of an actor-network, especially as there are often several alternative actor-networks, which are still connected to each other.[399] Despite all this criticism, ANT remains a very useful approach to studying new situations in which individuals, organisations, politics and technology play an important role and cannot be disentangled a priori.[400]

Holmström/Truex (2003) warn IS researchers against combining different social theories too hastily. Although one single social theory might not be sufficient for a certain IS topic, there is usually good theoretical reason why two social theories are not yet combined.[401] I will not here integrate ANT with another social theory. Some approaches, however, should be mentioned. Besides ANT, Giddens' structuration theory is the most frequently used social theory in IS research.[402] Walsham (1997) argues that ANT and Giddens' structuration theory might complement each other, as ANT contributes human/non-human aspects while Giddens offers concepts of social structure.[403] Atkinson/Brooks (2003) integrate both into their

---

[395] See Markus/Robey (1988) and the introduction to this chapter.

[396] See Callon (1999), p. 181.

[397] See Underwood (1998).

[398] See Monteiro/Hanseth (1996), p. 207.

[399] See Monteiro/Hanseth (1996), p. 208.

[400] See Tatnall/Gilding (1999), p. 963.

[401] See Holmström/Truex (2003), p. 2853.

[402] See Jones (2000), Monteiro/Hanseth (1996), Orlikowski/Robey (1991).

[403] See Walsham (1997), p. 473.

'StructurANTion' framework.[404] Others try to combine ANT with Luhmann's theory of social systems.[405] Stalder (1997) here sees a promising approach to drawing the boundaries of actor-networks: any entity "which is directly needed to achieve a certain goal is inside the network".[406] Thompson (2003), however, stresses that ANT is not a systems theory, as the concepts of systems are too deterministic.[407] Finally, the recent attempts to integrate stakeholder analysis into ANT are worth mentioning. This approach helps to better identify all the relevant actors in an actor-network.[408]

The further use of ANT in this study is as follows. First, I will describe two case studies without an a priori theoretical framework and without separating technical and social aspects (see sections 5.2 and 5.3). Then I will use the concepts of ANT to analyse and compare the cases and to derive a generalised model (section 5.4).

4.6   Summary and Conclusions

This chapter has discussed the theoretical ground for answering the second research question:

Why and how are interorganisational standards developed?

It has analysed the general nature of standards and reviewed theoretical approaches to standards and standardisation. In a strict sense, a standard is a broadly adopted specification document that orders repeated activities through unambiguous rules. Products, semantics, processes and performances are the main objects of standards. Governments, consortia, markets and communities are alternative ways of coordinating standardisation. There are three main theoretical perspectives on standards: technical design, economic decisions and social construction. Technical approaches discuss the importance of effective development processes and sufficient resources. Neo-classical economics is focused on product standards, to

---

[404] See Brooks/Atkinson (2004) for a first application of this framework.

[405] See Stalder (1997).

[406] Stalder (1997).

[407] See Thompson (2003), p. 79.

[408] See Pouloudi/Gandecha/Papazafeiropoulou, et al. (2004).

which market mechanisms are applicable. Neo-institutional economics stresses the importance of transaction costs caused by bounded rationality and opportunism. Political markets negotiate institutions such as standards in order to lower the transaction costs in economic markets. Social construction approaches reveal that standards are to a large extent shaped by the interests and perceptions of all participants. Understanding the development of standards thus means understanding negotiations between the actors involved. Actor-network theory deepens this approach and offers a process theory of negotiations, including human and non-human actors. The three concepts of translation, inscription and stabilisation serve to analyse the dynamics of such actor-networks. The examples of the hotel key and the 'EDIFACT mafia' illustrate the application of actor-network theory. Despite some obvious weaknesses of actor-network theory, its strengths justify its use for the analysis of two standards case studies in the next chapter.

5   The Development of Interorganisational Standards

> "IOS solutions are now collaboratively developed, structured around discretely defined cross-company business process standards and able to be distributed via the web. Compared with EDI technology from the past, the notions of open standards, modularity, scalability, and interorganisational business process reengineering have become embedded in modern-day IOS development."[409]
>
> *Matthew L. Nelson and Michael J. Shaw*

Drawing on the theoretical insights from the previous chapter, this chapter will answer the second research question:

Why and how are interorganisational standards developed?

Broadly accepted standards for information systems such as HTTP and XML are necessary, but not sufficient for the quick and loose coupling of firms in supply chain networks. The participants have to align many organisational issues before business processes across the organisational boundaries can operate smoothly. Setting up the supporting systems and processes can be costly if done differently with every single business partner. It thus seems to be more efficient to standardise technical and organisational aspects to align the business interfaces of firms for loose coupling. Such standards are called interorganisational standards. While this idea is convincing, many obstacles complicate the development and broad adoption of interorganisational standards. Several successful initiatives, however, demonstrate the general possibility of reaching this ambitious goal.

This chapter analyses the current situation from a theoretical perspective and derives a generalised process model. Section 5.1 discusses the foundational concepts of Web-based interorganisational standards and gives an overview of existing initiatives. Sections 5.2 and 5.3 provide in-depth case studies of the initiatives RosettaNet and ebXML. Using actor-network theory, section 5.4 discusses both cases and derives concepts for a process model of the development of interorganisational standardisation.

---

[409] See Nelson/Shaw (2003), pp. 258ff.

5.1 Concepts of Web-Based Interorganisational Standards

Since the first EDI systems back in the late 1960s, the basic EDI technology has not changed much. At the same time, the first Internet technologies and since the 1990s the World Wide Web have emerged and now offer an alternative platform for interorganisational communication and data interchange. The main advantages of the Internet are low costs, ubiquity, the existence of many experts, and the quick development of new standards. The next subsection introduces the latest technological developments of the Web that are relevant for interorganisational information systems. Subsection 5.1.2 then discusses the notion of interorganisational standards and the challenges involved in developing and using such standards.

5.1.1 The Emergence of Semantic Web Services Standards

Without any doubt, the World Wide Web is among the most important technical innovations of recent decades. It has influenced many different aspects of public, corporate and private life.[410] Interorganisational information systems (IOS) are no exception. Thus, this subsection introduces the main specifications and standards that have the greatest impact on existing and future IOS.

Strictly speaking, the Internet and the Web are not the same. The Internet is a set of standards that enable the coupling of heterogeneous networks, regardless of their size or underlying technology. The Web is another set of standards that use the Internet to enable distributed applications.[411] The core standards of the Internet are the Transmission Control Protocol (TCP) and the Internet Protocol (IP). One important aspect is the root of these standards. When researchers transmitted data based on Internet technology back in 1969, this could also have been done via the conventional lines of the existing telephone system. In the context of the Cold War, however, the military realised that having communication networks controlled by telecommunication companies offers a target easily destroyed in the event of attacks. The fundamental idea of the Internet was thus to enable data communication without centralised control.

---

[410] See, e.g., Zerdick/Picot/Schrape, et al. (2004) and Zerdick/Picot/Schrape, et al. (2000).
[411] See Tanenbaum (2003), p. 16.

Recognising the growing importance of data communication, the International Telecommunication Union (ITU) and the International Organisation for Standardisation (ISO) also engaged in standardising data communication. However, both X.25 from ITU and Open Systems Interconnection (OSI) from ISO lost the race against TCP/IP, which the Internet Engineering Task Force (IETF) maintains today. Many researchers have tried to explain the success of TCP/IP.[412] The main reasons for the failure of OSI are seen to reside in its overambitious objectives, which were planned to result in an all-embracing standard.[413] This led to delays in development and to defective specifications, which were difficult to implement and caused lengthy revision cycles. Finally, ISO charges fees for its standards, which further hinders adoption.[414] Even so, the conceptual model of OSI still serves as reference model for other data communication standards. ITU's X.25 and its successor Frame Relay were adopted to a considerable extent in business data communication and still serve as transport technology for EDI Value Added Networks (VANs). Egyedi (1996), however, sees the main reason for the disappearance of X.25 and Frame Relay in the so-called 'telephone paradigm' which ITU follows in its standards development. Essentially, it emphasises central control over network connections, while the 'data communications paradigm' is based on decentralised control (see Table 5.1).[415]

---

[412] See, e.g., Egyedi (1996), who also gives an overview of other works.

[413] See Egyedi (1996), p. 233.

[414] E.g., the OSI Reference Model costs CHF 150. Although this does not seem too much, it can prevent interested programmers from using it. Especially in the face of open source software, even low fees quickly prevent broad adoption of a standard, as the programmers do not (directly) earn money with their software.

[415] See Egyedi (1996), p. 181.

Table 5.1: Telephone vs. Data Communication Paradigms[416]

Paradigmatic aspects	Telephone	Data communications
Management domain	Public	Private/personal & organisational
Location of network control	Central	Decentralised
Concepts of network design	Hierarchical	Symmetrical
Focus & sources of revenues	Transmission	Applications
Interest groups	Public Telecom Operators	Private & experimental network operators, computer manufacturers, computer users
SDOs	ITU-T	ISO/OSI, IETF

TCP/IP standardisation, by contrast, followed the data communications paradigm. Its academic roots fostered the modularity, simplicity and openness of Internet standards. To this day, the work of the IETF responsible for it has reflected this. For instance, even if an IETF specification has reached de facto standard status, it is still called a Request for Comments (RFC), demonstrating the voluntary and open character of the standard.

However, the transition from the telephone paradigm to the Internet paradigm of standards is more difficult than might appear at first sight. Large telecommunication operators in particular still struggle to accept their fading control of telecommunication networks because of the broad acceptance of IP. Computer firms, on the other hand, embrace the Internet paradigm and actively contribute to open software and open standards. For example, IBM builds its strategy on both open source software such as Linux and Eclipse, and open Web standards such as XML, SOAP and WSDL. As the latter play a significant role for IOS, they deserve more attention.

---

[416] Shortened version of Egyedi (1996), p. 183.

It took almost three decades from the first Internet transmission to its broad acceptance. One of the key technologies to foster its adoption was HTML for Web pages. However, the roots of HTML go back to the late 1960s too. Based on other conceptual work, the IBM employees Goldfarb, Mosher and Lorie developed a structured tagging language published as Generalized Markup Language (GML) in 1969.[417] In 1986, ISO approved the successor Structured Generalized Markup Language (SGML) as ISO 8879. SGML is a meta-language using Document Type Definitions (DTDs) to describe the structure, elements and attributes of a document. When Tim Berners-Lee developed the first set of specifications for the Web at CERN, he used SGML and a DTD to define HTML.

In October 1994, CERN and MIT founded the World Wide Web Consortium (W3C) to coordinate the development of Web specifications such as HTML. It aims at the 'data communication paradigm' with decentralised organisation, open development and simplicity of specifications, sometimes also called the 'Spirit of the Web'.[418] This also resembles the development of open source software, which follows a similar spirit stressing democratic arguments and emancipation from dominating software vendors.[419] Indeed, some champions of open source software recently became involved in transferring the open source principles to the field of standardisation.[420]

As the early versions of HTML were quite limited, browser developers such as Microsoft and Netscape used proprietary extensions of HTML. To defend the original 'Spirit of the Web', this incited the W3C to improve and extend HTML continuously. The complexity of SGML, however, proved very inconvenient and slowed down the evolution of HTML. As a consequence, a group led by Jon Bosak from Sun Microsystems developed a reduced version of SGML. The W3C published this more 'Web-like' standard as eXtensible Markup Language (XML) in 1998. The HTML version defined with XML is now called XHTML, while the W3C will not further maintain the original HTML specification.

---

[417] See Mintert (2004), p. 10. The acronym also stands for the initials of the developers' surnames.

[418] See Nickerson/zur Muehlen (2003) discussed in subsection 3.3.2. For a comprehensive discussion of the 'Spirit of the Web' see Rowland (1999).

[419] For a discussion of open source software see, e.g., Brügge/Harhoff/Picot, et al. (2004).

[420] See Perens (2004). See also section 4.1 for a short discussion of open standards.

As XML is highly versatile, it can serve for the definition of almost any kind of structured data. The W3C thus uses it not only for XHTML, but also for the definition of other specifications, such as MathML for mathematical expressions or Scalable Vector Graphics (SVG) for graphics representation. Moreover, other developers have recognised the benefits of XML and started to use it for the definition of their own document structures, as is the case with the Organisation for the Advancement of Structured Information Standards (OASIS) (see section 5.3).[421]

While XML gained attention, the 'classic' EDI standards suffered from shortcomings such as cryptic syntax, inflexible and fragmented standards, highly specific software, and expensive VANs. Hence it was mainly large companies that used EDI for automated data exchange.[422] In contrast, the Web was cheap, ubiquitous, and content could be exchanged with minimum effort. While HTML was too specific for human-readable documents, XML appeared to be the perfect choice for electronic data interchange via the Web. However, there is often some confusion about the relation of EDI and XML. As this is a central point of my study, I will illuminate it in more detail.

An exemplary fragment of an EDI document looks like this:[423]

```
PAT+1'
DTM+273:2000070120000930:718'
MOA+873:506444.14'
MOA+870:456446.28'
NAD+OFF
MOA+860:3757.45
NAD+SUM
MOA+856:1155
MOA+860:8044.65
MOA+858:344.63
FTX+ZZZ+++ENDELIG'
```

This reveals the byte-orientation of EDI, which has two major disadvantages. First, it is hard to read for humans without any further support. Second, the order and position of all bytes have certain semantics, which

---

[421] OASIS (2004a) also gives an overview of 593 XML initiatives (updated November 2004).

[422] See Threlkel/Kavan (1999), p. 347.

[423] Kolar/Speicys/Aleksandrova (2001), p. 2.

are 'hard coded'.[424] If a single data element had to be added, both the EDI standard and all implemented systems would have to be adapted too. The case is somewhat different with XML. Below is an XML fragment coding the same content as above:[425]

```
<?xml version="1.0" encoding="ISO-8859-1"?>
<repayment_nl>
   <repayment start_date = "20000701" end_date =
"20000930"/>
      <repayment_total interest = "3757.45"/>
      <repayment_support interest = "8044.65"
            repayment = "1155"
            contribution = "344.63 "/>
      <repayment_rest bond_rest_payment = "506444.14"
            cash_rest_payment ="456446.18"/>
</repayment_nl>
```

While EDI documents are serialised byte-streams, XML documents have a tree-structure using so-called 'tags' to delimit data fields. It is possible to add or remove new elements without changing the semantics of the fields. In other words, the software does not derive semantics from the position of a data field, but rather from the name of a tag.[426] Moreover, the use of so-called 'name spaces' enables data fields from several different specifications to be combined within a single XML document. This apparently technical detail makes a significant difference to the flexibility and modularity of the data XML can describe. Additionally, the similarity to HTML syntax and the availability of cheap software fostered the quick adoption of XML. Today XML is without any competing technology, as there is no serious alternative and no successor on the horizon. In the terminology of Table 5.1, EDI belongs to the telephone paradigm, developed by governmental SDOs and transported by large telecommunication companies via expensive VANs. In contrast, XML represents the 'Spirit of the Web' that falls within the data communications paradigm.[427]

---

[424] See Weitzel/Harder/Buxmann (2001), p. 69.

[425] Kolar/Speicys/Aleksandrova (2001), p. 3.

[426] A software component called a 'parser' analyses the XML document, extracts the data fields, and makes their content available as variables to other applications.

[427] For further details on XML see Buxmann/Ladner/Weitzel (2001), Weitzel/Harder/ Buxmann (2001), and Böhnlein/vom Ende (1999).

Compared to a natural language, however, XML only standardises the 'characters' of an electronic language, but no words and no grammar. Defining this semantics is exactly what EDI standards such as EDIFACT do, although based on highly byte-oriented 'characters' and not a universal standard like XML.[428] Thus, the idea of migrating EDI semantics to the open and flexible XML is obvious,[429] and several initiatives have tried this.[430] These include Ariba with xCML, CommerceOne with xCBL, the XML/EDI Group, and ebXML, a joint effort by UN/CEFACT and OASIS. As only the latter is still of significance, section 5.3 will analyse it in more detail.[431]

It might be surprising that none of these approaches has so far been able to replace EDI systems, though empirical surveys show the superiority of 'Web-based EDI' over traditional EDI.[432] One reason is that a straight migration from traditional to XML-EDI may only be of marginal value.[433] Indeed, the high costs of implementing such a solution and coupling the software used with the trading partners' systems is still a significant obstacle for short-term relations and for smaller companies. Accordingly, several large software vendors developed the concept of Service Oriented Architectures (SOA), which is an approach to reducing the general problem of software integration. In the prevailing Object Oriented Architecture (OOA), software consists of local objects that are tightly coupled via method calls. The idea of SOA is to bundle a set of object methods within a component and offer them as a service to other components, independent of their location. An important element is a service registry, in which a service provider registers the services offered (see Figure 5.1). A service user can search for services in the registry and directly request the service required from the provider. This architecture promises to lower software

---

[428] See Reimers (2001).

[429] See Threlkel/Kavan (1999), pp. 348ff.

[430] See Huemer (2001), pp. 17-26.

[431] E.g., the Web sites of the XML/EDI Group had their last update in 2001: http://www.xmledi-group.org/.

[432] See Downing (2002). However, as this paper does not define exactly what is meant by 'Web-based EDI', the results should be judged carefully. WebEDI can also resemble Web browser-based access to an EDI system. This human-to-machine communication is not EDI in the original sense, but useful for connecting small enterprises to existing EDI systems.

[433] See Kanakamedala/King/Ramsdell (2003).

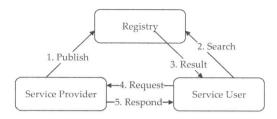

Figure 5.1: Service Oriented Architecture[434]

integration costs significantly, as the discovery and coupling of other services can be largely automated.

By now, all larger software vendors support a certain XML-based realisation of SOA called Web Services.[435] Berners-Lee briefly characterises the main idea of Web Services as "program integration across application and organisational boundaries".[436] As the official standards development organisation (SDO) of Web Services, the W3C provides this definition:

> "A Web service is a software system designed to support interoperable machine-to-machine interaction over a network. It has an interface described in a machine-processable format (specifically WSDL). Other systems interact with the Web service in a manner prescribed by its description using SOAP-messages, typically conveyed using HTTP with an XML serialization in conjunction with other Web-related standards."[437]

This emphasises that Web Services are not designed for direct human use, but for machine-to-machine communication. Besides HTTP and XML, the two basic W3C specifications for Web Services are SOAP and WSDL.

SOAP originally stood for Simple Object Access Protocol. As it is neither simple nor serves it for object access, W3C now uses its acronym without further reference to its original sense.[438] SOAP essentially specifies how XML messages are exchanged between service provider and user, how the

---

[434] See Kreger (2001), p. 7.

[435] See, e.g., Microsoft's .NET, which will play a central role in future versions of the Windows operating system, and SAP's Enterprise Services Architecture, which all new SAP products will support (Bacheldor/Ewalt (2003)).

[436] Berners-Lee (2003).

[437] World Wide Web Consortium (2003). For further definitions see Ratnasingam/Pavlou (2002), p. 2240.

[438] See Hauser/Löwer (2004), pp. 39ff.

messages are structured, and what the elements contain. Based on existing work, IBM and Microsoft jointly developed SOAP and submitted it to W3C in April 2000.[439]

The Web Services Description Language (WSDL) enables an unambiguous description of the methods a Web Service offers. As it is machine-readable, an automatic import of remote methods into the system of the service user is possible. It too was mainly developed by IBM and Microsoft and has been maintained at the W3C since March 2001.

UDDI (Universal Description, Discovery and Integration) offers a way of building a machine-readable registry, in which Web Services can be easily discovered as in 'yellow pages'. Again, IBM and Microsoft were the main developers of UDDI, which they submitted to OASIS in 2002.[440]

Figure 5.2 depicts how these three specifications form the Web Services stack that sits on top of the usual Internet/Web stack. Since their publication, the Web Services specifications have attracted considerable attention not only from experts, but also from the public.[442] Noteworthy is the quan-

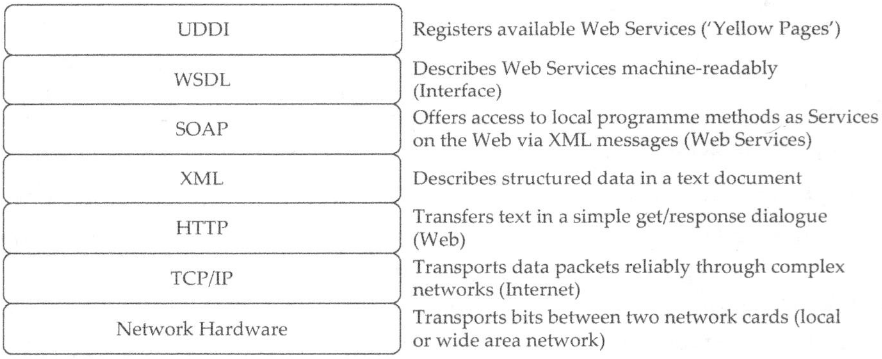

UDDI	Registers available Web Services ('Yellow Pages')
WSDL	Describes Web Services machine-readably (Interface)
SOAP	Offers access to local programme methods as Services on the Web via XML messages (Web Services)
XML	Describes structured data in a text document
HTTP	Transfers text in a simple get/response dialogue (Web)
TCP/IP	Transports data packets reliably through complex networks (Internet)
Network Hardware	Transports bits between two network cards (local or wide area network)

Figure 5.2: Web Services Stack[441]

---

[439] For a detailed introduction to the Web Services specifications see Hauser/Löwer (2004).

[440] The submission to OASIS and not to the W3C has several reasons discussed in the next subsection.

[441] Adapted from Bussler/Fensel/Maedche (2002).

[442] See, e.g., Kerstetter/Hamm/Ante, et al. (2002), Web Services lösen Investitionsschub aus (2002), Schmidt (2002), Schulz (2002), Fritsch (2001), Kerstetter (2001), and Kuschke/Wölfel (2001).

tity of books already available, most of which cover actual implementations and technical guidelines.[443]

All the Web Services specifications are essential for the dynamic configuration of value chains based on existing services, which is the vision of many Web Services protagonists.[444] This requires what Jones et al. (2001) call the self-integration of applications:

> "Ability of applications to find one another, to establish a dialogue, to exchange information, to understand that information, all more or less automatically"[445]

To come closer to realising this vision, however, it is not sufficient to standardise general mechanisms for the communication of software components. Rather, the definition of domain-specific semantics in machine-readable formats is also required. This is what EDI standards provide for business transactions on the basis of byte-oriented specifications. Despite the XML/EDI efforts already mentioned, widely accepted semantic definitions based on XML and usable with Web Services are still lacking.[446] One reason might be that there is no standardised way of defining domain-specific semantics using XML. Aiming at this gap, the Semantic Web initiative at the W3C is currently developing a set of Web-based technologies to describe data in a machine-readable way. Berners-Lee, the inventor and main proponent of the Semantic Web concept, briefly describes its main idea as "data integration across application and organisational boundaries."[447] In contrast to Web Services, which offer syntactical mechanisms to couple remote applications via Web-based remote procedure calls, the Semantic Web initiative aims at establishing a broadly accepted way of representing data and its semantics.[448]

---

[443] A search on Amazon.com in January 2004 retrieved about 300 English books with the term "Web Services" in the title. One English example of a practical guide is Glass (2002). A German example is Hauser/Löwer (2004).

[444] See, e.g., Hagel (2002). For early examples of Web Services use in practice see Picot/Breidler (2002).

[445] Jones/Ivezic/Gruninger (2001), p. 404.

[446] See Hauser/Löwer (2004), pp. 211ff., Bussler/Fensel/Maedche (2002), and Paolucci/Kawamuar/Payne, et al. (2002).

[447] Berners-Lee (2003).

[448] For the difference between syntax and semantics see Figure 2.1 on page 15.

The official definition by the W3C reads as follows:

"The Semantic Web provides a common framework that allows data to be shared and reused across application, enterprise, and community boundaries. It is a collaborative effort led by W3C with participation from a large number of researchers and industrial partners. It is based on the Resource Description Framework (RDF), which integrates a variety of applications using XML for syntax and URIs for naming."[449]

Besides RDF, Uniform Resource Identifiers (URIs) and XML more elements are needed to achieve the vision of the Semantic Web as described in the seminal article by Berners-Lee et al. (2001). Figure 5.3 shows the Semantic Web layer model. Representing fundamental parts of the existing Web, the three lowest layers are largely available. RDF is specific to the Semantic Web and allows the description of resources in a machine-understandable manner.

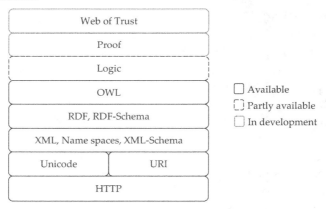

Figure 5.3: Semantic Web Stack[450]

Based on RDF, the Web Ontology Language (OWL) serves for the modelling of ontologies.[451]

"An ontology defines the terms used to describe and represent an area of knowledge. Ontologies are used by people, databases, and applications that

---

449 World Wide Web Consortium (2004).

450 See Neumeier/Löwer/Picot (2003), which is adapted from Fensel/Patel-Schneider (2002), p. 17.

451 The term 'ontology' is rooted in philosophy. In general, it is "the science of what is, of the kinds and structures of objects, properties, events, processes, and relations in every area of reality"; see Smith (2003).

need to share domain information (…). Ontologies include computer-usable definitions of basic concepts in the domain and the relationships among them (…). They encode knowledge in a domain and also knowledge that spans domains. In this way, they make that knowledge reusable."[452]

RDF has already found some widespread applications such as RSS (RDF Site Summary), which serves as specification for content syndication.[453] OWL has been an official W3C recommendation since the beginning of 2004, but still lacks broad support in actual implementations. The logic, proof and trust layers are in an early stage or are just concepts. Increasing academic and practical interest, however, make the Semantic Web a serious attempt to move the storage of meaningful data to the Web.[454] Although it qualifies especially for knowledge management, it will also play a major role in the coupling of IS.[455] The complementary nature of Semantic Web and Web Services technologies thus makes their convergence a logical step. Indeed, several research initiatives are concerned with the integration of Semantic Web and Web Services.[456] Although it is too early for concrete results, two quotations illustrate the directions the research efforts are aiming at:

> "Semantic Web Services (SWS) is the convergence of Web Services and Semantic Web. SWS is the next major generation of the Web, in which e-services and business communication become more knowledge-based and agent-based."[457]
>
> "Semantic Web Enabled Web Services will allow the automatic discovery, selection and execution of inter-organisation business logic making areas like dynamic supply chain composition a reality."[458]

---

[452] Heflin (2004).

[453] 'RSS' meant RDF Site Summary. As it is quite simple and does not implement many concepts from RDF, the latest version stands for Really Simple Syndication. See Hauser/Löwer (2004), p. 223.

[454] A query on Amazon in January 2004 retrieved about 20 books containing the term 'Semantic Web' in the title.

[455] See Fensel (2001).

[456] See, e.g., the Semantic Web Services Initiative (http://www.swsi.org/), the Semantic Web enabled Web Services project (http://swws.semanticweb.org/), W3C's Semantic Web Services Interest Group (http://www.w3.org/2002/ws/swsig/).

[457] Grosof (2004).

[458] Bussler/Fensel/Maedche (2002), p. 24.

Overall, we are witnessing a major shift in the architecture of IS in general and IOS in particular. The evolution of IS architectures from early mainframe-based, fully integrated systems to highly distributed semantic and service-oriented IS is illustrated in Figure 5.4.

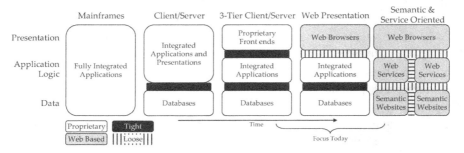

Figure 5.4: Paradigm Shifts in IS Architecture

Gebauer/Shaw (2002) see a delay in IS research regarding these recent developments. Not surprisingly, the literature on Semantic Web Services is primarily concerned with solving technical challenges and not yet with the management of actual Semantic Web Services implementations.[459] A certain amount of other literature is available on the Semantic Web. While one contribution from the IS community sums up serious obstacles to the broad adoption of the Semantic Web and sketches possible solutions,[460] papers rooted in computer science demonstrate successful applications and ways of further improving them.[461] The key message, however, is that Semantic Web technologies will initially play a significant role mainly in closed application domains and less in the open Web. One reason for this is the difficulty of defining Web-wide agreed ontologies and domain specifications in general.[462] As will be shown below, these difficulties are often less technical in nature than caused by managerial and political conflicts.

Below I will focus on the application domain of interorganisational relations, especially the exchange of business-related information in supply chain networks. I will review existing specifications, how agreements on

---

[459] See, e.g., Bussler/Fensel/Maedche (2002).

[460] See Benton/Kim/Ngugi (2002).

[461] See Angele (2003), Davies/Fensel/Harmelen (2003), and Singh/Iyer/Salam (2003).

[462] See Neumeier/Löwer/Picot (2003), pp. 82ff.

them were achieved, and how further domain specifications can be developed.

5.1.2   Web-Based Interorganisational Standards

Sections 3.1 and 3.2 showed that interorganisational (IO) relationships cover more than just exchanging commodity goods or services via market mechanisms. Today's supply chain networks (SCNs), for example, rely on concepts such as 'build-to-order', 'capable-to-promise', and 'efficient consumer response'. If all of these concepts were specifically modelled for each IO relationship, connecting many partners and switching between them would be prohibitively expensive. The main vision in IO standards is thus to standardise the interfaces between firms in order to enable loosely coupled IO relationships. Although the efforts at standardisation described in the previous subsection already aim to provide such standards, the Semantic Web and Web Services specifications are only fundamental technologies. They do not model business-related facts. This leads to the definition of interorganisational standards as I am using the term in this study:

> *Interorganisational standards are broadly adopted specifications that formally define or support business-related semantics and processes, which are made accessible to other organisations' information systems, usually via Web-based technologies.*

If such a specification is not yet broadly adopted, I will speak of a (Web-based) interorganisational (IO) specification.[463] Additionally, several initiatives also pursue the goal of the standardisation and automation of all transaction phases, i.e., initiation, negotiation, execution, monitoring and adjustment.[464] As many standardisation initiatives, are still far from achieving such extensive support, however, I recognise this goal, but do not see it as a required element of the definition.

---

[463] For a short discussion of the differences between standards and specifications, see section 4.1.

[464] See, e.g., ebXML as discussed in section 5.3.

Hepp (2003) lists several aspects an IO standard would have to specify unambiguously:[465]

- Time, quantities and currencies
- Physical places
- Goods and services
- Organisations and individual roles
- Business processes
- Agreements and Contracts

Most of these aspects are not stable, but subject to frequent change. Jacucci et al. (2003) claim that formalisation of (inter-)organisational domains will never come to full closure because of the unpredictable side-effects of human action.[466] Such semantic change demands permanent 'reparation' of formal specifications.[467] It would be inefficient to cover all aspects of business semantics within one specification, as it would be changing almost permanently, leading to instability and confusion. Accordingly, a modular approach seems to be superior, with a set of specifications each focused on a certain topic. Hepp (2003), for example, argues that permanently adapting the formal descriptions and classifications of goods and services is already a major challenge. Moreover, RosettaNet assesses almost 90 different specifications that all aim to offer at least some elements for a complete IO standards solution and most of which can be combined within the same IOS.[468]

One possible way of classifying formal specifications is the distinction between fact-based and rule-based models. In their philosophical analysis of information systems development, Hirschheim et al. (1995) see two radically different ways of data modelling. The fact-based approach is similar to the epistemology of positivist research:

> "Designing a language which would faithfully and clearly depict states and invariances of a reality which is presumed as objective".[469]

---

[465] See Hepp (2003), p. 68. He also lists risk and trust, which I exclude, as they are almost impossible to specify unambiguously.

[466] See Jacucci/Grisot/Aanestad, et al. (2003), p. 158.

[467] See Franck (1991), pp. 51ff. and the short discussion in section 3.2.

[468] See subsection 5.2.3.

[469] Hirschheim/Klein/Lyytinen (1995), p. 232.

The rule-based approach resembles the epistemology of interpretive research:

> "Cyclical hermeneutic processes by which reality is socially constructed through language as to make significant acting possible in that constructed reality."[470]

Here the focus is not on projecting the real world into a data model. Rather, the developers agree on certain rules through social processes, which they formalise in data models. This concept can be transferred to specifications, as these are also a kind of data model. Developers thus shape rule-based specifications according to their beliefs and needs. Examples are technical specifications such as SOAP and WSDL. Fact-based specifications have to represent a part of the real world as well as possible. Examples are product catalogue specifications such as BMEcat.[471] The distinction, however, is not always clear, as socially constructed rules can be mixed with real-world facts in one specification. One example is an EDIFACT order, which on the one hand represents a paper-based order (fact-based), but on the other hand, changes order management practices in the real world (rule-based).

Several other frameworks aim to categorise different interorganisational specifications.[472] On the basis of the Business Internet Consortium Framework,[473] I propose to use the interorganisational specifications stack as depicted in Figure 5.5. Although it would need to be even more detailed to show all the differences between the specifications, it offers a good compromise between detail and clarity.

The lowest layer is the network transport layer. It consists of all technologies commonly used for Internet connections, such as TCP/IP and HTTP. XML and several related technical standards such as XML Schema Definition (XSD) form the next layer. So far, the specifications serve in almost any kind of modern computer system and are not specific to IOS.

---

[470] Hirschheim/Klein/Lyytinen (1995), p. 232.

[471] See BMEcat (2004).

[472] See, e.g., Albrecht/Dean/Hansen (2003), p. 192, Gosain (2003), p. 10, and Jain/Zhao (2003), p. 213.

[473] See He/Wenzel/Thomasma (2001), p. 8.

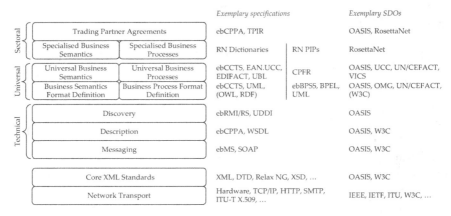

Figure 5.5: Interorganisational Specifications Stack[474]

Messaging specifications serve for the exchange of XML-based messages between the IOS of business partners. While SOAP is broadly accepted as a messaging specification for different kinds of applications, it lacks security mechanisms. ebXML's ebMS augments SOAP with security and adds further mechanisms needed for the business-specific use of SOAP.[475] The description layer offers specifications for the machine-readable description of the IO interfaces. Again, W3C's WSDL is a generic specification, while ebXML's ebCPPA also includes business aspects. Discovery comprises specifications for building central registries to make it easier to find business partners. Although UDDI is one of the basic Web Services specifications, here it differs from SOAP and WSDL, as it includes business-specific semantics and is maintained by OASIS. So far, the stack is similar to the Web Services stack depicted in Figure 5.2. As these specifications focus on technical aspects of IOS, I will further subsume them under the term 'technical IO specifications'.

The next layers are divided into two halves. Specifications concerned with business semantics are on the left and those concerned with business processes are on the right in Figure 5.5. Business semantics unambiguously describes the structure of business documents, their elements and their meanings. A typical example is an order, that contains the customer

---

[474] Based on ISO/IEC (1997), He/Wenzel/Thomasma (2001), p. 8., and Bitkom (2004), p. 5.

[475] For a detailed discussion of ebXML see section 5.3.

address, the order date, the products ordered, the quantities ordered, and the prices. For a successful transaction it is crucial that both business partners should have a common understanding of these data elements. Products, quantities and prices in particular are sources of misunderstandings: for example, products often come in different variations that are not obvious from the product name, such as different colours. A standardised product number system supports the unambiguous identification of products. By contrast, business processes describe the sequence and events of business document exchange. One example is the reaction to an order. The business process can specify when a supplier has to acknowledge an order and whether he has to send regular status information on the order. It can also specify whether the customer is allowed to change the order and within which limits (for example, the complete cancellation of the order or only the adjustment of quantities or shipping modalities). This short introduction to business semantics and processes illustrates that both fields can become quite complex.[476] Modelling both in different specifications is thus an appropriate approach to keeping these complexities separated.

Moreover, I distinguish three layers of business semantics and process specifications. The lowest layer comprises formats of how to define business semantics and processes. The Unified Modeling Language (UML) specification, for example, does not specify actual business semantics or processes. However, it offers several formal and graphical concepts that support these. Today almost all business-related specifications rely on UML.[477] While UML is a universal approach to modelling almost any kind of information system, specifications such as Resource Description Framework (RDF) and Web Ontology Language (OWL) offer ways of formally describing the semantics of entities and their relationships, that computers can automatically interpret. Similarly, the Business Process Execution Language (BPEL) and the Business Process Specification Schema (ebBPSS) offer concepts and elements for defining business processes that information systems can automatically execute. None of these specifications, however, provides readily defined semantics and processes, only the methods for doing so.

---

[476] For more details, see van der Aalst/Kumar (2003), Hess (1996), Smith/Fingar (2002), Hepp (2003).

[477] See, e.g., RosettaNet PIPs or UN/CEFACT's ebCCTS.

Specifications on the next layer comprise actual business semantics and processes that interorganisational scenarios can directly draw on. For instance, the EAN.UCC system globally defines unique numbers for the identification of products. CPFR is an industry-independent specification for collaborative forecasting developed by the SDO Voluntary Interindustry Commerce Standards (VICS). However, such universal business semantics and processes cannot usually meet all the requirements of a particular application domain. As a result, industries often develop specialised specifications based on the universal ones. For example, RosettaNet's collaborative forecasting Partner Interface Processes (PIPs) are based on CPFR, but customised to the needs of the electronics industry. If there are no universal specifications for a certain scenario needed in an industry, then SDOs usually develop specialised specifications, which can be transferred to other industries later. RosettaNet follows this approach, as it is a leader in developing IO business processes, but is also open for other industries to adopt them.[478]

The last element of the IO specifications stack is the definition of formal trading partner agreements. In the ideal case, such a trading partner agreement (TPA) comprises all technical, organisational and legal details and can be processed automatically by the IOS of the partners involved. Further complexity is added by the fact that such agreements also have to consider the details of the specification used on the other layers, as the on-top position in Figure 5.5 indicates. Several SDOs use TPA specifications in their architecture to support (quasi-)automatic discovery, negotiation and agreement via IO standards too.[479] However, the high complexity and the many different specifications used for IO scenarios will leave many issues unresolved until this vision is achieved on a broader scale. If this succeeds, autonomic software agents could play an increasing role in dynamic supply chain networks.[480]

To differentiate between the specifications that can be generally applied and specifications developed for a certain industry, I will call the former 'universal IO specifications' and the latter 'sector IO specifications' (see Figure 5.5).

---

[478] See the use of the RosettaNet specifications in CIDX and PIDX as shown later.

[479] See, e.g., ebXML's ebCPPA.

[480] See the existing research on this topic, e.g., Choi/Dooley/Rungtusanatham (2000), Swaminathan/Smith/Sadeh (1998), Singh/Iyer/Salam (2002).

All these different specialisations, however, face the threat of fragmentation and incompatibility, as happened with the many different EDIFACT derivates. A major challenge for specification development today is thus to use modern computer science concepts such as modularisation and inheritance to resolve the trade-off between specialisation and compatibility. Compared to the binary document approach of EDI, XML is a first step in this direction. Even so, the issue is not resolved and poses several challenges to standards development organisations (SDOs), on a technical as well as on an organisational level.[481]

The number of different SDOs with similar visions and unclear status confuses potential users and even experts in the field.[482] It appears to be a hopeless task to capture and classify all existing SDOs without missing some out.[483] Nevertheless, I have compiled a list including the most relevant SDOs for IO specifications. This only includes SDOs developing specifications meeting the definition of IO specifications. I have analysed the respective specifications using the stack in Figure 5.5 (see the result in the table of appendix C). The analysis reveals strong interconnections between the specifications. It is possible to combine them in many different ways, often not explicated in the specifications or supporting documents. The identification of explicated interconnections, however, results in the matrix depicted in Figure 5.6.[484] The two axes list all SDOs, separated into sectoral SDOs (upper part of the vertical axis) and technical or universal SDOs (lower part of the vertical axis). The '1s' in the matrix signify that the SDO on the left is using at least one specification from the respective SDO on the top. For example, RosettaNet uses specifications from eight other SDOs, while CEFACT's specifications are used by 10 other SDOs. The many '1s' in the upper right-hand part of the matrix reveal that the sectoral SDOs often rely on the technical/universal specification, while these are also highly interconnected (lower right). Two noticeable exceptions are RosettaNet and SWIFT. API's PIDX and CIDX's Chem eStandards use the messaging infrastructure of RosettaNet and some RosettaNet concepts for

---

[481] See, e.g., Graham/Pollock/Smart, et al. (2003), p. 7 and Nelson/Shaw (2003), p. 295.

[482] See Kotinurmi/Nurmilaakso/Laesvuori (2003), p. 143.

[483] An almost complete, but unstructured list of XML-based specifications is offered by OASIS (2004a).

[484] This excludes the use of core technologies such as XML and UML, as these are not specific to IO specifications and used by almost all SDOs.

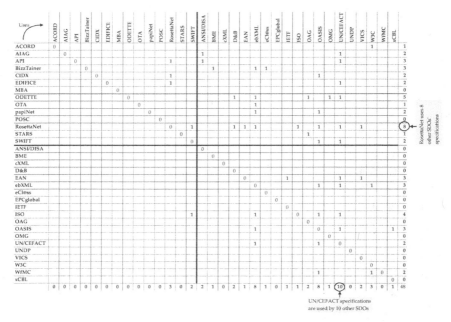

Figure 5.6: Interconnections between Standards Development Organisations

their semantics and process definitions too. EDIFICE, formerly developing an EDIFACT subset for the electronics industry, now organises the migration of its members from EDIFICE-EDI to RosettaNet. As the dominant specifications in the financial industry, SWIFT standards are indirectly used in almost any industry. RosettaNet started to integrate them into its specifications for financial processes, while ISO approved them as ISO 20022.

As all these IO standards are highly interwoven with the day-to-day business of the user firms, it is generally difficult to isolate their direct benefits.[485] In particular, as Web-based IO standards have only started to emerge since 1998, no comprehensive surveys of their impact are yet available. Nonetheless, several case studies show the benefits of these standards. For example, the use of RosettaNet PIPs for forecasting, inventory management and invoice/payment between Intel and its supplier Shinko resulted in a work-time reduction from 1668 hours to 316 hours,

---

[485] See, e.g., Niggl (1994), pp. 65ff.

i.e., 81%.[486] The situation before was completely manual, however, which explains this high improvement. Direct comparisons between EDI and Web-based IOS are still very rare. Downing (2002), for example, concludes that the operational impact of Web-based IOS is not very different from that of EDI-based IOS, but that the strategic measures of customer satisfaction and cooperation intensity show a clear advantage for Web-based IOS.[487] Despite the low number of IOS researched in this study, it indicates that the main benefits of Web-based IOS do not simply lie in replacing EDI. Rather, they aim at processes that were not automated until today, whether because there were no suitable EDI standards or because the setup costs were too high for short-term IO relationships. Moreover, several large companies such as Intel, Nokia and Sony have shown a strong commitment to Web-based IO standards. Intel, for example, has communicated a clear intention to switch off all EDI-based IOS and turn to RosettaNet-based IOS by 2006. As early as 2002, Intel already transacted five billion US$ worth of business via RosettaNet.[488]

All these points have motivated recent research to analyse IO standards in more detail, ranging from ROI calculator tools for practical use[489] to adoption and diffusion studies[490] and economic analyses. Kotinurmi et al. (2003) offer one of the latter, conducting short case studies on ebXML, RosettaNet and xCBL to analyse whether their findings support the main propositions of the common economics of standards:[491]

"(1) If the costs of compatibility fall more heavily on some than others, the free-rider problem biases away from compatibility.
(2) If the information is incomplete, an obsolete standard may prevail, although a better alternative is available.
(3) Standardisation by market is faster, but standardisation by committee causes fewer errors. A hybrid system of committee and market outperforms both. (...)
(4) Adoption dynamics work to the advantage of large networks and against small networks.

---

[486] See RosettaNet (2003c), p.

[487] See Downing (2002) and section 3.3 for an overview of impact measures.

[488] See Barlas (2003).

[489] See Peleg/Rajwat (2002).

[490] See Nelson/Shaw (2003).

[491] Their propositions are based on Katz/Shapiro (1985), Farrell/Saloner (1985), Farrell/Saloner (1988), Arthur (1989), Shapiro/Varian (1999). See the discussion in subsection 4.3.1.

(5) Expectations are vital to obtaining the critical mass necessary to fuel growth.
(6) Introducing new products faces a trade-off between performance and compatibility.
(7) Introducing new products faces a trade-off between openness and control."[492]

Their case studies support propositions (2), (3), (5) and (6). (1) is not necessarily supported. As large companies benefit greatly from interorganisational standards, they are willing to pay for the standardisation even if there are 'free-riders'. (4) is not necessarily supported, as interorganisational standards used intensively by a few companies can be of more value than standards used less intensively by many companies. (7) is not supported, as openness seems to be a critical factor for the adoption of all the interorganisational standards analysed. Kotinurmi et al. (2003) see the main reason for these differences in the fact that the end-users are companies and not individuals consuming a standards-based product.

Despite these differences with respect to the usual economics of standards and the practical importance of interorganisational standards, the actual organisational and political processes in the development of such standards were rarely a topic of research.[493] Moreover, Nelson/Shaw (2003) call for more research on these SDOs after conducting a comprehensive survey on the adoption of IO specifications. What follow accordingly provides two in-depth case studies on the development of RosettaNet and ebXML, which are considered the two most important SDOs for interorganisational standards, but have not yet been analysed in detail.[494]

5.2   The Case of RosettaNet

The electronics industry is one of the most dynamic industries.[495] As new technologies are invented and introduced into markets within short periods, supply chain networks are constantly evolving.[496] Grove (1996) de-

---

[492] Kotinurmi/Nurmilaakso/Laesvuori (2003), p. 136.

[493] See the overview in subsection 3.3.1.

[494] See also the interconnections in Figure 5.6.

[495] Here, the electronics industry mainly comprises computer and telecommunications hardware. These two sectors make up more than 60% of the 700 billion US$ electronics industry, which includes other segments such as automotive, measurement, medical and military electronics (see Norberg/Banavige (1999), p. 20).

[496] See Thomas (1999).

scribes the transformation of the electronics industry from a vertically integrated industry with few companies to a horizontally specialised industry with many specialised players.[497] Similarly, Afuah (2003) identifies the tendency for firms to grow horizontally but shrink vertically. In this process, IOS play a crucial enabling and driving role.[498]

Like other industries, the electronics industry for many years used to rely heavily on EDI solutions to connect supply chain partners. The several disadvantages of EDI, however, led to the formation of the RosettaNet consortium. Its notable success and its particular approach make Rosetta-Net an important case for research on interorganisational standards. Although RosettaNet is mentioned in the literature quite often, no in-depth research case studies on its standardisation practices are available yet. This section thus fills this gap and analyses RosettaNet in detail with the focus on the development of its standard specifications. First, the reasons for the formation of RosettaNet are described. The following subsection shows the growth and organisational structure of RosettaNet. Subsection 5.2.3 discusses its technical architecture and the Foundational Programs, while subsection 5.2.4 is dedicated to the process specifications and Milestone Programs of RosettaNet.

5.2.1 Formation

The roots of RosettaNet are closely bound up with one man, Fadi Chehadé. As an impecunious Egyptian boy, he migrated alone to the United States, studied at Stanford, and finally became responsible for e-commerce activities at the electronics distributor Ingram Micro.[499] There he developed a Web-based extranet solution for connecting hundreds of suppliers and thousands of resellers.[500] In 1997, Chehadé led a project to establish a more advanced connection between Ingram Micro and its supplier 3Com. However, not only the incompatibility of the respective systems, but especially the different business processes of the two companies made the project very time-consuming and expensive.[501] After its successful completion,

---

[497] See Grove (1996), p. 44.
[498] See also the discussion in section 3.2.
[499] See Anderson (2001).
[500] See RosettaNet (1999a)
[501] See Medina (2000).

another of Ingram Micro's partners asked for a similar solution. In the light of the agonising integration involving 3Com, Chehadé was wary of such projects and had the idea of reusing the solutions already developed wherever possible. The basic idea of standardised interorganisational processes for the electronics industry was born.[502]

As such an ambitious plan calls for broad support, Chehadé had to convince other companies of his ideas. In February 1998, he gathered together representatives from 26 major companies linked to the electronics industry, including Compaq, EDS, Federal Express, Hewlett-Packard, Intel and Microsoft,[503] and presented his vision of a "common XML-based machine-to-machine e-business standard."[504] To develop and promote it, he proposed to found a non-profit consortium, which would be supported by lending top executives and financial contributions from the member companies. Not surprisingly, he could not convince the participants, who regarded the plan as too ambitious to be feasible. The meeting ended without a decision being taken.[505] Nevertheless, Chehadé did not give up and finally won the endorsement of another major company, which he refuses to name publicly.[506]

Eventually, Chehadé managed to gather sufficient support from industry and an impressive list of firms officially founded the non-profit consortium RosettaNet: ABB, American Express, CHS Promark Electronics, Cisco Systems, CompUSA, Compaq, Computacenter, Computer 2000, Deutsche Financial Services, EDS, Federal Express, GE Information Services, GSA, HP, IBM, Ingram Micro, Insight, Intel, MicroAge/EC Advantage, Microsoft, Netscape, Oracle, PC Order, SAP, Tech Data, Tech Pacific Holdings, Toshiba and United Parcel Service.[507] The list includes companies as diverse as manufacturers, distributors, shippers, financial institutions and software vendors.

The name RosettaNet is taken from a stone found close to the Egyptian city of Rosetta in 1799 by a soldier from Napoleon's army. Dating back to 196 B.C., the stone carried the same message in Greek and two Egyptian

---

[502] See Medina (2000).

[503] See Sullivan (2003), p. 26.

[504] Sullivan (2003), p. 26.

[505] See Sullivan (2003), p. 26.

[506] See Sullivan (2003), p. 26.

[507] See RosettaNet (1998b).

languages. With the help of what became known as the Rosetta Stone, scholars were able to decipher the Egyptian language.[508] This historical background serves primarily as a metaphor, as RosettaNet supports the translation of one company's language into another's. Additionally, it recalls the Egyptian roots of RosettaNet's founder Fadi Chehadé.

The mission statement stresses the fact that RosettaNet was not only perceived as a technical initiative, but rather as a huge management effort as well:

> "RosettaNet will adopt, promote, and facilitate the deployment of open content and open transaction rules for increasing IT supply chain and electronic commerce efficiency. Its mission is to provide common business interfaces for supply chain trading partners and their customers to exchange information and transactions."[509]

This mission is also reflected in its initial organisational structure. All the founding companies sent top executives to RosettaNet's Managing Board.[510] This was responsible for the further development of the RosettaNet organisation and its specifications. Moreover, three types of partners supported this work. While Architect Partners contributed to the specifications, Coalition Partners supported the marketing, and Execution Partners assisted in actual RosettaNet implementation projects.[511] Right from the beginning, a Web-based platform helped to coordinate the efforts of all participants.

The operational work of RosettaNet started with four projects. One was concerned with general product information such as identification numbers, product descriptions, product classification and product shipping data. Three others defined technical attributes and determined sample values for the technical specifications of software, memory, and laptops.[512] Standardising all these aspects is a crucial prerequisite for the unambiguous selection of products and thus for the automation of interorganisational processes.[513]

---

[508] See RosettaNet (2004a), p. 4.

[509] See RosettaNet (1998b).

[510] See RosettaNet (1998b). To mark official RosettaNet concepts, they begin with a capital letter and are spelled in the original American English way.

[511] See RosettaNet (1998b).

[512] See RosettaNet (1998a).

[513] For a discussion see section 5.1.2.

5.2.2   Growth and Organisational Structure

RosettaNet's current organisational structure is best understood by tracing the major events since its founding. Table 5.2 summarises the milestones in its history, which I will further discuss in this subsection.

Table 5.2: Milestones in RosettaNet History[514]

Year	Regional Expansion	Organisational Change
1998	Americas	Founding Fadi Chehadé from Ingram Micro as CEO Information Technology Board
1999	Europe	Electronic Components Board
2000	Japan Singapore Taiwan	Jennifer Hamilton from Quantum as CEO Semiconductor Manufacturing Board Head for Asia activities
2001	Korea	Solution Providers Board Marketing Leadership Council
2002	Malaysia	Merger with Uniform Code Council
2003	Philippines China	Telecommunications Council Alliance with OASIS
2004	Australia	Logistics Council Architecture Advisory Committee Herman Stiphout from Siemens as CEO

Originally, RosettaNet was structured as a Managing Board and several kinds of partners. In 1999, it became obvious that companies delivering electronic components to the founding information technology firms should also be included in the standardisation efforts. In order to keep a separation of interests and responsibilities, RosettaNet was restructured as an industry-independent Executive Board and two industry-specific Managing Boards for information technology and electronic components.[515] The main goal was to transfer the specifications already developed to the new industry and to extend them only where needed. To avoid duplicate

---

[514] Based on RosettaNet (2004a), p. 4.

[515] See RosettaNet (1999c).

efforts, both boards had representatives on the Executive Board, which was led by Chehadé and defined the overall RosettaNet strategy. Besides the challenge of covering industry-specific demands, the specifications developed also have to cover regional differences. In the same year a European Office thus opened as a first step towards ensuring the global applicability of the RosettaNet specifications.[516]

At the beginning of 2000, Dell joined the Information Technology Board. This is noteworthy, as the tremendous growth of Dell to become the largest computer supplier in the world is attributed to the excellent management of its supply chain.[517] The hesitation of Dell in joining RosettaNet can be interpreted as a strategy not to share its supply chain management expertise with its main competitors and thus lose its competitive advantage. The pressure from important suppliers (e.g., Intel) was probably too great to ignore RosettaNet, and Dell had to adopt it too. Today Dell is still an active member, but only with Associate Partner status, indicating its cautious participation.[518] Nevertheless, most other large players in the electronics industry have remained clearly committed to RosettaNet. For instance, the Fadi Chehadé's successor in leading the consortium was Jennifer Hamilton, an on-loan executive from Quantum, at the time a large hard disk supplier.

In 2000, RosettaNet experienced the highest member growth in its history (see Figure 5.7). The main reason for this was the strong expansion into Asia, where many companies in the electronics industry have their headquarters. In March 2000, RosettaNet Japan was formed as an affiliate of RosettaNet with its own organisational sub-structure and Web presence.[519] This is different from the European Office, which was highly integrated into the US organisation. It is a tribute to the greater differences between Western and Asian business culture that also explains RosettaNet's partnership with CommerceNet Japan.[520] Similarly, the Infocom Development Authority (IDA), an agency of the Singapore government, supported the formation of RosettaNet Singapore. Simultaneously, RosettaNet

---

[516] See RosettaNet (1999d).

[517] See Magretta (1998).

[518] See RosettaNet (2004m).

[519] See RosettaNet (2000a).

[520] CommerceNet Japan is a non-profit organisation promoting electronic business in Japan.

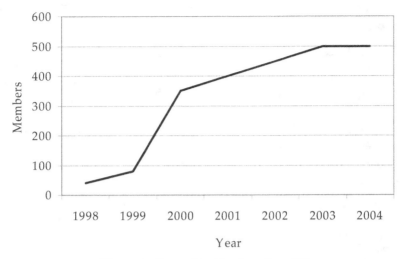

Figure 5.7: RosettaNet Members Growth[525]

Taiwan was founded with the semi-governmental Institute of Information Industry (III) and the Taiwan High-Tech Industry CIO association.[521] The main mission of these Asian affiliates is "to address regional differences in business practices and how they will conform to or influence modifications and/or enhancements to global RosettaNet standards."[522] To prevent too much divergence between global and Asian specifications, RosettaNet appointed a vice president for Asia, to whom the Asian affiliates have to report.[523] Moreover, as many of the new Asian companies were manufacturing semiconductors, a separate Semiconductor Manufacturing Board was established in 2000. Since then, RosettaNet has been covering the whole electronics supply chain "from silicon to desktop".[524]

Partnering with the Korea Institute for Electronic Commerce, in 2001 RosettaNet Korea was created as another affiliate in a country with a strong electronics industry.[526] Moreover, a newly established Solution Provider Board aimed at tightening the partnerships between supply chain

---

[521] See RosettaNet (2000b).

[522] See RosettaNet (2003j).

[523] See RosettaNet (2000b).

[524] RosettaNet (2000b).

[525] Based on the rough numbers in RosettaNet press releases.

[526] See RosettaNet (2001b).

companies and solution providers. Enterprise application and middleware developers, system integrators, consultancies, service providers and other intermediaries are coordinated to improve software solutions and implementations.[527] Since the same year, the Marketing Leadership Council has bundled all activities related to communicating RosettaNet's success and to recruiting new members.

In 2002, RosettaNet Malaysia was founded as yet another Asian affiliate with strong governmental support from the National IT Council.[528] Even more important was the merger with the Uniform Code Council (UCC). Having already been cooperating from an early stage, its merger with UCC clearly aimed to expand the RosettaNet specifications to other industries. At that time, UCC was already present in 23 industries, but with a strong focus on retail and grocery. The merger was also intended to reduce the confusion in the face of the many different standards development organisations available.[529]

In 2003, two further Asian countries joined RosettaNet: first the Philippines, supported by Semiconductor and Electronics Industries in the Philippines, Inc.[530]; second RosettaNet China, which had already been in preparation more than two years before,[531] when Hamilton had negotiated with China's SDOs and top executives from electronics companies.[532] Eventually, she even won over the governmental Ministry of Science and Technology for an official alliance with RosettaNet. Moreover, Siemens led a group of firms to establish a new board for the telecommunications industry.[533] Finally, having been cooperating before, RosettaNet and OASIS formed an official alliance to develop interorganisational specifications jointly. This was intended to avoid a duplication of efforts, with OASIS keeping industry-neutral and RosettaNet focusing on electronics-industry-specific standards.[534]

---

[527] See RosettaNet (2001c).

[528] See RosettaNet (2003h).

[529] See RosettaNet (2002b).

[530] See RosettaNet (2003j).

[531] See RosettaNet (2003i).

[532] See RosettaNet (2001a).

[533] See RosettaNet (2003b).

[534] See RosettaNet (2003e).

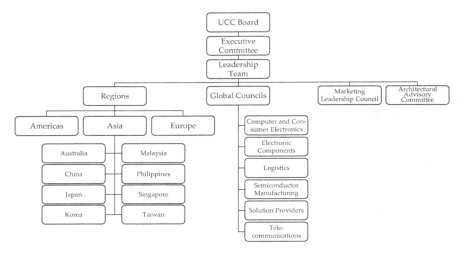

Figure 5.8: RosettaNet Organisational Structure[535]

In 2004, the formation of RosettaNet Australia together with EAN Australia was the latest expansion of RosettaNet's regional coverage.[536] Furthermore, Singapore's IDA fostered the creation of the Logistics Council to better adjust specifications to the requirements of the logistics industry.[537] Having six different industry boards and councils led to a renaming of the industry-specific Managing Boards as Global Councils and the Executive Board as Executive Committee.[538] Moreover, the information technology board is now called the Computer and Consumer Electronics Council. As it became increasingly difficult to coordinate the development of the basic technological architecture within the Industry Councils, this was concentrated in the newly formed Architectural Advisory Committee.[539] Figure 5.8 summarises the current RosettaNet organisation based on the discussion so far. Also in 2004, the UCC named Herman Stiphout from Siemens as president of RosettaNet, succeeding Hamilton.

---

[535] Based on RosettaNet (2004a), press releases, Web site information.

[536] See RosettaNet (2004g).

[537] See RosettaNet (2004k).

[538] See the comparison of RosettaNet (2003a) and RosettaNet (2004a). The redesign of RosettaNet's corporate identity including the official slide layout indicates further internal re-organisation.

[539] See RosettaNet (2004h).

An important topic for the development of standards specifications is the different kinds of participation options, as these have a great influence on the costs and benefits a firm can draw from developing and adopting a specification. RosettaNet offers four kinds of participation options: Associate Partner, Partner, Premier Partner and Council Member. Associate Partners have member access to the Web site, where they can publish what is known as a Business Profile with basic information about their organisation. They can participate in regional seminars and forums and can use some RosettaNet implementation support and services. In addition to this, Partners have access to implementation resources and to the Connectivity Profiles of Premier Partners. They can participate in training seminars and use more advanced services. They can also use the RosettaNet partner logo to be recognised as a RosettaNet partner in public presentations. Status as a Premier Partner adds the ability to publish Connectivity Profiles, which enables the automated exchange of trading partner configuration information. Moreover, they have the opportunity to participate in Industry Councils. Finally, being a Council Member is the only way to vote on standards decisions or to sponsor development programmes. Council Members can also participate in several councils at the same time. In 2004 the annual fee for a single council membership was 50,000 US$ and for two or more council memberships 100,000 US$. Comparatively cheap are regional memberships for plain Partner status, which range from 900 US$ for RosettaNet Philippines to 5,000 US$ for RosettaNet Japan.[540]

These fees ensure that firms only participate in councils if they have a strong interest in the respective benefits. It is no surprise that only 11 of the 28 companies that founded RosettaNet are still council members today: Cisco Systems, Compaq (as HP), Federal Express, Hewlett-Packard, IBM, Intel, Microsoft, Oracle, SAP, Toshiba and UPS. All the other founders have left their council status, including Ingram Micro, which no longer has member status, though it is still listed as a user of RosettaNet standards.

In 2003, RosettaNet had more than 500 partner members, with 158 in America, 46 in Europe, and 351 in Asia.[541] The latter contributed about 51 million US$ in the form of infrastructure, member funds and on-loan em-

---

[540] See RosettaNet (2004e).
[541] See RosettaNet (2003a), p. 23. Note that some companies are counted twice due to memberships in multiple regions.

ployees.[542] RosettaNet has about 25 full-time employees and more than 100 business and technical on-loan employees.[543] The on-loan employees usually spend two years working for the consortium, dedicating 25-100% of their working time.

5.2.3 Architecture and Foundational Programs

The RosettaNet architecture consists of three main parts:[544]

- RosettaNet Implementation Framework (RNIF)
- Dictionaries
- Partner Interface Processes (PIPs)

RNIF offers a technical platform for exchanging documents between business partners. It defines a XML-based message format including authentication, authorisation, encryption, and non-repudiation for reliable message exchange via the Internet infrastructure.[545] The dictionaries define common business semantics for unambiguous messages. The RosettaNet Business Dictionary defines business properties and business data entities, while the RosettaNet Technical Dictionary provides common properties for describing products. Both use standards from other SDOs. The Data Universal Numbering System (DUNS) provided by Dun and Bradstreet is a worldwide standard for the identification of business entities and locations. The United Nations Standard Products and Services Code (UN/SPSC) serves for the classification of products and services. Additionally, the Global Trade Item Numbers (GTIN) administered by UCC and EAN International enable the direct identification of products and services. Based on RNIF and the dictionaries, the Partner Interface Processes (PIPs) specify business processes for the quick coupling of supply chain companies.

As the business environment is changing permanently, it is obvious that all these specifications have to be revised and adapted frequently. RosettaNet thus coordinates formal 'Programs' for their further development. It

---

[542] See RosettaNet (2003i). A rough estimation of RosettaNet's budget might thus be 80-100 million US$ per year.

[543] See RosettaNet (2004a), p. 16.

[544] See Robson/Stern-Peltz/Tearnen (2003), p. 27.

[545] See Yendluri (2000), p. 3.

would not be a standards organisation if it had not standardised the applied development methods. In general, the Global Council members propose, execute and monitor such a Program. Each participating council member has to contribute resources to a Program. When a Program gets started, the Program Team operates independently of the Global Councils and is supervised by Commitment Leaders from the Program Sponsors and advised by the central RosettaNet Program Office.[546]

A Program Director manages the day-to-day activities of a Program Team, which always includes four further positions: a Program Scheduler, a Program Communicator, a Focus Process Leader and a Standards Product Manager. While the Program Scheduler manages dates and dependencies using a Web-based schedule, the Program Communicator handles the communication with other members and maintains related presentations and Web content. The Focus Process Leader manages a team of 5-10 experts developing the actual specifications. The Standards Product Manager has a pivotal role, as he is responsible for the specifications developed meeting the business requirements. Depending on the Program type, a Standards Engineer from the RosettaNet Architecture Office, a Technical Manager and/or further Engineering Resources complete the Program Team. After the completion of the specification development, the Program Team is transformed into a Validation Team, consisting of some former team members and some new team members especially from solution providers and early adopters, which do not necessarily have to be council members. This team tests the specifications in at least three prototypes connecting actual trading partners.[547]

Depending on their background, the participants, they represent different interests during the development process. Three types can be differentiated:

- The most neutral is the RosettaNet staff, which consist of full-time employees of the consortium. These fill the Program Office, the Architecture Office, and provide the Validation Manager.
- Although expected to refrain from lobbying, the on-loan resources may naturally be biased towards their sponsoring company. Nevertheless, RosettaNet urges them to act as neutrally as possible. Program Direc-

---

[546] See RosettaNet (2003f).
[547] See RosettaNet (2003f).

tors, Program Schedulers, Program Communicators and Focus Process Team Leaders are staffed with on-loan resources.

- The program participants clearly represent the interests and requirements of their individual companies. These fill the post of Commitment Leader, and include a member of the Focus Process Teams during development, and/or an Implementation Expert in the validation phase.[548]

RosettaNet gives several reasons why firms benefit from participating in a specification development program. As a program sponsor, a council member can direct RosettaNet resources to a concrete interorganisational problem in whose solution it is highly interested. If other partners experience similar problems, they can join resources to develop a solution. Besides this direct benefit, program sponsors attract public awareness as supply chain leaders through press releases, speaking engagements and company logos on official RosettaNet Web pages and materials.[549] Additionally, sponsors and all other participants that send on-loan resources benefit from gaining employees with in-depth knowledge of RosettaNet specifications. Even if companies only send Focus Process Team members or simple Program Participants, they still improve their skills in resolving real implementation issues. The RosettaNet Web-based Intranet platform offers detailed postings of open positions needed for forming Programs. Even in later phases companies can participate in a Program, e.g., to validate and implement the specifications in prototypes.[550]

To avoid conflicts resulting from different opinions on the individual contributions to a specification, RosettaNet follows a clearly formulated intellectual property rights policy. It covers only "business methods, business process, data structure, and data format specifications",[551] which are the main products of the consortium's efforts. The major goal of the policy is the protection of the specifications and their users from the claims of contributing participants. Consequently, RosettaNet specifications are generally royalty-free and their use will not be charged. The policy, however, allows royalty-bearing specifications in 'extraordinary circumstances', which have to be approved by the applicable council and are

---

[548] See RosettaNet (2003f).

[549] See RosettaNet (2004c).

[550] See RosettaNet (2003g).

[551] See RosettaNet (2002a).

labelled accordingly.[552] Since June 2002, all Program participants have formally had to agree to the intellectual property rights policy or formally withdraw if they do no longer agree.

Besides the organisational structure of Programs, RosettaNet members also use a standardised specification method, which evolved in nearly 50 Programs and is sketched in Figure 5.9. In the first phase, opportunities and restrictions for a new Program are identified, including the industry situation and affected stakeholders. Then a prospective RosettaNet Program Director interested in starting a new program presents his ideas to other members in various RosettaNet user meetings all around the world.[553] Having gained sufficient support from other members, they give a recommendation to the council in question. If this decides to pursue the initiative further, sponsoring council members are assigned as the proposal owners. In the Program Forming phase, these develop a detailed program plan and promote their ideas in order to raises awareness among other partners. The Program Sponsors and their provided resources are secured through formal agreements to the intellectual property rights policy and through the staffing of teams. If all governance guidelines are met and the council has agreed, the Program can be initiated.

The Investigation and Requirements Gathering is probably the most critical step, which explains why only formal partners have the right to participate. The first activity is to scan existing RosettaNet and other specifications to ascertain whether they already offer solution approaches to the targeted problem. Then the program team develops scenarios and use cases, and conducts surveys among the participating companies to identify

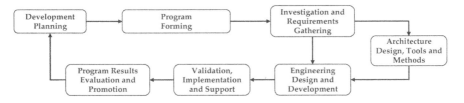

Figure 5.9: RosettaNet Development Process[554]

---

[552] See RosettaNet (2002a), p. 2.

[553] See, e.g., the 87th EDIFICE Plenary in Munich in November 2003, where a Program Director on loan from HP came from the US to promote a Milestone Program Proposal aiming at the enhancement of PIP 3B2. See HP (2003).

all requirements. These are analysed, consolidated and finalised in several feedback loops. Depending on the type of Program, additional elements for the architecture, supporting tools and/or new methods are then developed. The Engineering Design and Development phase comprises the writing of the actual specifications. The Focus Process Team develops UML models of the processes, generates XML Schemas, writes supporting documents, and revises this output in several loops including feedback from the participating firms. Before publication of a specification such as a PIP package, the consortium has to accept it formally.

For the Validation, Implementation and Support phase, the Program Team is transformed into a Validation Team, including new team members in particular from solution providers. This team tests the specifications in prototypes and improves them if they do not meet the original business requirements. When the specifications are mature, RosettaNet Implementation Guidelines (RIGs) are created, and both specifications and guidelines are published on the Web site.[555] The Program Results Evaluation and Promotion phase completes a Program. The adoption of the specification is evaluated and its benefits are estimated. Moreover, the Program results are systematically promoted to foster further adoption. For instance, ROI metrics are defined and results published, on-loan resources are recognised, quotations from satisfied executives are cited, and Web casts are conducted. Ideas for additional initiatives are systematically collected and lay the ground for follow-up Programs. Finally, the Program is closed.

The RosettaNet method distinguishes between two basic types of Programs: Foundational Programs providing formal definitions and methods, which Milestone Programs then use to specify business semantics and processes. Foundational Programs are thus concerned with the evolution of architectural and methodical parts of the RosettaNet specifications. Milestone Programs focus on the development of the actual interorganisational standards, i.e. Partner Interface Processes (PIPs).[556] This subsection gives an overview of Foundational Programs, while the next subsection analyses the Milestone Programs in more detail.

---

[554] Based on RosettaNet (2003d).

[555] Note that the RIGs are not available to the public, only for members.

[556] See RosettaNet (2003g).

Table 5.3: Completed RosettaNet Foundational Programs[557]

Program	Description
Global Company Identification	Addressed issues surrounding the use of the Data Universal Numbering System (DUNS) as a Global Company Identifier in PIPs.
Interoperability	Improved software and implementation interoperability within the RosettaNet trading network through collateral, education and testing activities.
Next Generation Architecture	Focused on enhancing RosettaNet's architecture, including its PIP specification architecture, to support modular PIP design as well as transactional, informational and collaborative business processes.
PIP Specification Format	Delivers methodologies for specifying PIPs in XML-Schema and BPSS and for producing accompanying implementation aids to PIP development.
Trading Partner Agreements	Created a TPA for RosettaNet transactions and for general electronic information exchange.

Table 5.3 shows the Foundational Programs completed by September 2004. The Global Company Identification was one of the first, as RosettaNet decided in 1999 to adopt DUNS instead of developing a new specification.[558] The Interoperability Program resulted in guidelines and testing tools to improve the interoperability of software solutions supporting RosettaNet specifications. The goals of the Next Generation Architecture Program to enhance RosettaNet's architecture proved to be quite complex. In 2002 it led to the Programs Dictionary Architecture, Domain Model, and PIP Specification Format. The latter developed a new PIP format based on XML Schema and ebXML BPSS aiming at more precise and machine-readable specifications and better support for a more modular PIP architecture. Besides RosettaNet, EDIFICE, ESIA and the UN/CEFACT Legal Working Group drove the Trading Partner Agreements Program. Drawing on existing work and experience with EDI, they created a multipurpose document template that "covers relevant legal aspects of any electronic

---

[557] See RosettaNet (2004f)..
[558] See RosettaNet (1999b).

information exchange [aiming at] removing many trust and psychological barriers normally associated with negotiating such agreements."[559]

Both the growing scope of RosettaNet and the fast evolution of information technology create the need for the RosettaNet architecture to be continuously adapted. Hence, there are always several Foundational Programs in an active state. Table 5.4 gives an overview of the different topics that were under development in September 2004. I will not discuss all of them, but highlight some.

The Constraint Description Program, for example, proposes to use Semantic Web specifications such as OWL to improve the consistency of information exchanged.[560] However, it is still at the stage of formation, as the RosettaNet Automated Enablement Program already covers some of the aspects. With its goal of significantly reducing the time and costs of PIP implementations, the latter is a crucial Program for the further development and adoption of RosettaNet specifications. It was submitted as a proposal to the councils in May 2003 and its investigation phase completed in October 2003. It had not been completed by September 2004, but was far advanced. The Program sponsors are Menlo Worldwide, HP, Intel, Micron Technology and Arrow Electronics. The Focus Process Team is staffed with employees from Adobe, the University of California, InSync Software, Cisco Systems, GridNode, E2open, Formfill, Fujitsu, Global eXchange Services, Nokia, ADOS, Texas Instruments, TIBCO Software, Motorola, National Semiconductor, NIST and ePromostandards Alliance (ePSA).

While the use of PIPs enables the automation of interorganisational processes, the implementation still involves a lot of manual work requiring project teams on both sides. These have to meet frequently to agree on details of the PIPs and test the implementations. The resulting set-up time and costs are prohibitive for connecting hundreds of partners and/or small and medium-sized enterprises (SMEs) using PIPs.[561]

---

[559] See RosettaNet (2001d), p. 4.

[560] See subsection 5.1.1 for a discussion of the Semantic Web approach.

[561] See Robson (2003).

Table 5.4: Active RosettaNet Foundational Programs[562]

Program	Description
Constraint Description	Leverage OWL and/or similar technologies to describe and check consistency of constraints at the message, document and information-model levels, which are general, industry-specific, or trading partner-specific.
Dictionary Architecture	Provides a scaleable architecture for RosettaNet dictionaries.
Domain Model	Provides the nucleus of the RosettaNet domain model (of reusable XML & UML objects), along with the documented processes by which PIP developers can make use of and extend the domain model.
Message Control & Choreography Program	Extend RosettaNet PIP architecture to support integrated multi-PIP and multi-party business interactions to enable long-running processes in dynamic trading networks.
Multiple Messaging Services	As RosettaNet architecture extends to support flexible, low-cost document exchange models and also evolves to support Web Services-based exchanges, enhanced messaging capabilities are required beyond current RNIF specifications.
RNBD Development	Enhances the RNBD for interaction with PIP specification development and publication processes.
RNTD Development	Provides ongoing development and management of the RosettaNet Technical Dictionary.
RosettaNet Automated Enablement	Proposal for RosettaNet to offer a scalable and flexible architecture that makes it a viable solution for even the smallest and least technically advanced trading partner.
RosettaNet Methodology	Focuses on RosettaNet process and methodology improvements, and is driven by the RosettaNet operations team.
RosettaNet Ready	Provides the tools and services required to measure software compliance with RNIF and PIPs specifications, and enable low-cost implementation testing solutions.

---

[562] See RosettaNet (2004f).

The main reason is the specification format of conventional PIPs. A PIP comprises a PIP package with human and machine-readable specification documents and a human-readable RosettaNet Implementation Guide. The latter describes in prose how to implement a PIP. For an actual implementation, several constraints usually have to be explicated that fully comply with the official specifications. It is important to understand this aspect, as users can tighten a specification, but – in order to guarantee compatibility – must never extend it. For example, a data field can be changed from optional to mandatory, but never vice versa. Put differently, implementations always have to be a logical subset of the official PIP specification. If extensions are needed, they have to be added via a Milestone Program to the official specifications.

The necessary constraints, however, have to be communicated to the partners via individual implementation documents, which are also only human-readable. The main idea of the RosettaNet Enablement Automation Program is to describe these customizing constraints in a machine-readable format dubbed 'Trading Partner Implementation Requirements' (TPIR). This replaces the RIGs and the individual implementation documents and can be automatically processed by appropriate software solutions. For small companies or other scenarios without full backend integration, an automatically generated TPIR presentation format enables manual communication with a PIP. Moreover, TPIRs can be stored in a central repository such as the RosettaNet Trading Partner Directory and serve as a Connection Profile. In the ideal case, a completely automated PIP set-up between new trading partners would be possible. Although this vision is not fully realised yet, the results of the RosettaNet Automated Enablement available in September 2004 were very promising. They are an important step towards the 'plug & play' of business partners, even for exchanging information that is more complex.

Finally, two characteristics of this Program are noteworthy. First, it draws a lot on the results of the new PIP Specification Format, i.e., XML Schema and BPSS. Second, the Program was split into two dependent parts, one as a Foundational and the other as a Milestone Program. This enabled the simultaneous development of the TPIR specification and new PIPs based on it, which lowered the total development time compared to a sequential approach that would have entailed first completing the Foundational Program before starting the Milestone Program.

Driven mainly by RosettaNet staff, the Methodology Program focuses on the improvement of central RosettaNet methods and processes. It comprises four different projects: Council methodology, Program management methods (e.g., on-loan resources staffing), standards development methods (e.g., maintenance of specifications), and standards convergence strategy. The results of the latter are made publicly available, which facilitates the positioning of RosettaNet compared to other standards initiatives.[563] First, RosettaNet distinguishes four roles in governing a specification attempt:

- "Build: RosettaNet to design, build, own and manage the total lifecycle of the standard
- Lead: Within RosettaNet governance, gathering and intellectual property (IP) rules, take a leadership role to develop standards that will be passed on to another organisation for long-term management
- Motivate: RosettaNet to participate with another organisation under their governance, gathering and IP rules to develop a standard
- Adopt: RosettaNet to use existing standards and integrate them into a new standard or solution"[565]

Second, RosettaNet distinguishes between a content view for business topics and an architecture view for technical issues. Both are further refined, as depicted in the resulting matrix in Figure 5.10. To maintain the

		Build	Lead	Motivate	Adopt
Content	Process	PIPs, TPIRs	eCustoms Declaration	SWIFT Payment	VICS CPFR
	Structure messages	PIPs			
	Data Dictionaries	RNBD, RNTD			
	Information Objects	RN USC, Class			(ebXML Core Components)
	Data Elements	RN Data Types			W3C Date & Time
	Code Lists	RN Payment Terms			UNSPSC Product Class
	Identification Keys				D&B DUNS
Architecture	Method	RN Implementation Guidelines			
	Content & Process Definition	RN Information Model	RN/EAN.UCC Key & Key Resolution Mechanism	IETF/ISO/EAN.UCC Universal Code List Map.	OMG UML, ebXML BPSS, W3C XML & DTD
	Content & Process Specialisation	RN Net Change Descriptions		(OASIS BPEL)	ebXML BPSS
	Registry & Repository	RN Repository & Registry Semantics			(ebXML RMI/RS, OASIS UDDI)
	Physical Connection Provisioning			ebXML CPPA Partner Profiling	
	Messaging	RNIF	RN Choreography Enforcement		IETF HTTP, ITU-T X.509 (ebXML ebMS)

Figure 5.10: RosettaNet Specification Governance Matrix[564]

---

[563] See RosettaNet (2004l).

[564] See RosettaNet (2004l). Only selected examples shown here. Specifications under discussion at RosettaNet are in brackets.

clarity of the figure, it shows only certain selected specifications. The publicly available version classifies about 90 different specifications and is regularly updated.

The Foundational Programs described so far lay the organisational and architectural ground for the Milestone Programs, which the next subsection analyses in more detail.

5.2.4 Partner Interface Processes and Milestone Programs

The Partner Interface Processes (PIPs) are the very core of RosettaNet. As the name indicates, they specify the interfaces between the processes of business partners. The formal specifications enable the full automation of such processes. A conventional PIP package comprises DTD documents specifying tags for the necessary XML files, HTML documents describing the tags used on the basis of the RosettaNet Business and Technical Dictionary, and text documents explaining the processes with UML diagrams. The latter offer three views.[566] The Business Operational View "[c]aptures the semantics of business data entities and their flow of exchange between roles as they perform business activities".[567] Derived from the Business Operational View, the Functional Services View specifies all required network components and their transaction dialogues. The Implementation Framework View defines the format of the XML messages that software systems exchange when executing a PIP.[568] Apart from the DTD, the PIP specifications are not machine-readable, making fast and accurate implementations more complicated. The RosettaNet Automated Enablement aims to solve this problem through fully machine-readable PIPs based on ebXML BPSS (see previous subsection).

In October 2004, the PIP directory listed 163 PIPs, of which 20% were not yet published, 17% on hold, 7% beta versions, 25% released, 27% validated and 4% obsolete.[569] Obsolete, on hold, and not yet published PIPs

---

[565] RosettaNet (2004l).

[566] The Business Operational View and the Functional Services View are derived from ISO's Open-edi reference model described in ISO/IEC (1997).

[567] RosettaNet (2004d), p. 1.

[568] See RosettaNet (2004d), p. 1.

[569] Numbers based on RosettaNet (2004f) with partner access. PIPs in early development phases (not yet published) are not shown to the public.

are either in the early stages of development or have been replaced by other PIPs. Beta versions are in advanced stages of development and have been submitted to RosettaNet members for voting. Released PIPs have been approved as official specifications, while validated PIPs have additionally have been successfully tested and implemented.

Figure 5.11: RosettaNet PIP Clusters[570]

All these PIPs are grouped into eight clusters, each concerning a certain area of business functions (see Figure 5.11). Cluster 0 offers PIPs for testing and failure notifications. Cluster 1 supports the selection of new trading partners and the exchange of basic information on products and services. Cluster 2 enables the periodic distribution of product and design information. For the future, it should also support collaborative design and engineering. Cluster 3 supports almost all issues concerning quotes and orders, including initiation, status reporting, discrepancy notification, invoicing, and payment. With 13 PIPs released and 18 validated it represents the core of RosettaNet's PIP family and is the most mature cluster. Cluster 4 facilitates collaborative forecasting and inventory management, including price protection and the allocation of constrained products. Cluster 5 supports the exchange of marketing information such as lead information, campaign plans, and design-win registration. Cluster 6 is concerned with after-sales support and services including technical support and warranty management. Finally, cluster 7 supports the exchange of information directly relevant for production such as design, configuration, process and quality information.

Each cluster is divided into several segments. For instance, Cluster 3, 'Order Management' comprises the segments 3A, 'Quote and Order Entry'; 3B, 'Transportation and Distribution'; 3C, 'Returns and Finance'; and 3D, 'Product Configuration'. Segments currently have between one (0A: Administrative) and 18 PIPs (3B: Transportation and Distribution). All PIPs have reached at least the beta stage are available and usable without RosettaNet charging any fee. To enlist support for implementing PIPs, however, one has to be a RosettaNet member. For example, the RIGs are

---

[570] See RosettaNet (2004f).

very useful for correctly implementing PIPs, but not available to the public.

In 1999, when RosettaNet first started its specification efforts, an outsourcing partner executed the development of PIPs.[571] As RosettaNet decided to treat the development of interorganisational standards as its core business, the Programs were formed. While the Foundational Programs are concerned with evolving the general RosettaNet organisation and architecture, the PIPs are developed in so-called Milestone Programs. Such a program does not usually focus on developing a specific PIP, but rather on solving a certain interorganisational business problem. Before developing new PIPs, the Program team has to check whether existing PIPs are applicable to the problem under consideration or can be modified with reasonable ease. This approach of reusing existing specifications is central to RosettaNet's overall goal of standardising processes wherever possible and deviating only where necessary.

The difference between PIP architecture and Milestone Programs is also reflected in the way RosettaNet structures the latter. Interorganisational business scenarios are categorised along a phase-oriented perspective with orders as the central element (see Figure 5.12). Usually, Design, Demand Creation and Forecast lead to an Order, followed by Manufacturing, Logistics and Payment. However, real business scenarios often deviate from this strict sequence and are much more intermingled, as the Figure 5.12 indicates. Nevertheless, an order is always the core, as it has the direct legal

Figure 5.12: RosettaNet Process Alignment[572]

[571] See RosettaNet (2004b), p. 1.

[572] See RosettaNet (2004a), p. 6.

and business impact.

Milestone Programs can be differentiated in terms of five different stages:[573]

- Pending programs concern general areas where the development of new PIPs might be beneficial.
- Proposed programs are in an early stage of formation and have to be approved by at least one Council before proceeding.
- After approval, a program is equipped with the necessary resources such as the staff for the team roles.
- Active programs have dedicated working teams on them, guided by strict implementation milestones, hence the term 'Milestone Program'.
- Finally, when a program has achieved its implementation milestones, its resulting specifications are published, and the program is completed.

Since starting its own PIP development in 2000, RosettaNet has completed 24 Milestone Programs. Table 5.5 gives an overview, including short descriptions of all the Programs.

Table 5.5: Completed RosettaNet Milestone Programs[574]

Program	Description
SM Work in Progress	Automation of inquiries and responses for work-in-process (WIP) on the semi-conductor manufacturing factory floor enables better WIP visibility - reducing inventories and allowing for more flexible operations.
Collaborative Fore-casting - Phase 1	Allows trading partners to improve the match between supply and demand.
SM Order Manage-ment	Addressed the unique order-management needs of the semiconductor manufac-turing trading network, expecting to reduce IT and order transaction costs and improve customer service.
SM Materials	Addressed unique semiconductor process manufacturing requirements, looking to reduce IT and ordering costs and improve customer service.
Basics & Express	Enables the affordable adoption of RosettaNet standards for small- to medium-sized companies.
Design Win - Phase 1	Automates registration and approvals to improve the effectiveness of the design win process.
iHub	Identified a set of business information needed to improve the match between supply and demand.
Order Management in Japan – Phase 1	Implements purchase order processes in Japan-based companies.

---

[573] See RosettaNet (2004f).

[574] See RosettaNet (2004f).

Table 5.5 (continued): Completed RosettaNet Milestone Programs[575]

Program	Description
Product Information Exchange	Access to technical information for all phases of electronic assembly, design and manufacture.
Ship from Stock - Phase 1	Developed the total ship from stock and debit/credit process and automated the first part of the business scenario in 2001.
Order Management - Phase 2 (SM)	Extends purchase order process capabilities and increases implementations by Semiconductor Manufacturing trading partners.
Manufacturing WIP - Phase 2	Automates manufacturing factory floor information exchanges to reduce inventories and allow for more flexible operations.
Forecasted Inventory Management	Improves the stability of inventory supply and reduces shortages and excessive stock.
Manufacturing Work Order	Provides the ability to release orders to the factory floor with the supporting manufacturing process information.
Design Engineering Information	Sends technical design information to reduce analysis and selection time and to improve product promotion efficiency.
Order Management in Japan - Extended	Extends order process capabilities to increase supply-chain effectiveness and accelerate RosettaNet standards adoption.
Ship From Stock - Phase 2	Automates the full business scenario to significantly reduce the number of manual transactions and improve days to payment.
Collaborative Forecasting - Phase 2	Extends the forecasting process capabilities to improve the match between supply and demand.
Ship Notice	Automates the advanced ship notice exchange providing early warning and improved cycle time.
Design Win - Phase 2	Deploys Design Win standards to improve channel efficiency, automate and expedite data collection and sharing.
Direct Ship/3PL	Supports both the outsourced manufacturer shipment and the direct shipment to the customer through a third party logistics (3PL) provider.
Global Billing	Adds functionality to existing RosettaNet invoicing and payment PIPs to support global billing.
Order Management Japan – Advanced	Continues and enhances the activities of OMJ(2001)/OMJ Extended(2002) for further acceleration of RosettaNet standards adoption in the global supply chain process of electronic components through strong leadership and collaborative resolution by member companies.
Price and Availability	Automates and standardises the process for requesting real time price and availability from suppliers (product providers).

In September 2004, 13 Milestone Programs were in an active state. Table 5.6 gives an overview of the basic goals of these active programs.

---

[575] See RosettaNet (2004f).

Table 5.6: Active RosettaNet Milestone Programs[576]

Program	Description
eCustoms Declaration	Customs import/export procedures traditionally have been a manual process in many countries. Usually it is bogged down by many processes. To facilitate faster movement of goods with enhanced efficiency, there is ample opportunity for improvement through automation and standardisation.
Engineering Information Management	Aims to migrate the exchange of engineering information from a paper to electronic format.
Material Composition	The high-tech industry needs to know the material composition of their products to satisfy legislation, drive environmental improvements in design, and be capable of providing information for customers and stakeholders when required.
Payment	Develops a simple payment process to streamline reconciliation of accounts receivable and improve the payment information flow for faster cash. Business and institution benefits will be achieved by this e-business process that has the objectives of reducing processing costs through automating accounts receivable reconciliation and improving the flow of payment information.
Product Catalog Information	Seeks to exchange product information to enable buyers to manage the procurement of a specific item from a seller.
RosettaNet Automated Enablement	Proposal for RosettaNet to offer a scalable and flexible architecture that makes it a viable solution for even the smallest and least technically advanced trading partner.
Sales Reporting	Aims to design a standard process for transmitting Product Sales information from single or multiple points of the sales chain. The objectives are to improve the information flow and reduce the costs of managing the associated business processes that generate and utilise the information.
Semiconductor Test Data Exchange	Aims to design a standards-based process for transmitting Semiconductor test data from manufacturing fabricators (FABS) to foundry customers: Fabless Semiconductor Companies (FSC). The objectives are to improve information flow, data integrity and to reduce the costs, for both the customer and the foundry, of managing the associated business processes that generate and utilise the data.
Service Contract Information Management	Drives development of an e-business process to automate the management of service contract information. Economic benefits are reduced parts-carrying costs, reduced logistics costs for mis-shipments, reduced data rework at time of service delivery, more accurate picture of contract start/end possibly leading to higher sales of renewed contracts to the service provider.
Shipment Booking and Status	Develops bi-directional communication between shippers, logistics providers and transportation providers in order to send initial pre-booking, acknowledgement, and confirmation of actual booking of shipments, booking cancellation, and shipment status.
Shipment Notification Management	Enables trading partners to deliver standardised shipment information. The purpose of this effort is to enable complex shipments and multiparty shipment notifications.
TC Order To Cash (Phase 1)	Applies Order To Cash e-business process model to the telecommunications industry.
Warranty	Automates the warranty claims process to eliminate redundant data entry and improve the warranty information quality.

---

[576] See RosettaNet (2004f).

Internally, seven further programs were at the proposal state (their preliminary names were eDistribution, eDiagnostics, Automated eTicketing, Material Release, Complex Product & Services, Freight Invoicing, and Semiconductor Process Data Exchange).

To illuminate which companies are the main ones driving the development of RosettaNet specifications, I have analysed the participation of RosettaNet Council members in Foundational and Milestone Programs. The data is taken from the RosettaNet Trading Partner Directory, including active and complete programs.[577] For an overview, Figure 5.13 shows the 15 most active Council members and the number of Programs each one has sponsored or participated in.

Although the many regional affiliates of RosettaNet in Asia might have implied a bias towards Asian firms, Figure 5.13 reveals a certain dominance of US companies in the RosettaNet Programs. Of these 15 firms, eight are US-based (Arrow Electronics, Cisco Systems, HP, IBM, Intel, Motorola, National Semiconductor and Texas Instruments), four Asian (Fujitsu, NEC, Renesas Technology, and Sony) and three European (Nokia,

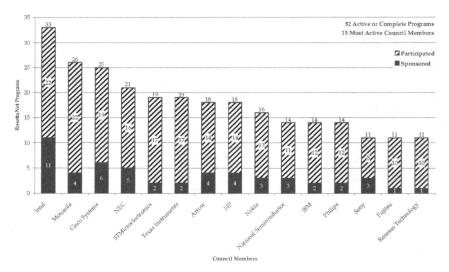

Figure 5.13: Participation of RosettaNet Council Members in Programs[578]

---

[577] See RosettaNet (2004m). The public access only shows participation in completed programs.

Philips, and STMicroelectronics). Taking the number of Council members that have participated in at least one Program yields similar results: 55% are US American, 22% Asian, and 22% European. These relations might change in the future, as RosettaNet has recently opened two development centres in Asia. One is the RosettaNet Asia Engineering Center in Penang, Malaysia, which focuses on PIP development.[579] The other is the Architecture Center of Excellence in Singapore, which concentrates on advancing RosettaNet's architecture within Foundational Programs.[580] However, even in the Asian activities American firms are highly involved. The vice-presidency for Asia, for example, has been staffed on three consecutive occasions by an on-loan executive from Intel. Also noteworthy is the exceptionally high Program participation of Intel, which has been a sponsor of 21% and a participant in 63% of all RosettaNet Programs.

Despite the interest they hold, these results have to be interpreted with care for three main reasons. First, the data is based on the (internal) Trading Partner Directory, which was not necessarily complete at the time of data extraction. Second, only companies that were Council members in September 2004 are considered. Some firms that were more active in previous years might no longer have been Council members by then. Third, while some companies have joined RosettaNet only recently – especially logistics and telecommunication firms as a result of the two new Councils – others have been members since its founding. The latter are naturally biased towards greater participation in Programs. Nevertheless, the results give a good indication of which players are leading the development of RosettaNet standards. In particular, all of the 15 most active firms are primarily users of the PIPs, showing that large solution providers such as Microsoft and SAP have only a very moderate influence on the specifications. Even IBM, which can be in both roles, as user and as vendor, is mainly active in Programs benefiting it as a user. It can be conjectured, moreover, that an indirect motivation for the active firms is the opportunity to sell their experience and products to firms in other industries. As IOS are critical for a firm's business, extremely powerful and reliable

---

[578] Based on RosettaNet (2004m), query at 2004-10-14, including active and completed programs.

[579] See RosettaNet (2004i).

[580] See RosettaNet (2004j).

hardware is required, which results in high profit margins for the hardware producers.

For an efficient set-up of a PIP-based IOS, appropriate software solutions are crucial. The RosettaNet Ready Foundational Program has already produced a free set of tests and tools for checking the solutions of software vendors as to their compliance with RosettaNet specifications. After passing all the tests, a software vendor can earn 'Software Compliance Badges', which indicate the proper support for RNIF and PIPs. This measure should also motivate new users to adopt RosettaNet specifications faster.[581]

5.2.5   Conclusions

RosettaNet is regarded as the most successful SDO for interorganisational standards.[582] The case study in this section revealed several likely reasons.

- The electronics industry is highly fragmented and dynamic, which forces the firms to cooperate with many and changing partners.
- The industry has a lot of experience in setting standards, as many electronic products are based on standards.
- The firms have a high level of expertise in information systems and do not have to rely on external providers. As there was no XML-based transaction platform available, for example, RosettaNet members simply developed their own (RNIF).
- RosettaNet has a clear focus on business value. It uses a top-down approach in the sense that first the business case has to be clarified (Milestone Programs), then the necessary processes are modelled (PIPs), and finally new technology is developed, if the existing is not sufficient (Foundational Programs). Another example is the Trading Partner Directory, which was built on a human-readable basis first, resulting in quick business value. Then it was gradually improved with new technologies to eventually make it a fully machine-readable discovery platform.
- RosettaNet seems to have a good balance between respecting the individual members' needs and developing neutral specifications. The main

---

[581] See Sengupta (2003).

[582] See Kotinurmi/Nurmilaaksco/Laesvuori (2003), p. 140.

reason for this is the mature and efficient development process, which includes a balanced mix of RosettaNet, on-loan, and user participants.

The next section analyses ebXML, which has a vision very similar to RosettaNet's, but approaches it very differently.

5.3 The Case of ebXML

With its vision and the results it has achieved already, the ebXML initiative is also a very important approach to interorganisational standards. As there are several good sources and case studies available on it, I will not discuss much technical detail.[583] Rather, this section focuses on organisational and political issues relating to ebXML.[584] The most obvious difference from RosettaNet is the origin of ebXML. It is not a newly formed organisation, but a joint effort undertaken by UN/CEFACT and OASIS. This section does not start with its formation, therefore, but rather with a short overview of both organisations and how they initiated ebXML. Next, the technical architecture is briefly described, while subsection 5.3.3 uncovers several political issues concerning ebXML. Finally, I give a conclusion of the main insights gained from the case of ebXML.

5.3.1 Organisational Structure of CEFACT, OASIS and ebXML

UN/CEFACT

The United Nations Economic Commission for Europe Working Party 4 (UNECE/WP.4) was responsible for developing the EDIFACT specifications, probably the most ambitious initiative to establish interorganisational standards ever undertaken.[585] It was part of the UN Economic Commission for Europe (UNECE), which is a commission within the UN's

---

[583] See Graham/Pollock/Smart, et al. (2003), Kotinurmi/Nurmilaakso/Laesvuori (2003), Beimborn/Mintert/Weitzel (2002), Kotok/Webber (2002) and Reimers (2001).

[584] Some of the findings of this chapter are based on Spicker (2004), a diploma thesis I was supervising.

[585] See, e.g., Reimers (1995), p. 223. For a short discussion of EDI and EDIFACT see section 3.2.

Economic and Social Council. In 1996, the Working Party 4 was reorganised under the new name UN/CEFACT.[586] Its mission is to support

> "(…) activities dedicated to improving the ability of business, trade and administrative organisations, from developed, developing and transitional economies, to exchange products and relevant services effectively. Its principal focus is on facilitating national and international transactions, through the simplification and harmonisation of processes, procedures and information flows, and so contribute to the growth of global commerce."[587]

To achieve these goals, it explicitly cooperates with the governmental SDOs International Electrotechnical Commission (IEC), International Organisation for Standardisation (ISO), International Telecommunication Union (ITU) and "selected non-governmental organisations".[589] The main elements of CEFACT's organisational structure are the Plenary, its Bureau[590], the Forum Management Group, and the Permanent Groups (see Figure 5.14). While the Plenary is the highest authority responsible for all of CEFACT's work, the Bureau mainly enforces the decisions of the Plenary. The Forum Management Group coordinates between the Plenary and the Permanent Groups, which execute the actual development of specifications. The Bureau and the Forum Management Group strictly

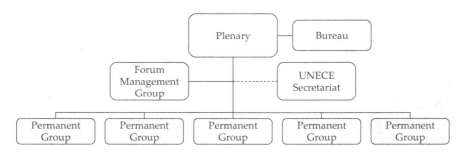

Figure 5.14: CEFACT Organisational Structure[588]

---

[586] See CEFACT (2004a), p. 2. In the further work, UN/CEFACT is usually abbreviated as CEFACT.

[587] CEFACT (2004a), p. 4.

[588] See CEFACT (2004a), p. 20.

[589] CEFACT (2004a), p. 4.

[590] Formerly called CEFACT Steering Committee (CSG)

control any creation or modification of Permanent Groups.[591] The latter

"(...) should endeavour to include representatives of all interested parties to ensure both sufficient expertise and broad visibility of their work products. (They) must be led and supported by relevant users and open to all organisations and bodies recognised by the Plenary."[592]

It has been of some discussion, whether 'all interested parties' can really participate in a reasonable manner.[593]

Since 2000, CEFACT has explicitly aimed at openness, worldwide participation, speed, compatibility and technical excellence with its formal Open Development Process (see Figure 5.15).[594]

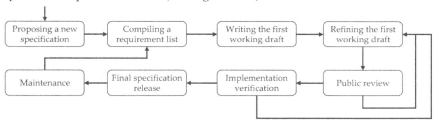

Figure 5.15: CEFACT Open Development Process[595]

Either within CEFACT or from the outside a proposal for a new specification is made. The proper Permanent Group takes over the responsibility and forms a small editing group consisting of one project editor and a few associate editors. The editing group gathers information from as many potential stakeholders as possible and compiles a requirements list. On the basis of this, it writes a first working draft serving as a foundation for further discussion. Members of the responsible Permanent Group and selected external organisations review it internally, resulting in a second working draft. This one is put on the CEFACT Web site for public review. Any individual interested can make comments on the specification draft. The editing group continuously refines the working draft, making all changes public. After several cycles, the Permanent Group makes a final

---

[591] See CEFACT (2004a), pp. 8ff. for more details.

[592] CEFACT (2004a), p. 15.

[593] See, e.g., LaMonica (2004), where it is claimed that CEFACT was for a long time hostile to vendor participation.

[594] See CEFACT (2000).

[595] Based on CEFACT (2000).

draft publicly available and calls for pilot implementations. Critical issues in the pilot implementations cause further updates of the specification. Finally, when the specification has reached sufficient maturity, the Permanent Group releases the official technical specification. It is available to everybody without CEFACT charging any royalties. At this point, the editing group disbands, while the Permanent Group receives any feedback on the specification. If major maintenance issues occur, a new editing group forms to rewrite the specification, starting by gathering new requirements.

OASIS

The Organisation for the Advancement of Structured Information Standards (OASIS) is quite a different organisation from CEFACT. In the early 1990s, the ISO standard SGML (Standard Generalized Markup Language) gained some momentum as a format for data exchange. To support each other, users and vendors of SGML founded the consortium SGML Open. In 1998, W3C published the simplified and improved XML.[596] To reflect its support of XML and its broader range of standardisation activities in general, SGML Open renamed itself as OASIS in 1999.[597] Today,

> "OASIS is a not-for-profit, global consortium that drives the development, convergence and adoption of e-business standards."[598]

This mission statement reflects the focus of OASIS on business-related specifications, usually based on XML and Web Services standards. However, OASIS also develops very technical specifications if there is a need from a business perspective.

OASIS consists of a Board of Directors, a Technical Advisory Board, Technical Committees (TC), and a TC Administration (see Figure 5.16). The Board of Directors runs OASIS and is supported by the Technical Advisory Board. OASIS members elect both for two years. The TC Administration supports the TCs, which conduct the actual specification development. The former also reports the TCs' activities to the Board of Directors, which only intervenes in the TCs' work in exceptional cases.[599]

---

[596] See subsection 5.1.1.
[597] See OASIS (2004e).
[598] OASIS (2004h).
[599] See OASIS (2003c).

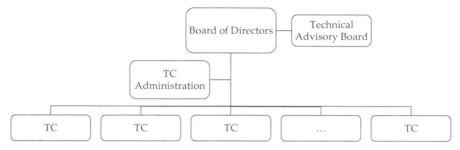

Figure 5.16: OASIS Organisational Structure[604]

OASIS receives its resources mainly from the members' contributions and membership fees. It offers several membership levels starting with individuals (250 US$ per year, no voting rights), smaller organisations (1,000 – 5,750 US$ per year, voting rights, contributor status) through to large organisations (13,500 US$ per year, voting rights, sponsor status, logo placements, naming in press releases).[600] OASIS also receives governmental support, e.g. from the US government.[601] In October 2004, OASIS had 83 sponsors, 356 contributors, about 3,500 developers from more than 100 countries, 14 completed or closed TCs, and 66 active TCs. Of the members, 51% are technology providers, 34% users, and 15% governmental and academic organisations.[602] The dominance of providers is also reflected in the Board of Directors (BEA Systems, e-Government Unit of UK Cabinet Office, Fujitsu Software, Nokia, HP, IBM, Intel, Microsoft, Oracle, Sun, and one full-time OASIS director) and the Technical Advisory Board (Entrust, IBM, SeeBeyond, Sun, one OASIS director, one individual member).[603] Moreover, OASIS cooperates with other SDOs, especially with IEC, ISO and ITU.

The structure of OASIS provides a stable organisational frame within which the members can form TCs to develop specifications for information systems with little administrative involvement from the consortium.[605]

---

[600] See Graham/Pollock/Smart, et al. (2003), p. 4.

[601] See Quantz (2002).

[602] See OASIS (2004f).

[603] See OASIS (2004c) and OASIS (2004g).

[604] Based on OASIS (2004e) and OASIS (2003c).

[605] See OASIS (2004h).

Nevertheless, a formal TC process and some guidelines ensure that the work environment for TCs is open, democratic and flexible.[606]

Openness is reflected in the relatively low barriers to starting up a new TC. Any three or more OASIS members can form a TC in an area of interest, the only requirement being to deliver a TC charter including the purpose, scope and schedule of the project. The spectrum of resulting specifications thus ranges from UDDI for building business registries to HumanML for representing human characteristics such as joy, fear, etc. Moreover, all TC work must follow the OASIS intellectual property rights (IPR) policy, which allows free use of OASIS specifications, yet does not completely exclude potential royalty claims from contributors in certain cases. Especially important for the openness of the TC work is the intensive use of Web-based tools to write the specifications. Besides public Web pages publishing drafts and completed documents, OASIS requires the actual discussions within the TCs to be public:

> "All TC business and technical discussions must take place on the TC email list, and all meeting minutes, or a reference to them, must be sent to this list so that all TC information is archived and publicly viewable."[607]

Democratic mechanisms for solving conflicts are important elements in OASIS work. In general, TCs should follow what is known as Robert's Rule of Order[608] and make decisions with majority votes of TC members. The Board of Directors only intervenes, if a TC cannot resolve a conflict itself. Moreover, all decisions are available to the public on the OASIS Web pages.

Flexibility of writing specifications within TCs is the third pillar of the OASIS philosophy. TCs can start at several entry points, from an early idea discussed in OASIS mail lists to almost finished specifications. TCs can be concerned with almost any kind of specification approach, as long as it is a structured information standard somehow related to business issues. TCs can form subcommittees, joint committees with other TCs, cooperate with other SDOs, and even work in another language than English.[609] Finally, they can publish a specification as a Committee Draft or as a more rigor-

---

[606] See OASIS (2003c), OASIS (2004h).

[607] OASIS (2004h).

[608] These are general rules on parliamentary procedures. See Robert III/Evans/ Honemann, et al. (2000).

[609] See OASIS (2004h).

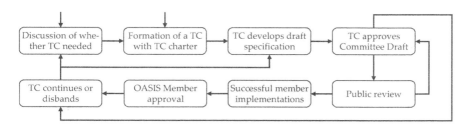

Figure 5.17: OASIS Development Process[611]

ously tested OASIS Standard. Figure 5.17 gives an overview of how this can be attained within the OASIS development process.[610]

OASIS members form a TC either by starting a preliminary public discussion on whether a TC is needed or directly submitting a complete TC charter to the TC Administration. The TC then develops a draft specification. The TCs have a great deal of flexibility in how they conduct this work in detail. They only have to follow certain general rules, make their discussions and decisions public, and use OASIS templates. If the work on the specification is finished, the TC can approve it as a Committee Draft, which requires approval from at least two thirds of all TC members and disapproval from no more than a quarter. TC Administration has to be notified and puts the specification on public Web pages under OASIS IPR policy. At this point, the TC can finish its work and disband. If the members are striving for an official OASIS standard, the specification has to be publicly reviewed for at least 30 days and successfully implemented by at least three OASIS members. Any changes to the specification break the Committee Draft status. The TC has to vote again for Committee Draft status before it can submit the specification to all OASIS members for approval. If more than 15% of the voting membership agrees, they accept the specification as an official OASIS Standard.[612] Finally, the TC either continues work on improving the specification or disbands. The TC Administration can shut a TC down, if it has less than three members, has no activities for six months, or makes no progress towards its goals. In October 2004, OASIS had 17 specifications in draft status and 16 in OASIS Standard status, of which four are ebXML specifications.

---

[610] See OASIS (2003c).

[611] Based on OASIS (2003c).

[612] For the voting details if members disapprove see OASIS (2003c), lines 623-641.

ebXML

In February 1998, W3C published the XML specification as a revised version of SGML. CEFACT recognised its importance for electronic data interchange between firms. As the official organisation for EDIFACT, the CEFACT members saw the need to get involved in XML-related activities too.[613] At the time responsible for relations between CEFACT and other SDOs, Klaus-Dieter Naujok contacted W3C to investigate options for common work on business-related XML specifications.[614] In a face-to-face meeting in the first half of 1999, Jon Bosak, the leader of the W3C XML effort, and Bill Smith, the president of OASIS, recommended working with OASIS. CEFACT approved this cooperation and the two organisations formed the ebXML initiative with two executives from OASIS and two from CEFACT (including Naujok as chair of ebXML).

In November 1999, they initiated an 18-month programme to develop a set of ebXML specifications.[615] The first result was a specification outlining the requirements for the ebXML architecture, including its vision:

> "The ebXML vision is to deliver: A single set of internationally agreed upon technical specifications that consist of common XML semantics and related document structures to facilitate global trade. This single set of ebXML technical specifications will create a Single Global Electronic Market."[616]

This vision could not be attained by just translating EDI into XML. Rather, the ebXML developers aimed to use business process perspectives and object-oriented modelling, which promised to overcome some of the drawbacks of EDIFACT.[617] During the 18-month programme several successful prototypes were developed, including the application of ebXML specifications on RosettaNet PIPs.[618] In May 2001, the ebXML team completed its programme on time and presented several specifications, all of which were approved by the usual CEFACT and OASIS procedures (see

---

[613] See Weitzel/Harder/Buxmann (2001), p. 14.

[614] For a more detailed discussion of the formation of ebXML, see the personal Weblog of Naujok: Naujok (2004a). Note the inconsistency in the claims made by Naujok and his former CEFACT colleague Glushko. Which one is right on the details is not important for my further analysis of ebXML.

[615] See Graham/Pollock/Smart, et al. (2003), p. 5.

[616] See Crawford (2000).

[617] See Weitzel/Harder/Buxmann (2001), p. 117.

[618] See ebXML (2000).

above): ebXML Technical Architecture, Business Process Specification Schema, Registry Information Model, Registry Services, ebXML Requirements, Message Service, and Collaboration-Protocol Profile and Agreement.

As it became clear that these specifications were not sufficient for achieving the ebXML vision, CEFACT and OASIS split up their responsibilities for further improvement. CEFACT was responsible for the business-semantic-related specifications, while OASIS maintained the technical specifications, and both were jointly to drive the foundational architecture and marketing of ebXML. A management committee consisting of three voting members from CEFACT and three from OASIS coordinated all these activities. An official Memorandum of Understanding fixed these agreements.[619] In June 2001, OASIS extended one existing TC and formed three new TCs for the advancement of the ebXML specifications.[620] One month later, CEFACT initiated the preliminary e-Business Transition Ad hoc Working Group for the same reason.[621] In September 2002, OASIS members approved the ebXML Messaging Services specification as the first ebXML OASIS Standard.[622]

In June 2003, the CEFACT plenary endorsed the ebXML specifications. All OASIS ebXML specifications had already reached version 2, while the Business Process Specification Schema (BPSS) managed by CEFACT was still at version 1.01 and the Core Component specification not yet finished.[623] In August 2003, CEFACT announced the successful completion of ebXML and the strategy to integrate other Web Services specifications too.[624] In October 2003, several developers left CEFACT to continue their work on BPSS within a newly formed TC at OASIS.[625]

In March 2004, ISO approved the OASIS ebXML Standards as technical specifications ISO/TS 15000.[626] This strengthens the perceived reliability of

---

[619] See Walker/Gannon (2001).

[620] See OASIS (2001).

[621] See ebXML (2001b). However, the planed e-Business Working Group was never formed. See later.

[622] See OASIS (2002).

[623] See ebXML (2003b).

[624] See CEFACT (2003a).

[625] See OASIS (2003b). For a further discussion of the tensions between CEFACT and OASIS see subsection 5.3.3.

[626] See OASIS (2004b).

ebXML specifications. Later in the year, CEFACT completed its work on the Core Components Technical Specification (CCTS) and submitted it to ISO, too.[627] In October 2004, CEFACT thus managed one group working on CCTS, while OASIS had five working on ebXML specifications (see Figure 5.18).

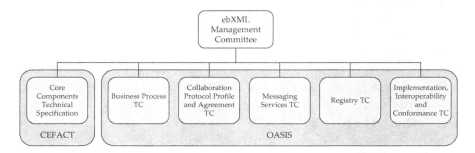

Figure 5.18: ebXML Organisational Structure

The actual development of the ebXML specifications follows the procedures of the SDO responsible as analysed above. Many different organisations participate in the development, including technology vendors (54%), users (30%), and the public sector (16%).[628] Noteworthy is the relatively strong support by governmental organisations and other SDOs ranging from ISO to RosettaNet.

5.3.2 Architecture

Since its first specification, the technical architecture of ebXML has comprised five components, which are also reflected in the TCs:[629]

- Messaging Service Functionality (Messaging Services TC)
- Trading Partner Information (Collaboration Protocol Profile and Agreement TC)
- Registry Functionality (Registry TC)
- Business Process and Information Modelling (Business Process TC)
- Core Components and Core Library Functionality (CEFACT)

---

[627] See CEFACT (2004c).

[628] See Gannon (2003).

[629] See Eisenberg/Nickull (2001), pp. 16ff.

What sets ebXML apart is the specification of this overall architecture before starting the development of the technical specifications. Most competing initiatives such as Web Services started by developing some technologies without formulating a comprehensive business vision first.[630] The following paragraphs briefly present the main ebXML specifications.

ebXML Message Services (ebMS) transports documents of almost any kind securely over the Internet infrastructure. It was intended thereby to replace the expensive VANs that are one of the main reasons why SMEs often refused to adopt EDI. Although ebXML developers originally developed a new solution based on HTTP and XML, they integrated this with SOAP as it became available and gained significant attention.[631] This is also the only ebXML TC in which Microsoft was involved. Some have speculated that Microsoft's engagement was mainly driven by its goal to further push SOAP, which was developed by Microsoft and later submitted to W3C.[632] Today, though it still has to compete with SOAP extended by Web Services security specifications, ebMS is the most widely adopted of the ebXML specifications.[633] In October 2004, the current OASIS version of ebMS was version 2.0 from April 2003, also published as ISO/TS 15000-2. The TC in question was working on version 3.0, including the integration of WS-Reliability, another OASIS specification.

The ebXML Collaboration Protocol Profile and Agreement (ebCPPA) specification is an important part of the ebXML vision of coupling information systems of business partners quickly, if not automatically. The main requirement for such interoperability is the clear definition of the partners' interfaces and how they are coupled. A collaboration protocol profile describes the interfaces, ranging from supported transport protocols through to business process specifications and the goods and services offered. A collaboration protocol agreement couples two or more such profiles, establishing an ebXML relation between all participants. In the ideal case, i.e. with interoperable software implementations and perfectly described profiles, this can happen automatically. This is one of the main differences of ebXML with respect to EDI, as EDI did not support the initiation of data interchange relationships, only the actual exchange of elec-

---

[630] See Virili (2003), p. 117.

[631] See Naujok (2004b).

[632] See Naujok (2004b), LaMonica (2004).

[633] ebXML (2003a), pp. 37ff.

tronic documents. The roots of ebCPPA lie in the Trading Partner Agreement Markup Language (tpaML) developed and patented by IBM. It took until May 2002 to clarify whether IBM would charge royalty-fees for its patent used in ebCPPA.[634] Eventually, OASIS convinced IBM to provide a royalty- free patent licence to all ebCPPA users.[635] In October 2004, the current OASIS version of ebCPPA was 2.0, also published as ISO/TS 15000-1, while the respective TC was working on the maintenance update version 2.1.

The two specifications ebXML Registry Information Model (ebRIM) and ebXML Registry Services Specification (ebRS) define the set-up of ebXML registries. Such registries permanently store different kinds of XML documents, non-XML supporting documents and metadata about the documents. In the context of ebXML, this might take the form in particular of Collaboration Protocol Profiles and Core Components. While ebRIM specifies the format in which its content is stored, ebRS defines how users can access it. With this basic concept, ebRIM and ebRS are clearly competing with UDDI. Ariba, IBM and Microsoft jointly developed the latter and submitted it to OASIS in 2002.[636] Since then, IBM has stopped its support for ebRIM/ebRS, but is still a sponsor of the UDDI TC. OASIS has given no explicit statement about how ebRIM/ebRS and UDDI relate to each other and whether if there are any plans to merge them. There is thus some confusion regarding the relation between them.[637] In October 2004, ebRIM and ebRS in version 2 had official OASIS standard status and are also accepted as ISO/TS 15000-3/4. The responsible TC has already approved version 2.5 and was working on version 3. To make matters more confusion, the OASIS members have approved UDDI as a standard only in version 2, although it has been contributed to OASIS as version 3.

The ebXML Business Process Specification Schema (BPSS) serves for the formal definition of public processes running between two or more business partners. Primarily, it offers a formal language to describe the roles of the participants, the associated messages, and the sequence of the message exchange. It does not, however, offer predefined business processes as RosettaNet PIPs do. Rather, the application of BPSS results in XML-based

---

[634] See Schüler (2002).

[635] See the discussion in Bosak (2002).

[636] See Hauser/Löwer (2004), p. 99.

[637] See Capell (2003).

business process definitions developed for specific use cases. For their modelling, the use of the UN/CEFACT Modeling Methodology (UMM) and the Unified Modeling Language (UML) is recommended, but not required.[638] The many different initiatives to establish a standard for the formal description of business processes emphasised the demand for such specifications. However, they also caused confusion, especially as several actors are involved in several initiatives. For example, Hauser/Löwer (2004) identify and analyse 12 different approaches to formal business process definitions.[639] Within ebXML, this turmoil in the field was one reason that the BPSS developers left CEFACT in October 2003 and have been continuing their work as an OASIS TC.[640] Again, this leads to a situation in which OASIS hosts TCs that are in some way competing with one another. In this case it is BPEL, driven by large vendors such as HP, IBM, Microsoft, Oracle, SAP and Sun, and BPSS, driven by Cyclone Commerce, Fujitsu and Sun. However, the BPSS TC explicitly cooperates with the BPEL TC and other related SDO efforts.[641] In October 2004, the current version was 1.01, dating from May 2001, but with the TC working on version 2.0.[642] Noteworthy, however, is the use of BPSS 1.01 as a central specification for all revised RosettaNet PIPs.[643]

The ebXML Core Components Technical Specification (CCTS) provides business semantics to be used in the other ebXML specifications. As the ebXML initiative aims at specifications usable for all industries, the Core Components only specify business semantics that are industry-independent. Obvious examples are date, time, time zones and currencies. More complex are concepts such as 'customer', which can refer to a passenger when using an airline, a guest when staying at a hotel, or a shipper when sending a product. In all these roles, the customer still has the same properties, such as a name, address, etc.[644] The Core Components unify these semantics and offer mechanisms to map them onto the specific se-

---

[638] See ebXML (2001a), p. 3.

[639] See Hauser/Löwer (2004), pp. 161ff. For a similar discussion, see Nickerson/zur Muehlen (2003).

[640] For further analysis, see the next subsection.

[641] See OASIS (2003b).

[642] See the next subsection for the discussion of UN/CEFACT BPSS version 1.1.

[643] See subsection 5.2.3.

[644] See Kotok/Webber (2002), p. 58.

mantics of an industry or individual company. As CEFACT had already carried out a similar effort in specifying EDIFACT, it was also responsible for CCTS. While few software vendors and users participated, large SDOs such as OAG, SWIFT and UCC supported CEFACT. In October 2004, the latest version of CCTS was 2.01, dating from November 2003. CEFACT will continuously revise this specification, as business semantics are always evolving.[645] However, there were some uncertainties about the work of CEFACT on ebXML, as I will discuss in subsection 5.3.3.

An overview of ebXML would not be complete without a short introduction to complementary specifications. While users can combine almost any other interorganisational specification with ebXML, some are more closely related to it than others.

The Universal Business Language (UBL) specifies the content of electronic business documents. It is not a formal part of the ebXML architecture, but complements it. While the CCTS is kept abstract from a concrete technology, UBL implements CCTS concepts in XML-based components. UBL consists of three main elements:

- "A library of XML schemas for reusable data components such as "Address," "Item," and "Payment" – the common data elements of everyday business documents.
- A small set of XML schemas for common business documents such as "Order," "Despatch Advice," and "Invoice" that are constructed from the UBL library components and can be used in a generic order-to-invoice trading context.
- Support for the customization of UBL in specific trading relationships."[646]

UBL draws on the experiences made with EDIFACT business content, but adds explicit mechanisms for the customisation of business documents without any loss of compatibility. A change in the binary format of an EDIFACT document always required adaptation on the part of the information systems involved. In UBL, changes are possible through additional data fields. Non-adapted systems can still use the documents, but simply ignore the additional fields.[647] In future versions of UBL, this inheritance mechanism will be further refined and automated where possible. UBL

---

[645] See subsection 5.1.2.

[646] OASIS (2004i).

[647] See Kettenmann (2004), pp. 113ff.

has its roots in the xCBL specification developed by CommerceOne, which converted EDIFACT semantics to XML.[648] The original idea was that a new OASIS CBL TC would further develop xCBL. CEFACT blocked this, as it also planned to develop an XML specification based on EDIFACT and the CCTS work. As these plans were never executed, OASIS formed the UBL TC to advance a universal XML-based EDIFACT successor.[649] Nevertheless, the UBL chair Jon Bosak, formerly responsible for developing XML at W3C, managed to get CEFACT and other UN initiatives closely involve in the UBL work. The main sponsors of UBL are Boeing, the US America's National Institute for Standards and Technology (NIST), Oracle, SeeBeyond, Sterling Commerce and Sun, with a growing membership from Asia, especially Korea. In November 2004, OASIS approved UBL version 1.0 as an OASIS standard and also planed the submission to ISO.

There is often a certain amount of confusion regarding the relation of Web Services specifications to ebXML. Table 5.7 juxtaposes the Web Services specifications BPEL, SOAP, UDDI and WSDL with roughly comparable ebXML specifications.

Table 5.7: ebXML vs. Web Services Specifications

	Web Services	ebXML
Semantics	–	CCTS (CEFACT) UBL (OASIS)
Processes	BPEL (OASIS)	BPSS (OASIS)
Discovery	UDDI (OASIS)	ebRMI/ebRS (OASIS)
Description	WSDL (W3C)	ebCPPA (OASIS)
Messaging	SOAP (W3C)	ebMS/SOAP (OASIS)

By October 2004 only SOAP and WSDL have already gained sufficient acceptance to speak of de facto standards. One reason might be their domain-independence, as they are implementations of the SOA programming approach and not specific to business needs. BPEL, UDDI, and the ebXML specifications at OASIS are as yet neither broadly accepted nor can

---

[648] See Kotinurmi/Nurmilaakso/Laesvuori (2003), p. 137.
[649] See Graham/Pollock/Smart, et al. (2003), p. 5.

they be sharply distinguished, as the TCs cooperate and influence each other.

Formed in early 2004, the OASIS Electronic Business Service Oriented Architecture (ebSOA) TC aims to clarify these relations. Moreover, it plans to improve the somewhat outdated ebXML Technical Architecture to reflect the recent developments in the concept of SOA.[650] The main sponsors are Adobe, Boeing, Cyclone Commerce, Fujitsu and Sterling Commerce. While many further organisations support this and the other ebXML TCs, the absence of the major business software vendors IBM, Microsoft and SAP is still a drawback for the future success of ebXML and ebSOA. However, this is not the only reason for the relatively slow adoption of ebXML, as I will discuss in the following subsection.

5.3.3 Politics

Some facts cited in the previous subsection have already indicated that the ebXML initiative was not free of political manoeuvring.[651] The analysis in this subsection treats an important facet of the difficulties faced on the path towards broadly adopted interorganisational standards. It is based on press releases from CEFACT and OASIS, mailing lists at OASIS, personal weblogs[652] and journal articles. Some statements may thus be highly biased towards the interests of the particular author. Nevertheless, a good picture of the actual events emerges through putting the pieces together.

The roots of the diverging opinions in the later ebXML development can be traced back to the late 1980s. Aware of the slow adoption of EDI by SMEs, the joint committee ISO/IEC JTC 1 developed the Open-edi Reference Model.[653] The main idea was to enable ad-hoc data exchange without long prior negotiations and agreements between trading partners. This was to be achieved by separating two views on business transactions. The Business Operational View (BOV) covered the semantics of business data and the rules for business transactions. The Functional Services View

---

[650] See OASIS (2004d).

[651] See Kotinurmi/Nurmilaakso/Laesvuori (2003), pp. 130ff.

[652] For a detailed discussion of weblogs and their role in the public relations of organisations, see Fischer (2006).

[653] See ISO/IEC (1997).

(FSV) was concerned with the technical aspects of functional capabilities, services interfaces and protocols.[654]

In 1995, UNECE/WP.4 created the ad-hoc committee AC.1 to investigate technologies for 'Next Generation EDI'. Based on the Open-edi Model, it focused on the BOV and recommended the use of business process modelling and object-oriented approaches. When UNECE/WP.4 became to UN/CEFACT in 1996, the Techniques and Methodologies Working Group (TMWG) continued the work of AC.1.[655] After the decision to use UML for business process modelling, TMWG developed the UN/CEFACT Modeling Methodology (UMM) based on the Rational Unified Process of the UML software vendor Rational Rose. The UMM aims to model interorganisational business processes independently of the underlying technologies. TMWG recommended that CEFACT work should focus on this modelling and the technological development be left to other organisations.[656]

When W3C's XML gained momentum in 1999, UN/CEFACT realised that it needed to get involved in XML to defend its EDIFACT expertise to other groups. As chair of UN/CEFACT's TMWG, Klaus-Dieter Naujok consulted W3C about cooperating on the development of an EDIFACT successor based on XML. Jon Bosak from Sun was leading W3C's XML effort and recommended working with OASIS. In November 1999, OASIS and CEFACT started the ebXML initiative. Bosak, who joined OASIS after the completion of XML and was leading the Technical Advisory Board, remembers how OASIS perceived the purpose of ebXML:

> "Our understanding was that UN/CEFACT and X12 members would provide the business expertise, and OASIS would provide the XML expertise, and when we were done, we would have basically a standard, cross-industry version of RosettaNet that would extend the known benefits of EDI to small and medium-size businesses. (…) that's what we thought ebXML would look like an XML version of EDI that would improve on 20 years of implementation experience with standardised XML formats for the messages, standardised XML machine-readable formats for the business process specifications and trading partner agreements, and a standardised XML registry/repository for registration and discovery. This is what we signed up for."[657]

---

[654] See ISO/IEC (1997), p. 6.

[655] See Naujok (2000).

[656] See Naujok (2000).

[657] Bosak (2003).

Remarkably, ebXML followed some of RosettaNet architectural designs, especially concerning business "(…) process context around the messages that EDI has always been missing." This was regarded as ensuring "(…) full interoperability between any process defined in terms of RosettaNet PIPs and processes defined in ebXML."[658] In September 2000, a discussion about the nature of 'business objects' revealed a 'fundamental disconnect' between the OASIS approach and the goal of CEFACT's TMWG. OASIS followed the concept of converting the existing EDIFACT into XML documents and adding aspects that were missing. The 'CEFACT vision', however, was to focus on business process and object modelling, from which the XML documents could automatically be generated. This concept is based on the Open-edi Reference Model and the subsequent work by TMWG as described above.[659] As the planned completion of the first ebXML version was only eight months away, it became unlikely that the two fundamentally different approaches would merge. A couple of days before an important ebXML executive meeting in Tokyo, Bosak proposed a compromise:

> "One group is focused on how we can completely automate electronic trade; the other is focused on how we can enable small businesses to engage in electronic trade and how we can help businesses of all sizes make the transition from legacy systems. I believe that both of these agendas can be accomplished if we recognize that complete automation is a long-term goal, whereas getting the small businesses online and beginning the transition from legacy systems is a short-term one."[660]

Nevertheless, the Tokyo meeting in November 2000 saw fierce arguments on this topic. Finally, the ebXML plenary consisting of several hundred participants decided not to include an obligatory business modelling method in the first version of ebXML.

On May 11, 2001, OASIS and CEFACT presented the first complete version of ebXML in Vienna. While the participants declared that their initial goals had been achieved, they also recognised the need to maintain the existing and to develop further specifications. They split up the responsibilities according to the Open-edi Reference Model. CEFACT was responsible for the BOV specifications, i.e. BPSS and CCTS, while OASIS was

---

[658] See Bosak (2003).

[659] See Naujok (2000).

[660] Bosak (2003).

concerned with ebMS, ebRIM/ebRS, ebCPPA, security and conformance matters. They were jointly to drive marketing and the evolution of the technical architecture. Ray Walker, chair at CEFACT, and Patrick Gannon, chair at OASIS, signed all this in a Memorandum of Understanding (MoU) at the Vienna meeting.[661] Virtually without delay, OASIS formed the appropriate TCs, and CEFACT's e-Business Transition Ad hoc Working Group followed shortly afterwards.[662]

In 2002, however, participants complained about significant political issues hindering smooth technical advancement. The main reason was seen to be weakness in the negotiation of the Memorandum of Understanding (MoU), which left too much flexibility for private 'agendas'. Moreover, a missing policy on the treatment of intellectual property rights (IPR) left participants and users unsure about the legal consequences of ebXML.[663] Uncertainty increased as rumours arose that CEFACT considered abandoning its ebXML efforts in order to focus on UMM, its technology-independent approach to interorganisational standards.[664]Additionally, ebXML developers were complaining about the condition of the UN/CEFACT Web presence, which was outdated, had missing links, and even gave incorrect information about ebXML:

> "CEFACT professes to set standards for 6 billion people yet hasn't had the civility within its own community to provide basic fundamental information about the ebXML undertaking, let alone, resources for dissemination of document and files. (...) Now, I suspect CEFACT does not actually support ebXML activities (as is apparent by their willingness to fund hundreds of megs of EDIFACT activities but nothing of ebXML). Is the CEFACT Forum then, a kind of trojan activity, a kind of sting, to lure hundreds of xml dissidents into an activity to stagger us, slow us down?"[665]

The ambiguous Web presence of CEFACT in 2002 and 2003 was critical, as at the same time many new Web Services-based specifications emerged. Several of them aimed at very similar goals to those of the ebXML specifications, e.g. BPEL, BPML and BTP.[666] In such a turbulent environment,

---

[661] Walker/Gannon (2001).

[662] See OASIS (2001) and ebXML (2001b).

[663] See Clark (2002).

[664] See Rawlins (2002).

[665] Boyle (2002).

[666] See Hauser/Löwer (2004), pp. 161ff.

reliable information on a specification is important for fostering its credibility. The confusion about ebXML made it easier for IBM and Microsoft to establish BPEL as an alternative approach to ebXML BPSS.

In May 2003, the UN/CEFACT plenary adopted the ebXML specifications as official CEFACT Technical Specifications. On August 20, 2003, CEFACT announced the completion of version 2 of CCTS, without mentioning the name ebXML in the specification. Among others, Naujok is noted as responsible for this press release. He is also jointly responsible for a press release dating from August 21, 2003, in which CEFACT declared the work on ebXML to be concluded. Moreover, it announced its plans to work on a technology-independent framework, while stressing CEFACT's new relations to the Web Services-centric OASIS BPEL TC and WS-I.[667] Christian Frühwald, then chair of CEFACT, is cited as saying:

> "Recognition that the next technology trend is just around the corner resulted in the recent UN/CEFACT Plenary meeting directing a new work programme to move UN/CEFACT closer to web services (...). This new work, known as UN/CEFACT Business Collaboration Framework (BCF), will allow UN/CEFACT to identify the growing needs of government, commercial and industrial organisations as they approach their global information exchange requirements."[668]

The same day, CEFACT responded to concerns from the UBL developers with another statement that it would "support only one document-centric approach to XML content and its desire is that UBL will be the foundation for that approach."[669]

In the first half of September 2003, a delegation from CEFACT, including Naujok and Walker, went on the so-called BCF-Tour to promote the BCF vision in Taiwan, Singapore, Kuala Lumpur, Hong Kong, Tokyo and Seoul.[670] They stressed the technology-neutral approach of the BCF. Some statements, however, could be interpreted as showing a strong preference of Web Services specifications over ebXML.[671]

---

[667] See CEFACT (2003a).

[668] CEFACT (2003a).

[669] CEFACT (2003c).

[670] See Techniques and Methodologies Group (2003).

[671] See Markoff/Schenker (2004) and also my participation in the BCF Seminar on September 4, 2003, in Singapore.

As a reaction to this policy of CEFACT's, OASIS announced the formation of an ebXML Business Process TC on September 19.[672] The purpose of this TC was to continue the work on ebXML BPSS, which the developers considered to be far from fully completed. On October 20, 2003, the TC was officially formed, mainly with developers that had previously been working on BPSS at CEFACT.[673] Because of legal disputes, the new OASIS TC had to continue its work on the basis of the flawed BPSS version 1.01, while CEFACT had already developed an improved version 1.1. All this forced CEFACT to make a position statement on ebXML the same day:

> "UN/CEFACT recognizes that ebXML is a very important technology solution which it will continue to actively maintain and support. UN/CEFACT recognizes the rapid pace of technology development and remains committed to the development of business content that can be used with any existing or future technological solution, such as UN/EDIFACT, XML and web services. In so doing UN/CEFACT remains open to cooperation and collaboration with all organisations sharing similar objectives."[674]

The migration of the BPSS developers to OASIS again caused a fierce discussion of ebXML's architecture and the responsibilities of the participants. Naujok, for example, reproached Sun for influencing the decision not to use UMM in ebXML because of vendor politics, while Bosak defended Sun by claiming that this decision was made by the full ebXML plenary and was not determined by vendors.[675] I interpret the essence of the discussion so far to be that the official strategy of CEFACT was to focus on BCF, CCTS and UMM independently of ebXML, while OASIS was to drive the technical development of ebXML, including BPSS, which is actually a technical specification.[676]

On November 15, 2003, however, CEFACT published version 2.01 of CCTS, now again officially termed part of the ebXML framework. This supports Bosak's assumption that many developers at CEFACT did not share the BCF vision, but rather preferred the ebXML approach.[677]

---

[672] Clark (2003).

[673] See OASIS (2003b).

[674] CEFACT (2003b).

[675] See Bosak (2003).

[676] See, e.g., Bosak (2003) and Naujok (2004a), entry from 2004-08-18.

[677] See Bosak (2003).

Up to October, the year 2004 was a successful one for the ebXML work at OASIS. First, OASIS formed the new Electronic Business Service Oriented Architecture (ebSOA) TC to work on the integration of ebXML and Web Services concepts. Second, ISO approved the OASIS/ebXML specifications ebMS, ebCPPA, ebRIM, ebRS as ISO/TS 15000. Finally, the ebXML TCs strengthened their work on improving the existent specifications, especially BPSS version 2.

The picture is different for CEFACT. In February 2004, the New York Times published an article titled "Microsoft Creates a Stir in Its Work with the UN".[678] The authors claimed that Microsoft contributed ideas to the BCF and sponsored the BCF-Tour in Asia to push its Web Services concept via CEFACT into the EDI/ebXML field. They also deduced that CEFACT "was privately turning its back on the ebXML standard". The complaints made by several CEFACT members about Microsoft's behaviour also supported these claims.[679] CEFACT officials responded that CEFACT's funding was always heavily dependent on the contribution of other organisations and Microsoft's portion was very small and in accordance with all applicable UN rules.[680]

On May 10, 2004, UNECE published a press release emphasising that CEFACT and OASIS had reaffirmed their commitment to cooperate on ebXML and strengthen their work on it:

> "In a joint statement, UN/CEFACT and OASIS stress that the proposed cooperation agreement should improve understanding and clarify the public perception of how the two entities work together. (…) Although it stands as a tremendous accomplishment, the original collaboration between OASIS and UN/CEFACT that created ebXML (…) was just the first step. The greater challenge lies ahead. The task before us now is to advance deployment of ebXML and work towards harmonization with emerging technology standards. UN/CEFACT's longstanding strengths in trade facilitation and e-business will be a key factor in this."[681]

As a first publicly visible step, on June 1 CEFACT submitted ebXML CCTS to ISO for approval as ISO Technical Specification 15000-5, as OASIS had previously done with the other ebXML specifications, apart from BPSS.

---

[678] Markoff/Schenker (2004).

[679] See Computerwoche (2004).

[680] Markoff/Schenker (2004).

[681] CEFACT (2004b).

Later in August 2004, Microsoft completely left CEFACT without any official statement. The unofficial reason was that the focus of CEFACT was shifting away from Microsoft's interests.[682] This could have been because of the renewed efforts by CEFACT to foster ebXML development.

Another reason could have been the intellectual property rights (IPR) policy of CEFACT. The fundamental purpose of such an IPR policy is to set a legal framework for any claims by contributors or users of a specification. On the one hand, contributors can charge royalties for the use of their patents included in a specification. On the other hand, users can sue an SDO or its contributors for damages caused by a specification. Since the first phase of ebXML in 1999, CEFACT had implicitly used the UN's IPR policy for ebXML work.[683] This included the full transfer of all IPR to the UN. In October 2002, CEFACT developed a new IPR policy, in which the participants have to grant an irrevocable, royalty-free licence to the UN but keep their IPR. Most CEFACT members regarded this approach as superior to the old one. The UN Office of Legal Affairs (OLA), however, was only prepared to accept this new IPR policy if it included an indemnity passage, which means that the contributors would have to defend the UN at their own expense against any third-party claims caused by a specification. If this was not accepted, CEFACT would have to return to the UN IPR policy. CEFACT sought advice at the World Intellectual Property Organisation (WIPO), which had also consulted OLA in IPR matters before. WIPO recommended following the CEFACT draft, without the indemnity passage, but OLA insisted on indemnity or the full transfer of IPR.[684] Ray Walker stated in early 2004:

> "The matter of IPR policy may seem arcane, but it is fundamental to standards work in the ICT area, and if not satisfactorily resolved may lead rapidly to a situation where UN/CEFACT cannot continue to develop or maintain eBusiness standards."[685]

Many large contributing members urged CEFACT to solve this IPR issue. As this did not happen until May 2004, SAP suspended its support for CEFACT until the IPR policy was on a solid basis. All this discussion

---

[682] See Computerwoche (2004).

[683] Naujok (2004a), entry from 2004-08-16.

[684] See Walker (2004).

[685] Walker (2004).

about IPR is likely to have been another reason for Microsoft withdrawing its support for CEFACT.[686] However, not only large companies struggled with the UN's IPR policy. Naujok too, who ran an electronic business consulting firm and was chair of CEFACT's Techniques and Methodology Group (TMG) (the successor of TMWG), tried to intensify the pressure on CEFACT to solve the IPR issue. On a personal weblog, he publicly discussed his view on the subject and stressed that the current IPR policy was too risky for most contributors. On September 1, 2004, the CEFACT chair dismissed Naujok as TMG chair because of several actions that "undermine the essential work undertaken by UN/CEFACT for the benefit of the user community, and are incompatible with the spirit in which the work of a United Nations Group Chair should be undertaken."[687] By way of response, Naujok wrote that he would stop the work on BCF and UMM, which was mainly driven by him.[688] This also included shutting down the web servers hosting resources for the TMG work, which Naujok's firm was running. Since October 2004, the domains unbcf.org and untmg.org, which many ebXML-related documents have links to, have not been accessible. Without going into the details of his conflict with CEFACT, Naujok has commented on the latest CEFACT election by pointing out that all the leaders elected as chairs are from European countries. It would be the first time that no nation from outside Europe has been represented with a CEFACT chair.[689] Moreover, he claims that most of the new chairs are very positive towards ebXML and have been publicly opposed to the BCF approach. In any case, this latest episode has seen CEFACT dismiss an expert in interorganisational standards who since 1989 has significantly contributed to EDIFACT and ebXML and been a driving force behind the vision of the technology-independent modelling of interorganisational processes.

In this study, I will not and cannot judge which party was right or wrong, as the whole story can be interpreted from at least two perspectives. One would be that CEFACT wanted to get rid of a 'weird visionary' who put the reputation of CEFACT at risk with unorthodox actions. The other would be that CEFACT is still stuck in its EDIFACT paradigm,

---

[686] See Computerwoche (2004).
[687] See Naujok (2004a), entry from 2004-09-01.
[688] See Naujok (2004a), entry from 2004-09-02.
[689] See Naujok (2004a), entry from 2004-09-16.

which it wants to continue with ebXML, and is not willing to switch to a technology-independent approach such as BCF.

5.3.4   Conclusions

The case of ebXML reveals several interesting points. First, its overall vision is certainly very demanding and even more ambitious than EDI-FACT's already was. From a theoretical perspective, therefore, it was an appropriate decision by CEFACT to ally with OASIS instead of developing ebXML on its own. The success of the joint 18-month programme supports this. Second, the cooperation in the following phase was almost a disaster. While no single reason can be identified, clearly the different opinions on the future course of ebXML played an important role. The business-oriented view and the technology-driven perspective could not be unified, and this caused a lot of friction in the cooperation between CEFACT and OASIS.

Third, while OASIS appears to be an SDO with clear rules and transparent processes, the picture of CEFACT, at least regarding the ebXML case, remains confusing. On the one hand, it displays tight control over bureaucratic processes, as the IPR policy debate illustrates. On the other hand, the somewhat chaotic appearance given to the public indicates that CEFACT did not have sufficient control over critical aspects such as an overall standards strategy (BCF vs. EDI-style), the influence of its participants (no clear membership fees, Microsoft's sponsoring, Naujok's public comments), and the inconsistent Web presence (contradicting press releases, confusing information on ebXML, shut down Web servers). It is obvious that none of these factors supports the establishment of standards in the sensitive field of interorganisational relationships. However, the major restructuring undergone by CEFACT in 2004 offers another chance to regain lost ground in its core business of interorganisational standards.

Assessing the future of ebXML is also difficult, as many factors influence it. OASIS seems to be a good organisational environment for the further development of the specifications. The tight coupling with UBL is another advantage of ebXML. Its broad adoption, however, depends on the software vendors. While IBM, Microsoft and SAP are not directly involved in the development of ebXML, they have to support it indirectly, as they all offer RosettaNet solutions, and all new PIPs are based on ebBPSS. Moreover, RosettaNet's leading position and ISO's recent approval could give ebXML further momentum, though they are no guarantee of success, as the Web Services standards are still severe competitors in several respects.

Table 5.8 summarises the ebXML and RosettaNet as described in the last two sections and reveals some major differences between the two of them. These are discussed in more detail in the next section, using the theoretical perspective of actor-network theory.

Table 5.8: Overview of ebXML and RosettaNet

	ebXML	*RosettaNet*
Vision	"ebXML enables enterprises of any size, in any global region, to conduct business using the Internet"	"E-Business Standards for the Global Supply Chain"
Focus	General electronic business infrastructure	Supply chain management in the electronics industry
Formation	Initiated to keep CEFACT's leading role in interorganisational data exchange	Initiated to solve concrete interorganisational integration problems in the electronics industry
Organisational structure	• Joint effort of CEFACT and OASIS; • OASIS Technical Committees lead the development; • Driven by governmental organisations (CEFACT) and software vendors (OASIS)	• Subsidiary of UCC; • Divided into regional affiliates and industry-specific councils; • Driven by Intel, Motorola, Cisco Systems, and several hundred other companies
Architecture	• Technical specifications for messaging, description and discovery; • Universal specifications for format definition, semantics and processes; • ebMS, ebCPPA, ebCCTS and ebBPSS as central elements, complemented with UBL; • Relations to other specifications confusing	• Sectoral specifications for business semantics, business processes and trading partner agreements; • Partner Interface Processes (PIPs) as central elements; • Clearly communicated strategy for the use of other specifications

Table 5.8 (continued): Overview of ebXML and RosettaNet

	ebXML	RosettaNet
Development processes	• Low (OASIS) to medium (CEFACT); • Open Development Process (CEFACT)	• Highly formalised; • Standardised RosettaNet Development Process
Intellectual Property Rights Policy	• Clear for OASIS, patents allowed; • Unclear for CEFACT	• Clear, patents allowed only in special cases
Politics	• Many public disputes, especially about long-term architectural strategy	• Few public disputes, long-term strategy seems consistent
Software support	• Only few major vendors	• Very good support by major vendors
Diffusion	• Low over all industries; • Future unclear, but used by RosettaNet; • Web Services partly as alternatives	• Medium in electronics industry; • Strong growth; • Few alternatives (e.g., existing EDIFICE specifications)

5.4   A Process Model for Interorganisational Standards Development

While establishing standards was regarded mainly as a governmental responsibility for a long time, it has become much more of an entrepreneurial task over recent decades.[690] Just as there is no single theory of entrepreneurship,[691] it is also unlikely that one theory can cover all the facets of developing and establishing standards. Moreover, in the development of

---

[690] See Picot (2001). For example, SWIFT is a profit-oriented firm developing interorganisational standards for the financial industry.

[691] In fact, there are many different theories explaining entrepreneurship and the functioning of firms, all covering very different aspects. See, e.g., Picot/Freudenberg (1997).

interorganisational standards, technical and organisational aspects are highly intermingled, making the creation of a simple theory difficult. In such a case, Markus/Robey (1988) propose an emergent perspective, which does not distinguish between technology and organisation, but rather analyses their mutual influence. Process theories promise to be an adequate approach to such emerging settings.[692] They do not predict which variables will cause which outcome. Instead, they describe the conditions that have to be met in one process step to enable the next step to be successful.[693] This section sketches such a process model for interorganisational standards.

Egyedi (1996) distinguishes three phases of standards development: the *formation* of a standards development organisation (SDO), its actual *organisation*, and the *development* of the specification within this organisation.[694] The IOS management framework described in section 3.3 comprises the phases *adoption, use* and *impact*. Combining all these phases results in the process chain depicted in Figure 5.19.

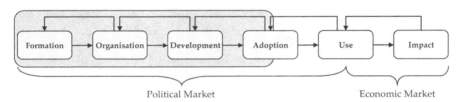

Figure 5.19: Standards Phases

The figure also indicates that all the phases are connected through feedback loops. For example, the formation of a standard initiative results in its organisation. If there are severe problems with the organisation, either the original initiative has to be reformed or a new one has to be started. Such a feedback mechanism works through the whole process chain. A stable organisation enables development of solid standards, whose adoption and use lead to certain impacts. If the actors are not satisfied with the impact, they challenge the use with new requirements. If use cannot be changed successfully, the adoption of other standards might be considered. If the available standards are not sufficient, new ones have to be developed, the

---

[692] See Markus/Robey (1988), p. 592.

[693] See section 4.5.

[694] See Figure 4.6 in subsection 4.4.2.

SDO organisation has to be changed, or even a new SDO has to be formed. Such feedback is especially important for IO standards, as the use domains often change permanently. In the terms employed by North (1990), all the latter are manoeuvres on the political market for interorganisational standards, while the use and impact represent the economic market where the benefits of the standards are received.

The further subsections focus on the phases *formation, organisation* and *development*, and their connection to *adoption* (see grey shade in Figure 5.19). I will interpret the dynamics of RosettaNet and ebXML in each phase from an actor-network perspective, using the case study data as presented in the sections 5.2 and 5.3.[695] A final subsection integrates all the findings into a generalised process model for interorganisational (IO) standardisation.

5.4.1 Formation

In the last decade, many new SDOs have emerged and disbanded because of the changing conditions for IO specifications. The formation of SDOs is thus an important element of standards development.

RosettaNet

Primarily, the formation of RosettaNet was a matter of translating other actors into its network, i.e., aligning their diverse interests. In the problematisation phase, the costly IOS integration project between Ingram Micro and 3Com uncovered the general problem of incompatible processes in different organisations (see Table 5.9). As a distributor with thousands of partners, Ingram Micro had a high interest in significantly lowering the integration costs. An ideal solution seemed to be the standardisation of the interorganisational business semantics and processes in the whole electronics industry. As the largest distributor in the industry, Ingram Micro expected to be an obligatory passage point for this vision, which could convince a critical mass of other companies. In the interessement phase, however, the representatives of the firms invited rejected the first presentation of the vision and concept the standard. The benefits of such IO stan-

---

[695] If no sources are given, this means that the facts under discussion were already mentioned in the case study sections.

dards were judged not to be worth the huge efforts needed and the political controversies expected. Nevertheless, Fadi Chehadé won the support of another powerful company, which was an even stronger obligatory passage point.

Table 5.9: Formation of RosettaNet from ANT Perspective

ANT Concepts	RosettaNet Formation Activities
Translation	→ Convincing
Problematisation	• Costly IOS integration project between Ingram Micro and 3Com • Need for standardisation of business semantics and processes • Ingram Micro as obligatory passage point (OPP)
Interessement	• Presentation of the standards vision and the concept for realising it • Refusal of the participating representatives • Winning of second company as an OPP convincing others to participate
Enrolment	• 28 companies related to the electronics industry eventually founded RosettaNet • Top executives formed the Management Board of RosettaNet
Inscription	→ Mission
Anticipation	• Further need for interorganisational standards • Mission: to "provide common business interfaces for supply chain trading partners and their customers to exchange information and transactions"
Irreversibilisation	• Press releases • Rosetta stone as a historical metaphor
Stabilisation	→ Strategy
Programmes	• Strategy with focus on electronics industry and implementation-driven specifications
Anti-Programmes	• No major changes to strategy

The inscription of the shared goals was reflected in the anticipation of the general need for interorganisational standards and the formulation of an appropriate mission statement. Irreversibility was strengthened by communicating the shared goals and the participating companies via press releases to the public. The metaphor of the ancient inscriptions of the Rosetta Stone can be interpreted as an inscript reflecting the intention of RosettaNet to also to break down language barriers and make history.[696]

The strategy of developing implementation-driven IO specifications with the focus on the electronics industry was the main programme stabilising the formation phase. As RosettaNet only adapted this strategy slightly, it can be seen as strong enough to have resisted all upcoming anti-programmes, i.e., requests to change the strategy.

ebXML

CEFACT realised that the increasing momentum of XML for structured data exchange posed a challenge to its core field of EDIFACT standards. In order to not lose significance, it decided to get involved in XML specifications by cooperating with a competent partner (see Table 5.10). In the interessement phase, consultation between CEFACT, OASIS and the W3C led to the decision to enrol OASIS. The anticipated goal was to combine EDIFACT concepts with XML technologies. The start of the 18-months-program to develop a first version of ebXML specifications aimed at the irreversibilisation of this goal. Despite some anti-programmes in the form of fierce discussion on the architecture of ebXML, the participants completed the 18-months-programme as planned. The original programme of combining EDIFACT and XML was stronger than the anti-programme of the process modeling approach.

---

[696] See RosettaNet (2004a), p. 4.

Table 5.10: Formation of ebXML from ANT Perspective

ANT Concepts	ebXML Formation
Translation	→ Convincing
Problematisation	• CEFACT did not want to lose significance in the face of the rising importance of XML • Plan to partner with external XML competence
Interessement	• Consultation with OASIS and W3C
Enrolment	• Formal ebXML initiative with CEFACT and OASIS
Inscription	→ Mission
Anticipation	• Mission: to deliver a "single set of internationally agreed upon technical specifications that consist of common XML semantics and related document structures to facilitate global trade."
Irreversibilisation	• Joint 18-months-programme
Stabilisation	→ Strategy
Programmes	• Main strategy to combine EDIFACT business concepts with XML technology
Anti-Programmes	• Discussion about the architectural strategy of ebXML (process model vs. document-centric)

A main difference with respect to RosettaNet is the reason for the formation of ebXML. While user firms founded RosettaNet to solve their own business problems, CEFACT initiated ebXML to defend its dominant position in the EDI field. Remarkable is the fact that CEFACT actively sought cooperation with another SDO. RosettaNet, in contrast, was independent of other SDOs, although it adopted existing specifications. Another difference is the architectural strategy. From the beginning, RosettaNet followed a process model approach, while ebXML members did not fully clarify their architectural strategy. The name 'ebXML' implies a strong focus on XML-centric aspects, while the ebXML architecture is partly independent of XML (especially ebCCTS). I suspect that the name 'ebXML' was intended to benefit from the considerable attention XML was receiving at the time. The founders of RosettaNet apparently anticipated the risk of referring to a particular technology in the SDO's name and chose one reflecting its overall mission.

Generalising the insights so far, I propose to use the term *convincing* for the translation phase of an SDO's formation. Here the driving actor has to convince other actors of the benefits of founding a new SDO. The inscription phase is called the *mission*, as it inscribes the main purpose of an SDO into a mission statement. The stabilisation phase of formation represents the *strategy*, as here it is revealed whether the main course of an SDO is successful or not (see Table 5.9 and Table 5.10).

5.4.2 Organisation

An SDO needs an appropriate organisation to put the standards strategy of the formation phase into practice.

RosettaNet

The main goal of RosettaNet is the coordination of different participants for the development of IO specifications (see Table 5.11). The main problem in reaching this goal is to secure the commitment of sufficient support and resources, especially from new companies and other organisations. As RosettaNet gained a unique position in its industry, it soon became an OPP without serious competition from any other SDO. Even so, it emphasises the task of interessement by clearly communicating its success via Web site and conferences. This is also a major task of the top executives at RosettaNet, as the tour of the CEO Hamilton to China shows. The Marketing Leadership Council is an organisational part of the consortium that concentrates on coordinating all these interessement activities. Another important factor for winning new support is the membership structure, which offers different participation levels ranging from Associate Partner to Council Member. Prospective members can start small and enlarge their participation level according to their needs. With these concepts, RosettaNet achieves commitment from many electronics companies and also regional organisations to expanding RosettaNet's structure and opening regional affiliates.

The anticipation of tasks to be executed is reflected in the organisational structure of RosettaNet. However, it has been important to adapt it to new requirements continuously. In this way, the consortium has been able to respect regional and industrial differences in its specifications. The irreversibilisation is reflected in the organisational structuring in terms of regions and industry councils, which have grown continuously in recent years. Also important was the merger with UCC, emphasising the reliability of RosettaNet's efforts. Moreover, the fact that executive and chief engineers are frequently named in press releases together with the goals they want to achieve reveals an aspect of inscription. This can be interpreted as a way of inscribing the company's commitments into press releases. As they are highly mobile and very durable,[697] press releases are inscripts with the programme that explicitly show RosettaNet's successful organisation and implicitly show the behaviour of its members.

The many successful Foundational and Milestone Programs[698] involving large numbers of participants, together with the fact that no affiliates have closed, have produced a high level of stabilisation in RosettaNet. Nevertheless, some anti-programmes can be identified. Not all new members saw their interests sufficiently represented, and some forced the RosettaNet organisation to adapt, for example by creating new councils. Moreover, several firms were cautious in sharing their expertise and thus lowered their level of participation or even left the consortium.

It will be interesting to follow RosettaNet's growth in the future. As one reason for its success is its sharp focus on the electronics industry, an expansion to other industries might threaten its effectiveness and efficiency. Currently, RosettaNet seems to be keeping its focus as it invests in developing additional value added services for the electronics industry. Nevertheless, there are vague plans to expand to other industries.

---

[697] They are available on the Web site, starting with the very first press release on RosettaNet's formation.

[698] Note the different meaning of Program in the RosettaNet sense (~development project) and programme in the ANT sense (~inscribed activities for reaching a given goal). In order to avoid confusing, I have stuck to the original notions. To mark the difference, RosettaNet Programs are capitalised and spelled according to American English.

Table 5.11: Organisation of RosettaNet from ANT Perspective

ANT Concepts	RosettaNet Organisational Activities
Translation	→ Relating
Problematisation	• Coordination of participants for developing IO specifications • Securing commitment of sufficient support and resources • RosettaNet soon gained position as OPP
Interessement	• Communication of success achieved via Web site and conferences • Tours of RosettaNet executives to different countries • Marketing Leadership Council • Different types of participation levels
Enrolment	• Achieving commitment from electronics companies to expanding structure and from regional organisations to opening affiliates
Inscription	→ Structure
Anticipation	• Clear organisational structure • Adapting RosettaNet organisation to new requirements • Respecting regional and industrial differences
Irreversibilisation	• Creating RosettaNet affiliates and councils • Merger with UCC • Press releases with executives named
Stabilisation	→ Participation
Programmes	• Resources like members fee and on-loan employees • Many participants in Foundational and Milestone Programs • No affiliate or council closed • Membership growth from a few dozen to more than 500
Anti-Programmes	• Interests of new members not represented in current organisation • Firms do not want to share their expertise • Firms leaving

ebXML

The consequences of not inscribing a clear architectural strategy in the formation phase, as well as other managerial issues became evident in the period that followed the 18-month programme (see Table 5.12). All the participants agreed that the development of the first version of ebXML specifications was a success, but was still far from completing the ebXML mission. As both CEFACT and OASIS were interested in continuing the work on ebXML while focusing on their core competencies, they split their responsibilities into technical specifications for OASIS and business concept specifications for CEFACT. Both enrolled to develop the specifications within their respective organisational structures, yet it was anticipated that the resulting specifications would fit closely together within a shared specification architecture. To secure this loosely coupled development approach, CEFACT and OASIS signed a Memorandum of Understanding (MoU). The programmes inscribed into the MoU and the respective TCs resulted in further improved specifications and ISO's approval of some of the specifications. However, several anti-programmes from different actors destabilised the ebXML actor-network and almost caused its collapse. First, the discussion on the right architectural strategy for achieving the ebXML mission came up once again. While the OASIS developers behaved quite neutrally, CEFACT members disagreed on whether to follow a document-centric or process-centric architecture. Bosak supported the former and Naujok the latter. Although they officially made several compromises, the highly ambiguous and inconsistent public policy and behaviour reveals severe leadership problems within CEFACT at the time. The most obvious result of a successful anti-programme against the organisation inscribed in the MoU is the migration of BPSS developers to a newly formed OASIS TC. Moreover, the tough negotiations between the UN OLA and CEFACT concerning a new IPR policy slowed down further development and drove away several participants. IBM's attempt to charge royalty fees for contributions to ebCPPA demonstrated the crucial role of a mature and balanced IPR policy.

Table 5.12: Organisation of ebXML from ANT Perspective

ANT Concepts	ebXML Organisational Activities
Translation	→ Relating
Problematisation	• After 18-month programme coordination of further development needed
Interessement	• CEFACT: continuing the development of business concepts specifications • OASIS: continuing the development of technical specifications
Enrolment	• Splitting of responsibilities • Development within respective organisational structures and development processes • ISO for approval of specifications
Inscription	→ Structure
Anticipation	• Split but coordinated work on a shared specification architecture
Irreversibilisation	• Memorandum of Understanding • Formation of OASIS TCs and CEFACT working group
Stabilisation	→ Participation
Programmes	• Improvement of specifications • ISO approval of OASIS ebXML specifications
Anti-Programmes	• Again discussion about the architectural strategy of ebXML • Ambiguous and inconsistent public policy and behaviour of CEFACT • BPSS team migrates to OASIS • IPR discussion at CEFACT

While RosettaNet has a strong vision and sharp focus well communicated on its Web pages, CEFACT showed severe difficulties. The political zigzag manoeuvres described above, combined with confusing Web pages and an ambiguous IPR policy, did not help to attract additional participants willing to invest significant resources in CEFACT's ebXML work. By contrast, OASIS maintains solid Web pages and a transparent IPR policy. However, the overall focus of OASIS is very broad, as it supports almost any kind of initiative as long as it is concerned with XML and meets the formal requirements. This leads to a situation in which OASIS TCs are working on competing, but also very different topics at the same time. Moreover, the names of CEFACT's ebCCTS and OASIS's UBL are very confusing. On the one hand, ebCCTS is (currently) an official part of ebXML, but completely technology-neutral. On the other hand, Universal Business Language (UBL) implies a neutral approach, but is in fact very XML-dependent and related to ebXML specifications. Logically, the specifications should be named the other way round. This shows the high irreversibility of a specifications name, as the renaming of an established specification would cause even more confusion among other developers and users.

An ANT analysis of the ebXML organisation reveals another important topic: control over resources and contributions. CEFACT has to rely primarily on voluntary resources. Every organisation or individual can contribute to CEFACT activities. CEFACT itself has only very limited resources for actively coordinating the ebXML development. The members even have to host CEFACT-related Web pages. The unreachable domains untmg.org and unbcf.org show the risk entailed by not owning them. CEFACT thus has only limited control over resources critical for developing and establishing specifications. In ANT terms, the anti-programmes of some actors can easily destabilise CEFACT's whole actor-network. By contrast, OASIS charges membership fees that depend on the size of the participating organisation. This enables OASIS to control its fundamental infrastructure, such as Web sites, the secretariat and several full-time employees. Moreover, it results in greater transparency regarding the participants' contributions, avoiding the accusations as seen in the debate on Microsoft's involvement in CEFACT's BCF effort. RosettaNet has even more full-time and on-loan employees that are directly involved in the development and adoption of RosettaNet specifications. It also controls activities more tightly through a highly formalised organisational structure and development process.

I propose to use specific terms for the three ANT concepts in the organisation phase. Translation comprises the management of relationships to all the organisations and individuals involved in an SDO. Thus, I will call it *relating*. During inscription, the *structure* of the SDO's organisation is fixed so as clearly to assign roles and responsibilities. The stabilisation phase reveals how well the structure fosters the appropriate *participation* of the members and other related organisations (see Table 5.11 and Table 5.12).

5.4.3 Development

The development of IO specification is the central element of an SDO's activities. Here I will first focus on the RosettaNet development and then discuss the major differences with respect to the CEFACT and OASIS development processes.

RosettaNet Development

As RosettaNet Foundational and Milestone Programs follow the same methods, I will analyse both at once. Table 5.13 summarises the insights discussed below.

The translation phase typically starts with the problematisation of a certain interorganisational scenario that one member would like to have solved. To assess whether a possible solution has a good chance of acceptance as an official RosettaNet Program, it is crucial to identify other potentially interested partners. To keep some control of the Program, the initiating member tries to become an obligatory passage point, for example by developing a preliminary solution approach and offering to be a sponsor of the Program. Several benefits aim to arouse the interest of other members in a new Program. First, they can benefit directly from developing the solution according to their needs. Second, the participating employees become highly trained experts in field of the Program. Third, their participation as a leading supply chain company is publicly communicated. This ANT phase of interessement also includes the formal RosettaNet phase 'Development Planning' (see Figure 5.20, which contrasts the RosettaNet phases with the ANT concepts). The prospective Program Director develops a Program proposal, which he presents on many different occasions to win partner support. When he has reached a critical mass of interest, the Council responsible decides on the continuation of the Program. This leads to the ANT phase of enrolment or 'Program Forming' in RosettaNet terms. All the necessary roles have to be staffed with appropriate employees. The resources promised by participants have to be secured and agreements to the intellectual property rights policy have to be signed.

Table 5.13: RosettaNet Development from ANT Perspective

ANT Concepts	RosettaNet Activities
Translation	→ Planning
Problematisation	• Solving a certain interorganisational problem • Identification of potentially interested partners • Developing a first solution approach and offering to sponsor a Program to become an OPP
Interessement	• 'Development Planning' • Direct benefits of developing a solution • Indirect benefit through trained employees and public awareness of supply chain leadership • Prospective Program Directors spread proposals • Council has to decide on Program
Enrolment	• 'Program Forming' • Open positions are staffed • Securing sponsored resources • Agreement to intellectual property rights policy
Inscription	→ Design
Anticipation	• 'Investigation and Requirements Gathering' • Standards strategy, reuse existing specifications • Gathering new requirements • Only formal partners are allowed to participate
Irreversibilisation	• 'Architecture Design, Tools and Methods' • 'Engineering Design and Development' • 'Validation, Implementation and Support' • UML models, XML schemas and supporting documents • Formal acceptance by consortium • High mobility, controlled durability • Testing and writing of RIGs
Stabilisation	→ Spreading
Programmes	• 'Program Results Evaluation and Promotion' • Measuring impact and winning new adopters
Anti-Programmes	• Specification does not fit to reality caused by new requirements • Unauthorised modification of specification possible • Start of new Program to adapt specification

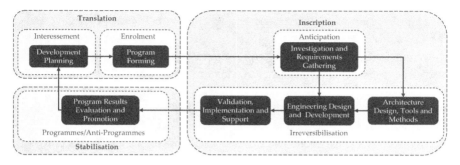

Figure 5.20: RosettaNet Development Method and ANT Concepts

Inscription resembles the main development activities. In 'Investigation and Requirements Gathering', anticipations are made as to what functionalities a new specification should cover. Existing specifications are reused, and requirements not yet covered are gathered. Only formal partners have permission to participate here, which emphasises the importance of this phase. Here the interests and goals of all the participants are formalised and will have a significant impact on the later specifications. The RosettaNet phases 'Architecture Design, Tools and Methods' and 'Engineering Design and Development' are concerned with irreversibility. UML models, XML schemas and all the supporting documents fix the interests and goals articulated before. The phase 'Validation, Implementation and Support' tests the specifications and produces the relevant supporting documents, weaving the interests into the specifications virtually irreversibly. Not only are the specifications highly mobile, as they are publicly available for no charge and include useful testing tools, but the consortium strictly controls changes to the specifications and makes older versions constantly available, which results in high durability. RosettaNet specifications are thus highly irreversible.

Stabilisation is primarily reached when the users can solve their problems by following the programmes inscribed in the specifications. 'Program Results Evaluation and Promotion' refers to the impact of specifications and the winning of new adopters. At this point, the actor-network around a specification stabilises and the specification becomes a standard. The RosettaNet Program can be closed.

However, it has to be re-opened if there are any successful anti-programmes. For example, a changing environment can lead to new requirements and render the specifications less valuable or even useless. Some users might modify the specification without the 'authorisation' of

RosettaNet. This might preserve existing implementations, but make them incompatible as well. If such anti-programmes become too strong, RosettaNet has to initiate a new Program in order to adapt the specifications to the changing needs. In all likelihood, there will always be some minor anti-programmes, i.e., implementations are often not 100% compliant with the specifications.

This analysis from the perspective of ANT reveals a very good fit between the ANT concepts and the official phases of the RosettaNet development method (see Figure 5.20). The most obvious deviation is before the interessement/'Development Planning' phase. This is because ANT also covers activities done before official planning starts, i.e., experiencing a problem or being forced to modify of specifications. Overall, the similarities between the ANT concepts and the RosettaNet Development Method are obvious.

CEFACT Development

The CEFACT Open Development Process shows several differences with respect to the RosettaNet process. An actor demanding a new specification submits it to a CEFACT Permanent Group, which forms a small editing group to develop the specification (see Figure 5.21). In RosettaNet, the enrolment phase of convincing others is a critical element for prioritising different specification proposals. In the CEFACT process, such decisions are not explicitly included and are done within a Permanent Group. The editor group consists of Permanent Group members, while RosettaNet staffs Program Teams with a blend of RosettaNet employees, on-loan resources, and employees from user firms. A CEFACT editor group consists of one project editor and usually two or three associate editors all from the CEFACT group's experts. RosettaNet defines a more differentiated struc-

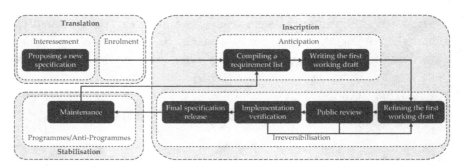

Figure 5.21: CEFACT Open Development Process and ANT Concepts

ture for its Program Teams, with a Program Director, a Program Scheduler, a Program Communicator, a Standards Manager, a Focus Process Leader, and between five and ten Focus Process Members, sometimes augmented with further specialised roles. Another important difference concerns the actual writing of the specification. While a CEFACT draft is refined and tested in a public process in which anybody can participate, RosettaNet keeps this phase closed within the Program and Validation Teams. Within the CEFACT process, the completed specification is published, and feedback for maintenance is gathered. RosettaNet also formalises implementation support, results evaluation, and Program promotion in order to stabilise the specification actively.

Summarising the differences, the CEFACT Open Development Process focuses on inscription that is open to many participants. The translation and stabilisation of the specification are hardly addressed. The RosettaNet method, in contrast, stresses open translation and stabilisation, while the actual inscription is closed from external influences.

OASIS Development

The OASIS development process shows several other remarkable differences with respect to the RosettaNet method. While it also has an intensive phase of interessement, this is additionally open to the public (see Figure 5.22). Everybody can join in the discussion on whether a new TC needs to be started. Unlike RosettaNet, OASIS has only a few rules on how TCs should organise the development process. One important element is the TC charter, a publicly available document on the enrolment details of a TC. Another is the requirement that all discussions and important decisions by the TC have to be accessible to the public. A TC has the choice of ending its work after approving a Committee Draft, which results in a specification of relatively low irreversibility. The process of public review, test implementations and OASIS member voting, by contrast, yields a higher degree of irreversibility. This can be further strengthened by ISO certification, as such a specification is very durable (not easily changed) and very mobile (high visibility and credibility of ISO standards). Finally, a TC can gather feedback from programmes/anti-programmes of specification use in order to further improve it. Alternatively, it can disband and leave the specification use and possible improvements to the users. A disbanded TC thus lowers the irreversibility of its specifications.

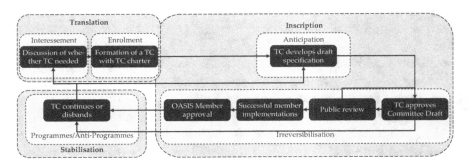

Figure 5.22: OASIS Development and ANT Concepts

Summarising the differences between RosettaNet and OASIS development, OASIS demands much greater public transparency in the actual
development processes, while also giving choices on how the TCs achieve
the irreversibilisation of specifications. RosettaNet controls this phase
more tightly.

In what follows, I call the translation in the development phase *planning*, as in all three development processes it comprises the planning of
tasks before starting the actual development. The inscription phase results
in the inscript *specification*. The stabilisation in the development phase is
best described as the *spreading* of the specifications (see Table 5.13).

5.4.4   Adoption, Use and Impact

When an IO specification is finally published, firms adopt it, use it in their
IO relationships, and profit from the impacts. Section 3.3 discussed the
mechanisms of these three phases, based on the large body of existing EDI
research. As revealed there, none of these works explicitly considers the
prior development of the IO specifications. To my knowledge,
Nelson/Shaw (2003) were the first to include any SDO concepts in their
empirical survey of IO standards adoption (see subsection 3.3.1).

Although adoption, use and impact are not the focus of this study, I will
briefly demonstrate the contribution made by applying ANT concepts to
them. Indeed, there are several attempts to better understand the adoption
and diffusion of new technologies from the ANT perspective.[699]

---

[699] See Tatnall/Gilding (1999) and Latour/Porter (1996).

As Table 5.14 shows, the concept of 'translation' refers to the process leading to the adoption of a specification. First, the user realises the need to use an IO specification or is forced by a more powerful trading partner to do so. The SDOs offer solutions with their specifications and promote them via Web pages, case studies, seminars etc. In this way they attract the interest of the potential user and try to convince him to adopt the specifications. If there are competing specifications, the user has to decide which one he will adopt. Once he has made his decision, he has become enrolled in the actor-network of the SDO in question. All these translation steps can easily be summarised by the term 'adoption'.

In the inscription phase, the user firm analyses its requirements, models its IOS, implements the specification, and finally couples its IOS with its partners' IOS. This resembles the 'use' phase. Stabilisation is reached when the IOS using the specification runs as planned and yields the expected benefits. The whole process can then be 'black boxed'. The 'impact', however, may deviate from the plans if the specification does not meet the requirements of the IOS (any more). A re-opening of the black box and an adaptation of the IOS or even the specification may then be needed.

Obviously, this is a very simplified description of the adoption, use and impact process. It reveals that an unsatisfactory impact can have several causes. The wrong use of a specification can be adjusted relatively easy. However, if the specification does not meet the requirements, several solutions are possible. First, the user firms can modify the specifications according to their local needs at the cost of losing compatibility with other firms that continue to use the original specification. Second, they can adopt an alternative specification that suits their needs better. Switching may be costly and is not possible if there is no superior specification available. Third, the user firms can contribute their proposals to the development of the specification. This closes the loop back to the previous subsection on the development of IO specifications. The next subsection thus integrates the insights attained so far into a process model for interorganisational standards.

Table 5.14: Adoption, Use and Impact from ANT Perspective

ANT Concepts	Adoption, Use, and Impact
Translation	→ Adoption
Problematisation	• User sees need to use IO specifications • Or he is forced by powerful partner
Interessement	• SDOs offer solutions with their specifications • Web pages and case studies to convince user
Enrolment	• User selects a specification
Inscription	→ Use
Anticipation	• Analysis of requirements, modelling
Irreversibilisation	• Implementation in software • Coupling with partners
Stabilisation	→ Impact
Programmes	• Implementation runs as planned and yields expected benefits
Anti-Programmes	• Changed requirements call for changes to the systems or of the specification

5.4.5 A Generic Process Model for Interorganisational Standards Development

In the previous subsections, I used actor-network theory (ANT) for an analysis of the case study data described in sections 5.2 and 5.3. Its concepts of translation, inscription and stabilisation, together with their respective sub-concepts, offered a robust framework for the processes taking place on different levels. This is comparable to the recursive pattern of the D-S-N standardisation model of Fomin et al. (2003), which also assumes similar processes on different levels of standardisation.[700] In the light of the concept of process theory, the very core of ANT is that translation is necessary for inscription, and inscription is necessary for the stabilisation of actor-networks. So far, this seems to be applicable to almost any process in

---

[700] See Fomin/Keil/Lyytinen (2003), p. 8.

which actors agree on something and fix it with an inscript stabilising the actor-network.

Fomin/Lyytinen (2000) stress the complexity of standards processes and structure them in different layers. Although they use actor-network theory, they do not explicate how the different layers of actor-networks are linked to each other. Thus, I propose the fundamental connections between layers as shown in Figure 5.23.

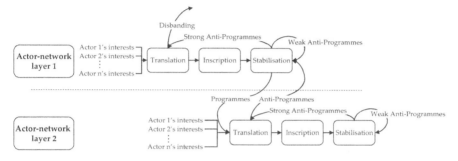

Figure 5.23: Connected ANT Layers

On actor-network layer 1 the different interests of the participating actors are translated, inscribed and stabilised. The stabilisation mechanism itself follows the ANT concepts again, only on a different layer. Programmes link the stabilisation of layer 1 to translation in layer 2. Thus, not only the different interests of the actors on layer 2 have to be translated, but also programmes from layer 1. The usual ANT phases inscription and stabilisation follow, in which the programmes of the first layer also influence the inscript of the second layer. Up to this point, everything has worked as smoothly as planned.

However, an important aspect of ANT is that it takes into consideration anti-programmes, i.e., actions not in accordance with the programme of the inscript. On layer 2, three things could happen with an anti-programme. First, it could be anticipated during inscription and simply be weaker than the inscript. In this case, the actor-network would be able to absorb the weak anti-programme and remain stable. Second, the anti-programme could be stronger than the inscript, which would give rise to a new translation in order to inscribe the new interests. Third, the anti-programme could again be stronger than the inscript, but this time cause a new translation that is not successful, i.e., the conflicting interests cannot be aligned. In this case, the strong anti-programme would go back to the stabilisation phase of layer 1.

On layer 1, the same three things could happen. First, the programme on layer 1 could be stronger than the anti-programme from layer 2. Second, the anti-programme could be stronger and cause a new translation that is successful. Third, the anti-programme could again be stronger, but the translation fail, eventually causing the disbanding of the actor-network on layer 1. In other words, the three possible cases of an anti-programme can be: it is weak and is ignored; it is strong, but resolved on the same layer; or it is strong and passed to the higher layer.

As described at the beginning of this section, three phases of standards development can be distinguished: formation, organisation and development. I propose to put each phase on a different layer of an actor-network of standards development, while including adoption, use and impact on a fourth layer. On the basis of the concept of interlinking actor-network layers, I combine these layers into one integrated model for a general IO standardisation process (see Figure 5.24). On each layer are the three main ANT concepts 'translation', 'inscription' and 'stabilisation', but each with the terms as given in the previous subsections.

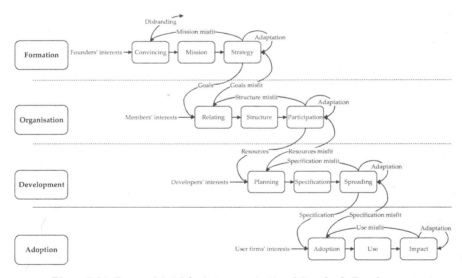

Figure 5.24: Process Model for Interorganisational Standards Development

On the formation layer, different actors interested in forming a new standards development organisation (SDO) come together. If they cannot convince each other to follow common interests, the initiative disbands before an SDO can be formed. If they are convinced of the new SDO's formation, the founders inscribe their interests into the mission of the SDO. A leadership team follows a certain strategy to achieve this mission. Several factors such as competing SDOs or unsatisfied members threaten the SDO's strategy. If the strategy cannot be adapted within the restrictions of the original mission, the actors have to agree on a new mission within a new phase of convincing. Otherwise, the SDO disbands.

On the organisation layer, the SDO brings the interests of its members into relation with its goals. The relationships to its members are then fixed in the organisational structure of the SDO. Within this structure, the members can participate in the SDO's activities. If they do not want to share their expertise or even plan to leave the SDO, adaptations have to be made to the incentives for participation. If this is not possible within the existing structure, the SDO's structure has to be improved through new kinds of relationships. For example, it could form new councils or committees. If this is not possible with the given goals (e.g., members from a different industry than the SDO is aiming at), the goals might have to be revised on the formation layer.

On the development layer, the planning combines the developers' diverse interests in a new specification with the available resources. In the specification phase, the developers try to channel all their interests into the specification. After completion, the SDO spreads the specification to the user firms. While minor flaws in the specification are quickly adjusted through updates, larger changes require new planning and specification phases.

On the adoption layer, potential user firms examine whether a specification meets their interests. If it does, this results in a decision to adopt. During the use phase, the actors implement the specification in their IOS and use it with trading partners. If the impact is not satisfactory and cannot be improved by minor changes, the whole implementation has to be questioned. If the problems cannot be resolved without changing the specification, the misfit is reported to the development layer.

Naturally, this process model cannot reflect all possible issues in the development of IO standards in reality. As it is based on ANT, moreover, it is a mainly descriptive model without claiming full explanatory or predictive rigour.[701] Nevertheless, it is an attempt to combine all crucial aspects within one model using the theoretical approach of ANT. It offers a 'map'

---

[701] For a discussion of ANT's theoretical claims see subsection 4.5.4.

that shows real-world standards issues and reveals their relations to other concepts.[702]

5.5 Summary and Conclusions

On the basis of the theoretical foundations of interorganisational relationships and standards as separately discussed in the previous chapters, this chapter has answered the second research question:

Why and how are interorganisational standards developed?

In a first step, I sketched the recent technical advancements in the field of coupling information systems across organisational boundaries (section 5.1). While firms have been using EDI-based technologies since the 1960s, the publication of XML in 1998 enabled new types of information systems architectures. The Service Oriented Architecture attracted significant attention, mostly implemented as Web Services and increasingly combined with Semantic Web concepts. The resulting information systems are highly modular and can easily be distributed across organisational boundaries. However, a complete solution for the loose coupling of firms via such interorganisational information systems requires more than technical specifications. Drawing on existing work, I proposed an interorganisational specifications stack, comprising messaging, description, discovery, universal semantics, universal processes, sectoral semantics, sectoral processes and trading partner agreements. Using this stack as a framework, I analysed 14 sectoral and 19 universal specification efforts. None was found to offer a complete solution, but most of these standards development organisations are highly interconnected and can be combined with each other. While this leads to some confusion for potential adopters, it is a result of the many different aspects that have to be covered for a complete interorganisational solution. Although there is some consensus in the existing literature that ebXML and RosettaNet are the most important initiatives, there are as yet no in-depth case studies on their organisational and development practice. This study thus focused on ebXML and RosettaNet in sections 5.2 and 5.3 with a view to deriving general insights.

---

[702] See Stalder (2001), pp. 48ff., who describes ANT as primarily a 'mapping device'.

While RosettaNet is the most mature standards development organisation, it is limited to the electronics industry. It offers sectoral specifications tailored to the business requirements of its industry and uses several dozen of technical and universal specifications from other organisations. Development projects called 'Collaborative Forecasting', 'Global Billing', or 'Order Management' emphasise the strong business focus. With this approach, RosettaNet established the topic of interorganisational standards as a managerial issue that deserves attention from both technical staff and top executives. The overall success of RosettaNet demonstrates the fundamental possibility of comprehensive interorganisational standards. To transfer this expertise to other industries, RosettaNet actively participates in the ebXML initiative.

ebXML is the most ambitious initiative to develop interorganisational standards. Backed by UN/CEFACT, which also develops the EDIFACT standards, and OASIS, which develops several other XML-based business specifications, ebXML is a joint effort by two organisations with unrivalled expertise in interorganisational standards. Its architecture covers all the technical and universal aspects of the interorganisational specifications stack. Several factors, however, have so far prevented ebXML from becoming a de facto interorganisational standard. First, from the beginning of the initiative, there were diverging goals regarding the long-term architectural strategy of ebXML. Essentially, one side wanted to use EDIFACT's document-centric approach and add missing elements such as XML syntax and process description, while others preferred a model-driven approach, following a very different paradigm. This resulted in fierce discussions, an unclear UN/CEFACT strategy, and the confusion at developers and adopters. Second, during this phase of ebXML confusion, the Web Services approach of several major software vendors attracted significant attention. While many perceive ebXML and Web Services as alternatives, they are closely related and are more complements than competitors. The large vendors, however, prefer Web Services, probably because these offer a greater differentiation potential than ebXML. Third, several conflicts regarding intellectual property rights in interorganisational specifications revealed the importance of a clear policy in this area. While OASIS agreed on a balanced intellectual property rights policy, UN/CEFACT struggled with this issue until recently, causing several firms to suspend their participation.

Using the perspective of actor-network theory, I analysed both RosettaNet and ebXML in section 5.4. On the layers of formation, organisation, development and adoption, this analysis revealed repeated patterns, always consisting of a translation, an inscription and a stabilisation phase. I introduced a model linking different layers of actor-networks together. Its main feature is a feedback mechanism differentiating three types of anti-programmes. Weak anti-programmes are resolved within the phase of stabilisation, while strong anti-programmes can be resolved either by new translation on the same layer or by passing the anti-programme to the actor-network layer above. Based on this idea, I proposed a descriptive process model of interorganisational standards that integrates the four layers formation, organisation, development and adoption. This model offers a generalised way of 'mapping' practical issues of interorganisational specification efforts.

6 Strategies for the Development of Interorganisational Standards

> "There is no standard way in which standards are developed."[703]
>
> *Stanley M. Besen and Garth Saloner*

This chapter will answer the third research question:

How should actors coordinate the development of interorganisational standards?

As this study has revealed so far, managing the development of interorganisational standards is a complex business with interwoven technical, economic and political aspects.[704] To offer a complete guide covering all these topics in sufficient detail lies outside the scope of this study. Nevertheless, this chapter integrates new insights from the previous chapters to recommend strategic options for the four most important stakeholders of IO standards. These are user firms, vendors offering compatible software, standards development organisations (SDOs) and governmental organisations (see Figure 6.1). While the original matrix of Besen/Saloner (1989) has some drawbacks for analyzing the adoption of standards[705], minor modifications make it very useful for distinguishing of the stakeholders' strategies. Combined with insights from the ANT-based process model of the previous chapter, it serves as an analytical framework in this chapter.

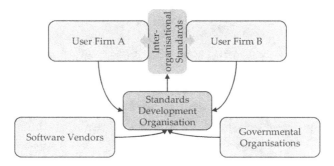

Figure 6.1: Stakeholder in the Development of Interorganisational Standards

---

[703] Besen/Saloner (1989), p. 2.

[704] Even in economic models with strict assumptions outcomes of standardisation processes are hard to predict. See section 4.3.1.

6.1   The User Firm Perspective

This perspective is concerned with firms that want to use IO specifications for connections with their business partners. It does not include software vendors or other organisations participating in an SDO.

The most general recommendation for such firms is to focus on specifications on the business operational view of the Open-edi Model.[706] In Figure 5.5 these are the specifications on trading partner agreements, on specialised business semantics and processes, and on universal business semantics and processes. As a top-down approach is recommended, the firms should start by gathering their business requirements and then choose or develop the necessary specifications. The emphasis should thus be on sector-specific semantics and processes, while universal specifications are already available for most requirements. Examples of universal specifications are CPFR, ebXML/ISO 15000 and UBL. Only in some cases can user firms benefit from directly contributing to these universal efforts. One example is Boeing, which actively participates in the ebXML initiative because it already has a large installed base of ebXML systems.[707] Developing technical specifications on the functional service view holds even less promise for user firms. A superior approach seems to be the development of specific semantics and processes with peer firms in an appropriate SDO. If there are universal or technical issues to be resolved, this SDO should gather the issues and pass them bundled to other SDOs. For example, few electronics firms are directly involved in the ebXML initiative. RosettaNet, however, strongly represents their interests through participating as an SDO in ebXML.

So how should a user firm get involved in a sectoral SDO? In general, it participates if the expected benefits from participation are clearly higher than its costs. Moreover, its engagement depends on the interests of all participants, which can be aligned or divergent. While the former dimension is idiosyncratic for each firm, the latter is a global dimension, which influences the strategies of all user firms. These two dimensions result in four generic strategies as depicted in Figure 6.2.

---

[705] See Niggl (1994), pp. 56ff.

[706] See ISO/IEC (1997).

[707] See OASIS (2003a), p. 8.

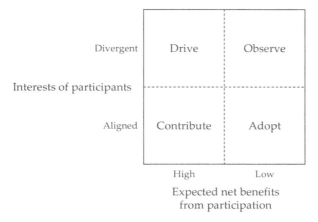

Figure 6.2: Generic Strategies for User Participation in IO Standardisation[708]

If the interests of the actors in an SDO are different from the interests of a particular user and the net benefits from participating are low for this user, then the best strategy for him is only to *observe* the initiative. If the benefits of participating are low, but the interests are aligned, the user should not participate, but simply *adopt* the specifications. If the benefits are high and the interests are aligned, the user should *contribute* to the SDO. Finally, if the interests are in conflict with other actors, but the benefits are high, the user should actively *drive* some of the SDO work in order to defend his interests. On such a general level, however, the recommendations of the matrix might lead to wrong decisions, as typical IO standardisation processes are complex and consist of several layers, each with different benefits and interests involved. Moreover, the continuous improvement and expansion of IO specifications require the constant reassessment of the decisions made. I will thus use concepts from the process model of the previous chapter to discuss the application of the four strategies in more detail. For all strategies, I am assuming a currently existing SDO for specifications related to the IO relationships and IOS of the user firm.

Observe

There are several reasons why the mission, the structure and/or the specifications of an SDO may not meet the interests of a firm. The mission

---

[708] Based on Figure 4.5 in subsection 4.3.2.

might deviate, for example, because no SDO exactly covers the industry of the firm in question, just as CIDX targets the chemical industry, but not the requirements of the related pharmaceutical industry. The structure might not be appropriate, just as RosettaNet has no council for automotive electronics. Further, the specifications may not meet the needs of the firm, just as ACORD mainly covers the needs of life insurance, but neglects the requirements of other assurance types. If the firm expects the costs of actively changing the situation to be higher than its benefits, it will decide only to observe the existing SDO's activities, while using proprietary solutions for its IO relationships.

A second situation could be that a firm wants to keep its proprietary solutions to itself and wants to prevent their standardisation. In a business web, for example, the shaping firm tries to control critical points that are sources of competitive advantage. Such control points are often specifications for accessing the resources of the shaping firm.[709] Amazon, for instance, offers direct access to most of its Web shop functionality via Web Services-based IO specifications, enabling other firms to integrate Amazon's services into their offers.[710] It is not in Amazon's interests to make these specifications available to its competitors, as this would make it easily interchangeable. By contrast, it aims to use specifications with features not offered by others. When following such a strategy, however, the firm should observe whether SDOs could threaten the proprietary solution through superior specifications.

There are several possibilities for observing the SDO's activities, very much depending on its openness. On the one hand are very open SDOs such as OASIS, which even offers public insight into the development process. On the other hand, there are more secretive SDOs such as ODETTE, which requires membership status to be able to access the specification documents. It might thus be an appropriate option to become a member of the critical SDOs just to observe their activities. Bold firms could even try participating in a development without intending ever to use the resulting specification. Although such behaviour can be seen in reality, it is difficult to judge in what situations it is genuinely beneficial. The SDOs, in turn, can control such members through several mechanisms

---

[709] See Steiner (2005), pp. 142ff.

[710] See Amazon (2004).

discussed below. Moreover, firms can always switch to one of the following strategies when the conditions have changed.

Adopt

If the mission, structure and specifications of an SDO already meet the
interests of a firm though it expects no benefits from influencing them, it
can simply adopt the specifications. In this 'free-rider' strategy, the firm
does not get involved in most issues concerning the SDO and just uses the
specifications for its IO relationships. While most SDOs publish their
specifications free of charge, they often provide additional services to their
paying members. For example, RosettaNet offers supporting documents
and discovery services only to partners. The firm can thus benefit from
being a member without participating in the specification development.
Moreover, the firm should also include observing activities in order to stay
informed of changes in the SDO's mission, structure or specifications (see
the Observe strategy).

As revealed in section 3.3, most existing IOS research studies typically
cover this situation. They identify several further factors influencing the
decision to adopt IO specifications. These are classified as environmental
conditions, IO relationships, organisational readiness and the perceived
benefits from use of the specifications (see Figure 3.4). If these factors are
not strong enough, a firm will not be interested in adopting IO specifications at all. In the discussion of the next two strategies, I assume that a firm
clearly wants to adopt, but also wants to participate in the development
activities.

Contribute

When the mission, structure and specifications of an SDO meet the interests of a firm, it might expect benefits from participating in the further
work of the SDO. The main benefits result from contributing one's own
ideas and from the knowledge transfer between the contributors, which
Xia et al. (2003) call the 'insider effect'.[711] The firm can contribute primarily
to the development of further specifications, but also to other of the SDO's
activities.

Contributing to specification development is the usual way of participating in an SDO's work. Most SDOs have structured and transparent

---

[711] See discussion in subsection 3.3.2.

procedures for the development process. RosettaNet, for example, uses its mature RosettaNet Standard Methodology with clear roles and transparent decisions. This keeps the coordination costs low and enables the efficient use of the contributors' resources.

However, the firm should pay attention to the intellectual property right policy of an SDO. Two fundamental cases can threaten a firm's contributions. First, the firm might completely lose the property rights for its contributions. This lowers the motivation to contribute, while also fostering 'free-rider' behaviour in other firms. At CEFACT, this issue caused some firms to stop their contributions to specification development. OASIS, by contrast, does not generally exclude patents. In certain cases, it might be an appropriate option to contribute patented concepts in order to keep greater control over a specification. However, this runs the risk of irritating other contributors, who are wary of becoming dependent on the patented specifications and probably having to pay royalties. Second, the firm might be sued for damages caused by a specification. It is thus important to check the rights of the adopting firms before contributing to a specification. For example, the UN's Office of Legal Affairs wanted to make CEFACT's contributors responsible for any claims from specification users. Obviously, such an IPR policy rarely motivates firms to participate in specification development.

Besides contributing to specifications, a firm can also participate in other SDO activities such as administrative tasks or promoting the adoption of specifications. The benefit from supporting the administration depends on the incentive system of the SDO. Usually greater administrative responsibilities are coupled with more decision rights. Moreover, a firm benefits directly from promoting the adoption of a specification through the typical impacts of IO specification use. In addition, many SDOs coordinate promotional seminars and case studies, to which the firm can also contribute. As most SDOs resemble user communities in which trust and reliability are important values, contributing to the activities usually results in indirect benefits such as easier knowledge transfer between the firms' experts.

Drive

In this situation, the mission, structure and/or specifications of an SDO do not fully meet the interests of a firm, but it expects high benefits from participating in the SDO. The best strategy then is to drive the SDO actively towards the firm's interests. Generally, this can be done on the three layers of formation, organisation and development.

The mission of an SDO is set during its formation. If some members desire a completely new mission, the founding of a new SDO might be more efficient than adapting the existing SDO.[712] In other words, if the mission of an SDO strongly deviates from the interests of a firm, the firm should consider founding a new SDO. When Ingram Micro discovered its need for Web-based process-oriented IO specifications, for example, it could have tried to develop these within existing SDOs such as ANSI/DISA or EDIFICE. However, as their mission was too focused on the specification of document semantics, Ingram Micro decided to drive RosettaNet with a completely new mission. The case study on its formation revealed the obstacles that can threaten such an attempt. Above all, convincing other firms of the mission and persuading them to contribute resources can be a daunting task. An alternative could be to establish a new group for IO specifications within an existing industry consortium originally dedicated to other tasks. For example, the members of the Mortgage Bankers Association (MBA) formed the Mortgage Industry Standards Maintenance Organisation (MISMO) largely within the existing association.[713] The attempt to change the mission of an existing SDO is still an option, providing the new mission is not too different. The driving firm has to convince a critical number of other firms to support the new mission. Such a change can be critical for the whole SDO, as other participants as well as the adopting firms can become confused and may withdraw their support for the SDO's specifications. This is exemplified by the internal differences at CEFACT concerning whether the future course should focus on ebXML or on a technology-independent framework. This almost cost CEFACT its credibility regarding its competence in setting IO standards.

Many conflicting interests also arise on the organisational layer. Although a firm may agree to the mission, it may not see its interests reflected in the organisational structure of the SDO. Its goal would thus be to adapt the structure to its needs, which is inherently supported by some SDOs. RosettaNet, for example, established several new industry councils because some partners demanded this. One such firm was Siemens, which had already participated in RosettaNet for several years. As it realised that

---

[712] Obviously, this depends on size and structure of the SDO.

[713] See Markus/Steinfield/Wigand (2003), p. 84.

the interests of its telecommunication business were partially conflicting with the existing industry councils, it convinced other RosettaNet members and several new firms to form the new telecommunications council. Only large corporations have the resources for such an organisational effort at RosettaNet, while OASIS supports a new TC whenever three members demand it and meet certain formal criteria. Compared to such prearranged organisational changes, unplanned ones are more difficult to achieve and may require larger reorganisation projects with all the typical opportunities and threats.[714]

The third layer where interests can be conflicting is the development layer. Two cases can be distinguished. First, a firm may be lacking proper specifications for its requirements, while no other firms see any benefit in developing such specifications. Then the firm has to drive a critical mass of others to participate in the development. This can be done by convincing others of the benefits of a specification, but also by urging dependent firms such as smaller business partners to participate. Second, conflicts can occur during the actual development. Depending on the severity of the conflicts, the driving firm might convince the others of its position. Otherwise, it is possible that some firms may abandon the development effort. It can thus prove difficult to push through one's own interests without losing the support of the other participants.

While a single firm rarely has the power to impose its interests on others, it often occurs that several groups with diverging interests form. As seen in the case of CEFACT, such a situation can escalate and threaten the whole SDO. If possible, the SDO should take measures to settle such conflicts. However, an SDO has no ultimate hierarchical power, as it depends on the contributions of its members and cannot afford to lose many of them. The community character of most sectoral SDOs can also prevent excessively harsh conflicts, as strongly opposing members can be excluded. Such an exclusion from an SDO with highly beneficial 'insider-effects' can constitute a threat to the competitive advantage of the firms excluded.

Obviously, the interests and expected benefits from participating can change over time. For example, a firm that used to only adopt a specification might experience new business requirements that are not yet covered by the specification it uses. If other firms have similar requirements and

---

[714] For reorganisation projects see Freudenberg (1999) and Gaßner (1999).

plan to modify this specification, the recommended strategy for the first firm changes from *adopt* to *contribute*. In doing so, it can ensure that its interests are reflected in the modification effort. If other firms, however, have contradictory plans, the first firm should *drive* the efforts in order to prevent the specification from being modified in an unfavourable way. Such strategic changes are not limited to these two examples, but can occur in all possible directions. Overall, the strategic options described are not static recommendations, but have to be reconsidered in the face of changing conditions.

6.2 The Perspective of the Standards Development Organisation

The overall goal of a standards development organisation (SDO) is to coordinate the development and adoption of specifications and thus to establish them as standards. Moreover, as a complete IO specification stack requires several specifications from different SDOs, and the field of IO SDOs is highly interwoven, a universal or sectoral SDO should also clearly manage its relationships to other specifications. An SDO thus has three main responsibilities: to coordinate the specification development, to participate in other SDOs, and to promote the adoption of its specifications. As the latter is not the focus of this study, I shall leave the discussion of it to other researchers such as Nelson/Shaw (2003), while this section focuses on the first two aspects.

The general participation strategies of an SDO very much resemble the participation strategies of a single user firm. It can *observe, adopt, contribute* to or *drive* the activities of another SDO (see section 6.1 and Figure 6.2). RosettaNet, for example, uses the matrix displayed in Figure 5.10 to show for which technical specifications (termed 'architecture' by RosettaNet) and which universal specifications (termed 'content') it follows the *Observe* strategy (~specifications in parentheses), the *Adopt* strategy (~'adopt'), the *Contribute* strategy (~'motivate'), or the *Drive* strategy (~'lead'). Obviously, a fifth strategy is to develop its own specifications. As this is the main responsibility of an SDO, I will discuss it in more detail.

Before doing so, it should be noted that clearly communicating one's relationships to other SDOs would very much help observers to classify an SDO. Few SDOs apart from RosettaNet do this on their Web pages. Often, hints are hidden somewhere within the actual specification documents.

The ideal would be a standardised way of categorising SDOs, which a universal SDO such as OASIS or CEFACT could develop and promote. This would require a global agreement on an IO architecture as I propose in subsection 5.1.2. While the disbanded Business Internet Consortium aimed to achieve just this, there have been no serious efforts in November 2004.

As the case studies of ebXML and CEFACT revealed, a reasonable intellectual property rights policy is a critical factor for an SDO's success. If contributors have to transfer all the rights of their contributions or can even be sued for damages caused by their specification, the motivation to participate will be very low. On the other hand, if the contributors dominate the specifications and claim royalties, other firms will avoid adopting them. This resembles the debate on software patents and their optimal embodiment for maximising their social value.[715] As it has not been the focus of this study, this is not the place for general recommendations on this complex and still not fully clarified topic.[716]

However, based on the four strategies open to user firms (see section 6.1), an SDO can determine its own strategies as regards how to manage the contributions (see Figure 6.3). As an SDO usually has very limited re-

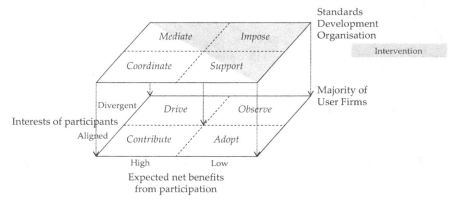

Figure 6.3: Generic Strategies for Managing User Firms Participating in an SDO [717]

---

[715] See, e.g., Brügge/Harhoff/Picot, et al. (2004), pp. 136.

[716] The complexity is demonstrated by the IPR discussions within UN/CEFACT, which lasted for years.

[717] Based on Figure 4.5 in subsection 4.3.2, Figure 6.2 in section 6.1, and Picot/Fiedler (2002), p. 249.

sources, it should only intervene in the actual specification development under certain conditions, which are shaded grey in the figure. If the majority of an SDO's user firms have different interests in a certain specification and expect few benefits from using it, they will choose the *Observe* strategy (see discussion in previous section). However, it is possible that such a specification is important for the further development of the SDO's specifications. In this case, the SDO should *impose* one specific solution on its members. RosettaNet, for example, chose to use the DUNS numbers for the unambiguous identification of user firms. As the benefits of alternative identification specifications were low, few arguments were made for using other ones, and RosettaNet could impose the DUNS system on its members.

If the interests of most user firms are aligned, but the benefits they expect from a specification are relatively low, they will follow the *Adopt* strategy of not contributing to, but only adopting a certain specification ('free rider'). This is often the case when the members decide myopically, not perceiving the long-term value of a development effort. Here the SDO should *support* the development in order to lower the costs of contributing and raise the net benefit for the participants. RosettaNet, for example, installed the Architectural Advisory Committee and two development centres in order to support specifications the members would not develop own their own. These are often Foundational Programs, as they do not yield direct benefits, but improve the overall RosettaNet architecture in the long run.

If the user firms' interests are aligned and they expect high benefits, then they voluntarily *contribute* to an SDO's effort. In this case, the SDO has to maintain a stable organisational environment for the developing groups. Usually, it should only *coordinate* the development process without much intervention. One exception could be to limit the number of contributors, as several theoretical insights suggest that too many contributors can result in inferior specifications.[718] Nevertheless, in the majority of practical cases SDOs do not have to intervene in the development of IO specifications. OASIS, for example, explicitly follows this strategy with most of its projects, as the Technical Committees have a lot of freedom in actual development processes and only have to follow certain fundamental rules relating to IPR policy, the voting mechanism and public mailing lists.

---

[718] See Niggl (1994), pp. 94ff. and Reimers (1995), p. 96.

In the fourth case, high expected benefits coupled with diverging interests cause the user firms to *drive* specifications in different and sometimes conflicting directions. While some differences are normal and important for motivating the search for innovative solutions, the SDO has to *mediate* fundamental divergence or conflicts. Otherwise, the integrity of the developed specifications would be threatened. RosettaNet, for example, formed its Asian affiliates in order to cover the different interests of the Asian firms. However, the vice president for Asia explicitly has to prevent too much divergence in the Asian activities. Indeed, RosettaNet aims to integrate all reasonable deviations into its official specifications, as these are supposed to be globally unified. Moreover, clear and transparent voting mechanisms are crucial to resolve conflicts between the contributors' interests. OASIS, for example, permits different TCs to follow conflicting goals, as with ebXML vs. Web Services efforts. However, all members are able to vote for the acceptance of a specification as an OASIS standard. Even a relatively small percentage of opposing votes can prevent a controversial specification from beeing accepted.

6.3   The Software Vendor Perspective

The main goal of software vendors is to sell their software products to user firms. According to usual product standards strategies, a software vendor very much prefers to have a proprietary specification that is broadly accepted. The network externalities of using this specification could result in a quasi-monopoly for this vendor. Microsoft's Office file format demonstrates the power of proprietary exchange specifications in terms of the market share of a software product. Indeed, as the leading vendor of business software, SAP offers an IO specification called IDoc. User firms, however, seem to have learned from MS Office and similar experiences and have not accepted the IDoc format as a dominant IO specification.[719] Today, the openness of specifications and the independence from software vendors play a crucial role in users' decisions regarding their information

---

[719] See Fricke/Weitzel/König, et al. (2002).

systems.[720] The chances of a vendor establishing its proprietary IO specifications as a broadly accepted standard are thus relatively low.

While a user firm has to consider only one or a few sectoral SDOs, a software vendor typically has to deal with many different SDOs, which are active in different specification fields. Especially large vendors that cover almost any industry should systematically decide on their participation in different SDOs. Essentially, they can follow the four strategies available to user firms as described in the previous section (see also Figure 6.2). These strategies result in different activities, however, as I will discuss below.

The *Observe* strategy is recommended when interests are divergent and benefits from participation are low. Obviously, this is the case when SDOs focus on sectors to which a software vendor does not sell its products. Moreover, universal or technical SDOs using a specification architecture not supported by the vendor's software should also only be observed. One reason that many vendors did not support the CORBA approach of the Object Management Group (OMG), for example, is that competing vendors developed it, and most did not want full interoperability between their products.[721] The category of SDOs to be observed also includes new initiatives trying to establish new technologies, such as the REST efforts that are trying to establish an alternative to Web Services standards. In general, software vendors offering IOS should systematically observe any initiative in the field of IO specifications, when not actively participating with one of the following strategies.

The *Adopt* strategy should be chosen if interests are aligned and benefits from participation are low. Sectoral SDOs with members served by the vendor belong to this category. In the ideal case, these SDOs use established universal and technical specifications and focus on the development of sectoral semantics and processes. Here, the software vendor does not benefit much from contributing, but has to integrate these specifications into its products to stay competitive. Being a member of such SDOs, moreover, the vendor can gain detailed insights into its customers' demands. For example, SAP is a member of several sectoral SDOs such as RosettaNet and CIDX. Additionally, it is an important element of the *Adopt* strategy to

---

[720] The broad adoption of Linux is another example of users trying to gain some independence; see Brügge/Harhoff/Picot, et al. (2004), p. 172.

[721] See Nickerson/zur Muehlen (2003), p. 340.

stress the specification support of one's products for marketing purposes.[722]

If interests are aligned and the benefits from participation are high, *Contribute* is the recommended strategy. This is often the case for technical SDOs, as a vendor knows best the limits of the technical specifications it uses and ways of improving them. Early and intensive involvement in development gives the contributors in-depth knowledge of the specifications and can result in a competitive advantage over non-contributors through earlier and better products. Contributing to the development of universal semantics and process specifications can also yield benefits for the vendor, as these can be used in products for a wide range of customers. However, as numerous SDOs are concerned with even more technical and universal specifications, it is an important task for the vendor to prioritise its contributions. As described above for the user firms, vendors also have to pay attention to the IPR policy of the SDOs to avoid legal conflicts caused by contributing to a specification. Again, it is also a marketing tool to announce one's active participation in a certain SDO. Most SDOs support this by placing the logos of active vendors on the home page of their Web presence.

If a vendor's interests differ from those of an SDO, but the vendor expects clear benefits from its contributions to a specification, it has to actively *drive* its ideas. Three general options exist. First, the vendor can develop a specification of its own without an SDO and try to push it through via its customers. This approach might work in other fields, but as described above, user firms are very cautious in adopting proprietary IO specifications. Without the legitimacy of an accepted SDO, they are unlikely to adopt a new IO specification. Second, the vendor can develop a specification without an SDO, but then submit it to an SDO as an official specification. IBM and Microsoft, for example, chose this option for their Web Services standards, which they jointly developed and then submitted to W3C and OASIS. Third, the vendor can develop the new specification within an SDO by forming a new working group. Whether such an approach is feasible within a particular SDO while conflicting with other of its specifications depends on the SDO policy.

---

[722] See, e.g., SAP's public announcement of supporting RosettaNet and CIDX specifications in Ashton/Rothenstein (2003).

OASIS, for example, hosts several TCs working on competing specifications, especially BPEL and UDDI vs. ebBPSS and ebRIM/RS. One reason may be the competition between certain SDOs, most prominently between OASIS and the W3C. While the W3C has a strict policy regarding the coordination of activities and intellectual property right policies, OASIS is open to almost any activities that meet the formal requirements. The general possibility of keeping the property rights on patented contributions to OASIS's specifications is one reason for the submission of UDDI to OASIS. Although this is an obvious way to charge royalties for a broadly adopted specification, user firms are unlikely to adopt such royalty-laden specifications. An opportunistic contributor could thus use the 'submarine patent' approach.[723] While contributing to a specification, he silently files his contributions for patents. After the specification has been broadly adopted, he claims royalties for the use of its patents.[724] OASIS could avert such a case by making a statement that it will not collect royalties, especially since IBM has been contributing patented concepts to ebCPPA.

Besides these legal issues, the vendors also have a great influence on the success of a certain specification's adoption. If some customers want to use a new specification, but large vendors do not support it, the adoption process can be slowed down significantly. For example, the relatively slow adoption of ebXML was caused in part by the weak support from some larger vendors' products, which favoured Web Services specifications. Many of these political manoeuvres by software vendors are fostered by the fact that comprehensive open standards lower the vendors' potential for differentiation and make them increasingly interchangeable.

---

[723] See Stix (2002) and Markus/Steinfield/Wigand (2003), p. 87.

[724] One widely discussed 'submarine patent' case is the claim by the UNIX firm SCO that it holds patents on Linux source code and thus has the right to charge royalties from all Linux users; see Kuri (2004). A recent case in the field of IO specifications was the bankruptcy of the software vendor Commerce One, which held 39 patents used in Web Services specifications. While several large companies were also very interested, these patents were finally auctioned to a 'mysterious bidder'; see Gilbert (2004).

6.4 The Governmental Perspective

This section briefly discusses the ways governmental organisations can intervene in the development of IO specifications. Essentially, they should consider two aspects. First, tight cooperation within SDOs always bears the risk of collusion between the participants, which could be a threat for free markets. Governmental antitrust divisions should thus observe especially sectoral SDOs for illegal collusion. Some SDOs try to prevent such collusion by explicitly prohibiting it within SDO activities.

Second, a government welcomes its national firms being able to improve their productivity through the broad adoption of IO standards. There exists academic consensus that governmental organisations usually lack the competencies for directly setting complex technology and IO standards.[725] However, this does not rule out the possibility that the government intervenes in privately organised SDOs. Based on the four strategies for an SDO discussed in the earlier section (see Figure 6.3), a governmental organisation can also decide on different intervention measures (see also Figure 4.5).

In the private good situation, the firms follow the *Observe* strategy. They all use their own solutions and only observe the specification activities of other firms. Nevertheless, one standard might be of high social value. In this case, the government has to intervene by *imposing* a specification as a norm and enforcing its acceptance.

In the public good situation, the firms follow an *Adopt* strategy. They do not expect a positive return from contributing to an SDO's effort, but benefit from using the specifications. One reason is the high cost of participating. The government should *support* the SDO to lower the costs of development. For example, the Chinese Ministry of Science and Technology helps its national industry to participate in RosettaNet activities.

In the coordination situation, all firms expect high benefits from *contributing* and have no preferences for a specific standard. This is usually the case if the coordination costs of agreeing on a specification are relatively low and the firms expect no differentiation potential in the standard regarding competitive advantage. In such a situation, firms will establish an SDO to coordinate their standardisation efforts. The government has no reason to intervene, as firms will agree on an efficient standard through

---

[725] See the short discussion in 4.3.1.

self-organisation. The only tasks would be to *coordinate* the SDOs and to prevent collusion between the firms.

In the conflict situation, all firms expect a high benefit from contributing to a specification. As they have conflicting interests, however, they prefer different specifications. This is usually the case if one firm or SDO holds the property rights of a specification and wants to establish it as a standard to improve its competitive advantage by leveraging network effects. The strategy of the firms or SDOs here is to *drive* their specification towards a common standard. As such competition is likely to establish the best standard itself, the government should only *mediate* if firms use unfair practices that distort the competition. One example is the competition between some ebXML and Web Services specifications.

6.5   Summary and Conclusions

This chapter has offered general answers to the third research question:

How should the actors involved coordinate the development of interorganisational standards?

As this study revealed in the previous chapters, the development of inter-organisational standardisation is highly complex and shows only limited determinism. It is thus impossible to derive a complete theory that could lead to a comprehensive management guide for interorganisational specifications. Nevertheless, this chapter has used the insights gained in the course of this study to derive recommendations for different stakeholders' strategies. The user firms can follow the *Observe, Adopt, Contribute* or *Drive* strategies for their SDO participation. The *Observe* strategy involves no participation at all, while the *Adopt* strategy uses the specification without contributing to its development ('free-rider'). In the *Contribute* strategy, firms actively contribute to the development, while the *Drive* strategy involves actively leading other participants despite the diverging interests in a specification. The software vendors have essentially the same strategic options. As their focus is on selling their products to user firms, however, the concrete actions are quite different. For example, they have to participate in a much wider range of different SDOs than the user firms in order to cover all the customers' requirements. When SDOs have to participate in other SDOs, they can also follow one of the four strategies. To organise their own specification development, SDOs also have four corresponding strategic options: *Impose, Support, Coordinate* and *Mediate*. If its members only observe, the SDO may have to impose specifications and if they only adopt, the SDO may have to support active participation. If the members contribute voluntarily, only coordination is needed, while members driving in conflicting directions have to be mediated. A governmental organisation has essentially the same strategic options for interving in specification development. Additionally, it has to prevent the collusion of firms through antitrust measures. Overall, this chapter has revealed that the two dimensions of 'interests in' and 'benefits from' specification development can be used to produce clear strategic recommendations for the different stakeholders.

7   Conclusions

"We are concerned with what happens when new devices are created, and with how possibilities for innovation arise. There is a circularity here: the world determines what we can do and what we do determines our world. The creation of a new device or systematic domain can have far-reaching significance – it can create new ways of being that previously did not exist and a framework for actions that would not have previously made sense."[726]

Terry Winograd and Fernando Flores

This concluding chapter gives a summary of the insights gained and then sketches potential fields for future research on interorganisational standards.

Summary and Insights Gained

As a trade volume of several trillion US$ is globally processed using interorganisational standards each year, they are a business topic of high importance. In the face of increasingly dynamic supply chain networks, which are configured in a 'plug & play fashion', interorganisational standards will gain further significance. Since most business environments are permanently changing, however, these standards cannot be developed just once, but have to be continuously adapted. To illuminate the development of such interorganisational standards, this study has followed three main research questions. The first question to be answered was:

Why and how do information systems support interorganisational relationships?

Although interorganisational relationships play an increasing role especially in industries with modular products, it is difficult to define them precisely. Essentially, they comprise the exchange of goods and services between organisations, whether organised via markets mechanisms or in long-term strategic alliances. This study has focused on interorganisational relationships called *supply chain networks*, which aim at high efficiency in vertical relationships through the coordination of resources in primary

---

[726] Winograd/Flores (1987), p. 177.

tasks. Moreover, these relationships are usually secured through neo-classical contracts, are highly formalised, and often comprise a set or network of participating firms.

As many mechanisms in such supply chain networks require speed and accuracy, they are enabled by interorganisational information systems. These are information systems sending information across organisational boundaries. For several decades, EDI-based systems have been the most important type of interorganisational information systems, as they use automatic data exchange to execute business transactions between firms. As a large body of research on managerial aspects of EDI systems already exists, I summarised the current state in what I termed an *IOS Management Framework*. This distinguishes the phases *adoption, use* and *impact* of interorganisational information systems. While it reveals independent and dependent variables for managerial activities, it neglects the development of interorganisational standards, which has emerged as an increasingly important topic over recent years. Thus, the second research question was:

Why and how are interorganisational standards developed?

To answer this extensive question, a general introduction to theories of standards had to be given. A standard is a set of broadly adopted rules for repeated activities, usually codified in a specification document. The objects covered by a standard can be classified as *products, semantics, processes* or *performances. Governments, consortia, markets* and *communities* represent different approaches to coordinating the development and adoption of standards. This study has focused on semantics and process standards organised by consortia. Three theoretical perspectives – technical, economic and social – aim to explain the emergence of standards. Theories on *technical design* cover the efficiency of development processes, the necessary resources, and the actual development of the specification documents. Theories based on *neo-classical economics* explain how product standards affect market mechanisms, while *neo-institutional theories* see a standard as an institution for lowering transaction costs in economic markets, and which is negotiated in a political market. Theories on the *social construction of standards* examine how participants act in political markets.

Actor-network theory is one such social theory that explains how actors form networks consisting of humans and artefacts in order to achieve their goals. It distinguishes three main phases to describe the dynamics of actor-networks: *translation, inscription* and *stabilisation*. In the translation phase, the actors negotiate on their interests and agree on shared goals. To fix these goals, they are inscribed as programmes into artefacts called inscripts. These inscripts aim to stabilise the actor-network. If so-called anti-programmes successfully attack the inscript to deviate from the negotiated goals, the actor-network destabilises. The actors thus try to create strong and irreversible inscripts in order to stabilise the actor-network. Standard specifications are such inscripts in which actors inscribe their interests, aiming to make other actors follow the inscribed programmes. Actor-network theory was then used to analyse the case studies conducted and derive a general process model.

While IS researchers have not yet been able to agree on a common term for standards such as ebXML, RosettaNet or UBL, I proposed to use 'inter-organisational standards' and define them as *broadly adopted specifications that formally define or support business-related semantics and processes, which are made accessible to other organisations' information systems, usually via Web-based technologies.* As a complete interorganisational standard has to cover many different aspects, I also proposed an interorganisational specification stack, consisting of the elements *messaging, description, discovery, universal semantics* and *processes, sectoral semantics* and *processes* and *trading partner agreements*. While Web Services standards for messaging and description have attracted considerable attention in recent years, specifications for the other elements are less known. They are, however, crucial elements for the coupling of organisations via interorganisational information systems. Moreover, the development of such specifications is highly complex and never fully complete, as the corresponding business environments are continuously evolving. Since user firms can become highly dependent on these specifications, it is important to understand their development and possible ways of participating in it. As there is little literature available on this topic, I conducted two in-depth case studies on RosettaNet and ebXML.

RosettaNet is a consortium that focuses on developing specifications for sectoral semantics and processes tailored to the electronics industry, while using dozens of technical and universal specifications from other organisations. It demonstrates that the development of comprehensive interorganisational standards is very complex and demands the coordination of many different standardisation efforts. RosettaNet's strong emphasis on the business needs of its members combined with its mature organisational structure and development processes are the main reasons for its remarkable success.

ebXML is a joint standards development initiative by OASIS and UN/CEFACT. The former has a lot of expertise in XML specifications, while the latter previously developed the EDIFACT standards. This background promised to make the ambitious ebXML initiative the main source for universal interorganisational standards. Indeed, the development of the first version of ebXML specifications was a success. As these versions still had potential to improve, OASIS and UN/CEFACT agreed to continue the effort in a second phase. This almost ended in a disaster, however, because of fierce discussions on ebXML's long-term strategy, an unclear intellectual property rights policy at UN/CEFACT, and the competition from the Web Services approach pushed by large software vendors.

Using the concepts of actor-network theory, I derived patterns of interorganisational standards development, resulting in a generalised process model. This consists of the four layers, *formation, organisation, development* and *adoption*. On each layer, the three phases of actor-network dynamics *translation, inscription* and *stabilisation* have to be passed through. Antiprogrammes are either resolved in stabilisation, in a new translation, or on a higher layer. For example, if a specification reveals minor flaws, it can be slightly modified so that it is not prevented from spreading. This is usually indicated by minor version changes. If the problems are more serious, a new development cycle has to be passed through, comprising planning (translation), specification development (inscription), and spreading (stabilisation), often indicated by major version changes. If the planning is not successful because the available resources no longer fit, the problem is passed to the organisation layer. Here the participants have to agree on whether organisational changes are to be made to enable the development of new specifications. This is the case, for example, when new OASIS Technical Committees or RosettaNet industry councils are initiated. The model I have proposed serves above all as a 'map' for placing concrete issues of interorganisational standards in relation to other aspects, supporting stakeholders in decisions on where to participate. This leads to the third research question:

How should the actors involved coordinate the development of interorganisational standards?

Given the early stage of the research field, I could not develop a complete theory of interorganisational standards in the previous chapters. On the basis of the insights from the case studies and the derived process model, however, I formulated generic strategies on how different actors should participate in the process of interorganisational standards development. A user firm can choose to *observe* the standards development organisations (SDOs), *adopt* the resulting specifications, *participate* in the development, or actively *drive* the SDO in the direction it desires. The options *contribute* and *drive* are especially recommended when sectoral SDOs are focused on the industry of the user firm, while it should prefer to *observe* or *adopt* for technical and universal specifications. Software vendors have the same strategic options, but this time with the focus on *contributing* and *driving* for technical and universal initiatives and *observing* or *adopting* for sectoral ones. SDOs have two fields in which they have to decide on their development strategies. First, when an SDO has to participate in another SDO, it has the same options to choose from as user firms or software vendors, depending on its overall standards strategy. Second, when the SDO has to coordinate its own participants, it can *impose* certain specifications, *support* the participants, *coordinate* voluntary contributors, or *mediate* between conflicting contributors. Governmental organisations also have these options when they have to decide whether to intervene in a nation's standards development activities.

Implications for Future Research

Several limitations to this study and ideas for further research should be mentioned:

– Due to resource restrictions, it focused on the two most important initiatives RosettaNet and ebXML considering other SDOs only in overviews. Although the interconnections between the SDOs were revealed, an appropriate actor-network theory analysis might result in further insights.
– The interorganisational standards covered in this study are limited to supply chain networks. Some insights can in all likelihood be transferred to other fields such as standards for human resources or business reporting, which are currently emerging. Moreover, the insights might also be fruitful for dealing with social and political aspects of the modelling of domain-specific ontologies, which are the basis for the upcoming Semantic Web Services.
– The goal of this study was primarily to provide a qualitative model. Further research could quantify important aspects, probably based on the work of Xia et al. (2003). Moreover, empirical surveys could prove these models and the derived strategic options.

- Two aspects for qualitative research also offer research opportunities. First, the issue of intellectual property rights was neglected until recently in standards research, but plays an important role in the motivation of firms to participate in standardisation efforts.[727] Second, SDOs for interorganisational standards can also be regarded as communities in which the exchange of best practices plays almost the same role as developing standards. An analysis from the perspective of knowledge-transfer could thus also be very fruitful.
- As this study has revealed, the actor-network theory is a useful approach to analysing situations in which technology and politics are highly interwoven. In my opinion, it has great potential to be developed towards a general theory of information systems, something the field is still searching for. However, its roots in the social sciences and its very heterogeneous application in information systems research make further improvement of the theory necessary. This study has offered a first step by clarifying the core concepts on the basis of the original literature, but tailored to information systems requirements. One possible direction would be to examine the similarities and differences with respect to neo-institutional economics. Both fields could enrich each other, for example, by regarding inscriptions as contracts or analysing the transaction costs of translations.

Overall, this study has contributed to the young field of interorganisational standards through two in-depth case studies, uncovering aspects rarely mentioned before. These are especially the different organisational aspects of SDOs and the strategic options for participating in standards development initiatives. Moreover, it has revealed the crucial role of intellectual property rights for the whole field.

Finally, I give a short outlook on how the field of interorganisational standards might develop in the coming years. I expect that the need for the 'plug & play' of organisations will continue to grow, increasing the demand for broadly adopted standards on all levels of the interorganisational specifications stack. As shown in this study, on all these levels usable specifications are already available. However, they are often not yet sufficiently mature for broad adoption. Moreover, the sectoral semantics

---

[727] See Blind/Thumm/Iversen, et al. (2004).

and process specifications in particular will never be fully completed, as they have to be constantly adapted to the continuously changing business requirements. In progressing towards broadly adopted interorganisational standards, therefore, we will probably witness a similar pattern as could be seen in the development of EDI. Back in the 1960s, the logistics industry developed the first EDI solutions, which were gradually transferred to other industries.[728] Today, RosettaNet is the leading SDO for a complete interorganisational specification stack. Its close relations to other SDOs make it very likely that universal interorganisational standards will emerge from these initiatives in the near future. Given the great impact of such standards, no firm can afford to ignore the recent progress made in the field of interorganisational standards, but should instead be preparing strategies for getting involved. This study offers a first starting point for doing so.

---

[728] See Killian/Picot/Neuburger, et al. (1994), pp. 269ff.

Appendixes

A Primary Data Sources

Date	Type	Organisation	Topic	Participants
October 2002	Conference	German Informatics Society (Gesellschaft für Informatik)	"WebServices - Integration im Netz"	Web Services technology officer of a German IT consulting company, Members of the German Informatics Society
June 2003	Interview	Global electronics company	RosettaNet	RosettaNet champion
July 2003	Conference	World Wide Web Consortium (W3C)	"Semantic Web Tour"	Two W3C directors, two IS professors, general audience
July 2003	Interview	Semantic Web software company	RosettaNet and Semantic Web	CEO of a Semantic Web software company
September 2003	Conference	Singapore EDI Committee	"The Business Collaboration Framework"	Chairmen of several UN/CEFACT groups, general audience
September 2003	Conference	RosettaNet Singapore, Infocom Development Authority Singapore	"Getting Ready for RosettaNet"	Several executives of Singaporean companies, general audience
September 2003	Interview	Medium-sized Singaporean electronics company	RosettaNet implementation and use	IS executive of medium-sized Singaporean electronics company
September 2003	Conference	Enterprise software vendor	"Facilitating Cross-Industry Supply Chain Integration With RosettaNet Standards"	Vice president RosettaNet, vice president of enterprise software vendor, two executives of global electronics companies, general audience

Date	Type	Organisation	Topic	Participants
October 2003	Interview	IOS solution provider	RosettaNet adoption and use	Consultant of IOS solution provider
October 2003	Interview	Enterprise software vendor	RosettaNet support by software vendors	Consultant of enterprise software vendor
November 2003	Conference	RosettaNet, enterprise software vendor	"The Collaboration Continuum"	CEO of RosettaNet, vice president of enterprise software vendor
November 2003	Conference	RosettaNet, global electronics company	"RosettaNet Architecture Seminar"	Vice president of standards management at RosettaNet, vice president of RosettaNet Europe, implementation support manager of RosettaNet, RosettaNet member representatives
November 2003	Conference	EDIFICE	"EDIFICE Plenary Meeting"	Vice president RosettaNet Europe, several EDIFICE member representatives
November 2003	Interview	Global electronics company	RosettaNet vs. EDI	EDIFICE member representative

B Theoretical Concepts for EDI Adoption, Use and Impact

Adoption

Source	Environmental conditions	Interorganisational relation	Organisational readiness	Perceived net benefits
Saunders/Clark (1992)		✓ (Dependency, trust)		✓ (Perceived benefits, perceived costs)
Premkumar et al. (1994)			✓ (Compatibility, complexity, communicability)	✓ (Relative advantage, costs)
Williams (1994)	✓ (Industry competitiveness, demand uncertainty)	✓ (Channel power)	✓ (Organisational size, organisational structure)	
Daugherty et al. (1995)			✓ (Organisational size, formalisation, decentralisation)	
Iacovou et al. (1995)	✓ (Competitive pressure)	✓ (Imposition by partners)	✓ (Organisational readiness)	✓ (Perceived benefits)
Premkumar/Ramamurthy (1995)	✓ (Competitive pressure)	✓ (Transaction climate, dependence, exercised power, organisational compatibility)	✓ (Internal need, existence of a champion, IS infrastructure)	
Walton/Miller (1995)	✓ (Market uncertainty, exchange concentration)	✓ (Asset specificity, information sharing, time, number of transactions)	✓ (Organisational flexibility, organisational assistance)	✓ (Previous outcomes)
Mackay/Rosier (1996)	✓ (Competitive necessity)	✓ (Told by customers, trade with auto sector)	✓ (Company size)	✓ (Strategic advantage, logical business decision)
Murphy/Daley (1996)		✓ (Customer resistance, customer training)	✓ (Corporate culture, compatibility of hardware/software, standard formats)	✓ (Awareness of EDI benefits, setup costs)
Bensaou (1997)	✓ (Technological unpredictability)	✓ (Perception of fairness, goal compatibility, switching costs, ownership ratio, contract length)	✓ (Scope of IT use)	
Bergeron/Raymond (1997)		✓ (Imposition)	✓ (Top management support, EDI structure)	
Hart/Saunders (1997)		✓ (Power of customer, trust)		

Source	Environmental conditions	Interorganisational relation	Organisational readiness	Perceived net benefits
Hart/Saunders (1998)		✓ (Supplier dependence, customer power, supplier commitment, supplier trust)		
Nault et al. (1998)				✓ (Adoption benefits, adoption costs)
Peffers et al. (1998)		✓ (Bargaining power of customers)		✓ (Cost reduction, interorganisational process redesign, strategic IORs)
Holmes/Srivastava (1999)		✓ (Relationship, collaboration)	✓ (EDI readiness)	
Lee et al. (1999)			✓ (Top management support, IT context)	
Ramamurthy et al. (1999)	✓ (Competitive pressure)	✓ (Compatibility, customer support)	✓ (Internal support)	✓ (Benefits, resource intensity)
Son et al. (1999)	✓ (Uncertainty)	✓ (Asset specificity, reciprocal investments, power exercised, trust)		
Chwelos et al. (2001)	✓ (Competitive pressure, industry pressure)	✓ (Dependency on TP, enacting TP power, TP readiness)	✓ (Financial resources, IT sophistication)	✓ (Perceived benefits)
Damsgaard/Lyytinen (2001)	✓ (Intermediating institutions)			
Maingot/Quon (2001)				✓ (Reasons for adopting EDI)
Teo et al. (2003)	✓ (Mimetic pressure, normative pressure)	✓ (Coercive pressure)	✓ (Organisation size, IT department size, extend of EDI applications implementation)	

Use

Source	Implementation management	Implementation extent			
		Breadth	*Diversity*	*Volume*	*Depth*
Banerjee/Sriram (1995)		✓ (Percentage of vendors using EDI)	✓ (Percentage of transactions using EDI)		
Massetti/Zmud (1996)		✓ (Breadth)	✓ (Diversity)	✓ (Volume)	✓ (Depth)
Bergeron/Raymond (1997)	✓ (Planning, testing, evaluation, training)	✓ (External integration)	✓ (Internal integration)		
Hart/Saunders (1998)			✓ (Diversity)	✓ (Volume)	
Peffers et al. (1998)	✓ (Selecting IOS standard, selecting hardware/software)		✓ (Structure of connections with trading partners)		
Williams et al. (1998)		✓ (Range)	✓ (Width)	✓ (Depth)	
Fearon/Philip (1999)		✓ (External diffusion)		✓ (Breadth and depth)	
Son et al. (1999)			✓ (Diversity)	✓ (Volume)	
Sriram et al. (2000)	✓ (Training of employees)				
Truman (2000)			✓ (EDI diversity)	✓ (EDI volume)	✓ (Interface integration, internal integration)
Maingot/Quon (2001)	✓ (Adequate resources, hardware/software selection, selling concept to employees, internal/external implementation staff, training of employees)		✓ (Activities to include in EDI system)		
Hill/Scudder (2002)		✓ (Depth)			

Impact

	Hansen/Hill (1989)	Pfeiffer (1992)	Neuburger (1994)	Riggins/Mukhopadhyay (1994)	Banerjee/Sriram (1995)
Strategic					
Competitive advantage		✓ (Ability to compete)			
Customer satisfaction	✓ (Customer service, sales)	✓ (Customer service)			
Cooperation intensity		✓ (Trading partner relationships)	✓ (Vernetzungsstrukturen)		✓ (Nature of vendor contact)
Organisational change			✓ (Reorganisationsprojekte, Entfallen von Bereichen, Fertigungstiefe)		✓ (Changes in organisational structure)
Efficiency	✓ (Administrative cost, manufacturing cost)	✓ (Operational efficiency, transaction costs)	✓ (Automatisierung, Kosteneinsparungen)		✓ (Simplification of purchasing procedures, ordering inefficiency, process automa-)
Operational					
Speed		✓ (Cash flow)	✓ (Schnellere Information)	✓ (Order cycle time, response time)	
Accuracy	✓ (Clerical error, control of data)	✓ (Information quality)	✓ (Bessere Qualität der Information)	✓ (Error generation, data integrity)	
Inventory costs	✓ (Inventory cost)	✓ (Inventory levels)	✓ (Reduktion der Lagerhaltung)		
Logistics costs					
Employee costs					✓ (Buyer retraining, reduction in purchasing personnel)

Source	Strategic					Operational				
	Competitive advantage	Customer satisfaction	Cooperation intensity	Organisational change	Efficiency	Speed	Accuracy	Inventory costs	Logistics costs	Employee costs
Mukhopadhyay et al. (1995)			✓ (Information handling cost)					✓ (Inventory holding cost, obsolete inventory cost)	✓ (Premium freight, transportation cost)	
Mackay/Rosier (1996)		✓ (Customer service)			✓ (Reduction in administrative costs, improved productivity)		✓ (Increased data accuracy)			✓ (Clerical staff savings)
Murphy/Daley (1996)	✓ (Staying ahead of competitors)	✓ (Customer service)	✓ (Communications)		✓ (Reduced paperwork, increased productivity, cost efficiency, improved billing)	✓ (Quick access to information, improved tracing and expediting)	✓ (Accuracy)			
Bensaou (1997)			✓ (Buyer-supplier cooperation)							
Bergeron/Raymond (1997)	✓ (Strategic advantage)				✓ (Administrative costs, operations management)	✓ (Transaction speed)	✓ (Information quality)			

Source	Strategic					Operational				
	Competitive advantage	Customer satisfaction	Cooperation intensity	Organisational change	Efficiency	Speed	Accuracy	Inventory costs	Logistics costs	Employee costs
Philip/Pedersen (1997)	✓ (Competitive advantage, survival of the business)		✓ (Trading relationships)		✓ (Reduction of paper documents, reduced costs)	✓ (Elimination of delays)	✓ (Improved information)	✓ (Inventory costs)		
Peffers et al. (1998)	✓ (Competitive advantage)	✓ (Sales)	✓ (Relationships with customers)		✓ (Costs)		✓ (Order processing errors)	✓ (Inventories)	✓ (Inbound logistics)	
Lee et al. (1999)								✓ (Inventory level, stock out level)		
Young et al. (1999)			✓ (Business relationship, balance of power)							
Truman (2000)					✓ (Claim payment time)		✓ (Claim error rate)			✓ (Number of professional employees, number of administrative employees)
Nakayama (2000)			✓ (Power shift)							
Sriram et al. (2000)	✓ (Remain competitive)	✓ (Customer service)	✓ (Communications)		✓ (Cost efficiency, productivity, convenience)	✓ (Speed, order entry processing, access to information)	✓ (Accuracy)	✓ (Inventory control)	✓ (Shipments tracing)	✓ (Manpower)

Source	Strategic					Operational				
	Competitive advantage	Customer satisfaction	Cooperation intensity	Organisational change	Efficiency	Speed	Accuracy	Inventory costs	Logistics costs	Employee costs
Ahmad/Schroeder (2001)				✓					✓ (Delivery performance)	
Iskandar et al. (2001)	✓ (Competitiveness, market share in the long run)	✓ (Customer services)	✓ (Information sharing with trading partners)		✓ (Administrative cost)	✓ (Response time, lead-time)	✓ (Clerical errors)	✓ (Customer inventory cost, own inventory)		✓ (Number of employees)
Lim/Palvia (2001)		✓ (Customer service, post-sale product support)	✓ (Distribution system flexibility, distribution IS)			✓ (Order cycle time)	✓ (Distribution system malfunction)	✓ (Inventory capability)		
Maingot/Quon (2001)	✓ (Competitive advantage)	✓ (Customer service, sales)	✓ (Supplier relationship, trade facilitation)		✓ (Administrative cost, manufacturing cost)		✓ (Clerical error, control of data)	✓ (Inventory cost)		

C Interorganisational Standards Connections

Last update: November 2004.

Bold letters: SDO develops these specifications

Normal letters: SDO uses these specifications

Not shown is the use of network transport protocols, XML core standards, and UML, as these are almost the same in all SDOs.

SDO	Messag-ing	Descrip-tion	Discovery	Business Semantics Format Definition	Business Process Format Definition	Universal Business Semantics	Univer-sal Business Processes	Specialised Business Semantics	Specialised Business Processes	Trading Partner Agree-ments
ACORD	SOAP							**XMLife**	**TXlife**	
API	RNIF					ASC X12 EDIFACT		**PIDX**		
ANSI/DISA						**ASC X12**				
AIAG						ASC X12 EDIFACT				
BizzTainer	ebMS					BMEcat eCl@ss open-TRANS				
BME						**BMEcat open-TRANS**				
CIDX	RNIF			UBL		UBL		**Chem eStandards** (based on RN Dic-tionaries	**Chem eStan-dards** (based on PIPs)	
cXML	**cXML**	**cXML**				cXML				
D&B						DUNS				
EAN	AS2		**GDSN**			EAN.UCC EDIFACT	CPFR	**EANCOM GPC GTIN**		
ebXML	**ebMS SOAP**	**eb-CPPA**	**ebRMI/RS**	**ebCCTS**	**ebBPSS**	**ebCCTS**				**eb-CPPA**
eCl@ss						**ecl@ss**				
EDIFICE						EDIFACT		**EDIFICE** RN Dic-tionaries	PIPs	
EPCglobal						**EPC** EAN.UCC				
HL7	**HL7**							**HL7 CCOW**	**HL7**	
IETF	**EDIINT AS2**									
ISO	**FSV 15000-2** ebMS	**15000-1** eb-CPPA	**15000-3/4** ebRMI/RS	**15000-5** ebCCTS	**BOV**	**15000-5** ebCCTS		**20022**	**20022**	**15000-1** ebCPPA

SDO	Messaging	Description	Discovery	Business Semantics Format Definition	Business Process Format Definition	Universal Business Semantics	Universal Business Processes	Specialised Business Semantics	Specialised Business Processes	Trading Partner Agreements
MBA								MISMO		
OAG	ebMS					BOD OAGIS				
OASIS	ASAP ebMS	eb-CPPA	ebRMI/RS UDDI	UBL ebCCTS	BPEL BTP ebBPSS	UBL ebCCTS xCBL				
ODETTE				CWM ebCCTS	UMM	BOD DUNS ebCCTS EDIFACT OAGIS		ODETTE	ODETTE	
OMG	CORBA	IDL		CWM	MDA UML					
OTA	ebMS							OTA		
papiNet	ebMS							PapiNet		
POSC								Energy eStandards	Energy eStandards	
RosettaNet	RNIF FSV	TPIR eb-CPPA	Trading Partner Directory		BOV ebBPSS	DUNS EAN.UCC UNSPSC EDIFACT	CPFR	RN Dictionaries GTIN UNIFI	PIPs	ebCPPA
STARS						BOD OAGIS				
SWIFT				UNIFI ebCCTS		ebCCTS		UNIFI ISO 20022		
UN/CEFACT				ebCCTS	UMM	ebCCTS EDIFACT UNTDED				
UNDP						UNSPSC				
VICS						EAN.UCC	BOL CPFR	VICS EDI		
W3C	SOAP	WSDL		RDF OWL	WS-CDL					
WfMC	ASAP SOAP				XPDL					
xCBL						xCBL				

List of Figures

List of Tables

Abbreviations

ABB	Asea Brown Boveri
ACORD	Association for Cooperative Operations Research and Development
AIAG	Automotive Industry Action Group
ANSI	American National Standards Institute
ANT	Actor-Network Theory
API	American Petroleum Institute
AS2	Applicability Statement 2
ASAP	Asynchronous Services Access Protocol
ASC	Accredited Standards Committee
ATP	Available to Promise
BMEcat	Bundesverband Materialwirtschaft, Einkauf und Logistik Catalog
BOD	Business Object Document
BOL	Bill of Lading
BOV	Business Operational View
BPEL	Business Process Execution Language
BPMI	Business Process Management Initiative
BPML	Business Process Modeling Language
BPSS	Business Process Specification Schema
BTP	Business Transaction Protocol
CEN	Comité Européen de Normalisation
CEO	Chief Executive Officer
CERN	Conseil Européen pour la Recherche Nucléaire
CIDX	Chemical Industry Data Exchange
COBOL	Common Business Oriented Language
CORBA	Common Object Request Brokerage Architecture
CPFR	Collaborative Planning, Forecasting and Replenishment
CSG	CEFACT Steering Committee
CWM	Common Warehouse Metamodel
cXML	Commerce XML
D & B	Dun and Bradstreet
DIN	Deutsches Institut für Normung e.V.
DISA	Data Interchange Standards Association
DRM	Digital Rights Management

DUNS.. Data Universal Numbering System

EAI .... Enterprise Application Integration
EAN .... European Article Numbering
ebCPPA .... ebXML Collaboration Protocol Profile and Agreement
ebMS .... ebXML Message Service
ebXML .... Electronic Business using eXtensible Markup Language
ebRIM ....ebXML Registry Information Model
ebRS .... ebXML Registry Services Specification
EDI .... Electronic Data Interchange
EDIFACT.. Electronic Data Interchange For
                                           Administration, Commerce and Transport
EDIFICE... EDI Forum for Companies with
                                           Interest in Computing and Electronics
EDS.. Electronic Data Systems
EPC .... Electronic Product Code
EPOR..Empirical Programme of Relativism
ERP..Enterprise Resource Planning
ESA.. Enterprise Services Architecture
ESIA ....European Semiconductor Industry Association
ETSI.............................European Telecommunications Standards Institute

FSV... Functional Service View

GDSN... Global Data Synchronization Network
GE...General Electric
GML..Generalized Markup Language
GPC... Global Product Classification
GSM ....Global System for Mobile Communication
GTIN .... Global Trade Item Numbers

HL7 ....Health Level Seven
HP .... Hewlett Packard
HTML .... HyperText Markup Language
HTTP.. HyperText Transfer Protocol

IBM...International Business Machines
IBP...Interorganisational Business Process
ICE ....Information and Content Exchange
IDL .... Interface Definition Language
IDoc..Intermediate Document
IEC... International Electrotechnical Commission
IEEE...................................... Institute of Electrical and Electronics Engineers

IETF .... Internet Engineering Task Force
IO .... Interorganisational
IOR .... Interorganisational Relationship
IOS .... Interorganisational Information System
IP .... Internet Protocol
IPR .... Intellectual Property Rights
IS .... Information System
ISO .... International Organisation for Standardisation
IT .... Information Technology
ITU .... International Telecommunication Union

MBA .... Mortgage Bankers Association
MDA .... Model Driven Architecture
MISMO .... Mortgage Industry Standards Maintenance Organisation
MIT .... Massachusetts Institute of Technology
MOST .... Ministry of Science and Technology
MoU .... Memorandum of Understanding
MS .... Microsoft

NEC .... Nippon Electric Company
NIST .... National Institute for Standards and Technology

OAG .... Open Application Group
OAGIS .... Open Application Group Interchange Specifications
OASIS .... Organisation for the Advancement of
Structured Information Standards
OBI .... Open Buying on the Internet
ODETTE .... Organisation for Data Exchange by
Tele-Transmission in Europe
OLA .... Office of Legal Affairs
OMG .... Object Management Group
OOA .... Object Oriented Architecture
OPEC .... Organisation of the Petroleum Exporting Countries
OPP .... Obligatory Passage Point
OSI .... Open Systems Interconnection
OTA .... Open Travel Alliance
OWL .... Web Ontology Language

PIDX .... Petroleum Industry Data Exchange
PIP .... Partner Interface Process
POSC .... Petrochemical Open Standards Consortium

RDF .... Resource Description Framework

REST.. REpresentational State Transfer
RFC .... Request for Comment
RIG .... RosettaNet Implementation Guide
RNBD... RosettaNet Business Dictionary
RNIF...RosettaNet Implementation Framework
RNTD...RosettaNet Technical Dictionary
ROI .... Return on Investment
RSS .... RDF Site Summary

SAP............................... Systeme, Anwendungen, Produkte in der Datenverarbeitung
SCM .... Supply Chain Management
SCN...Supply Chain Network
SCOR ....Supply Chain Operations Reference
SCOT.. Social Construction of Technology
SDO.. Standards Development Organisation
SGML...Standard Generalized Markup Language
SME...Small or Medium Enterprise
SOA.. Service Oriented Architecture
SOAP ....Simple Object Access Protocol
STAR...................................Standards for Technology in Automotive Retail
SVG ....Scalable Vector Graphics
SWIFT .... Society for Worldwide Interbank Financial Telecommunications
SWS.. Semantic Web Services

TC... Technical Committee
TCP ....Transmission Control Protocol
TDCC..................................... Transportation Data Coordination Committee
TMWG...Techniques and Methodologies Working Group
TPA ....Trading Partner Agreement
tpaML .... Trading Partner Agreement Markup Language
TPIR .... Trading Partner Implementation Requirements
TSMC... Taiwan Semiconductor Manufacturing Company

UBL ....Universal Business Language
UCC .... Uniform Code Council
UDDI.. Universal Description, Discovery and Integration
UML...Unified Modeling Language
UMM...UN/CEFACT Modeling Methodology
UN/CEFACT.......................United Nations Centre for the Facilitation of Procedures
                                            andPractices for Administration, Commerce & Transport
UNDP .... United Nations Development Programme
UNECE ....United Nations Economic Commission for Europe

UN/EDIFACT ....United Nations Electronic Data Interchange for
Administration, Commerce and Transport
UNIFI...UNIversal Financial Industry message scheme
UNSPSC..................................United Nations Standard Products and Services Code
UNTDED ....United Nations Trade Date Element Directory
URI ....Uniform Resource Identifier
US..United States
USC .... Universal Structures Content

VAN .... Value Added Network
VICS .... Voluntary Interindustry Commerce Standards

W3C..World Wide Web Consortium
WfMC... Workflow Management Coalition
Wf-XML..Workflow XML
WI..Wirtschaftsinformatik
WIPO.. World Intellectual Property Organisation
WP.4.. Working Party 4
WS-CDL........................ Web Services Choreography Description Language Version
WS-I..Web Services Interoperability Organisation
WSDL... Web Services Description Language

XBRL .... eXtensible Business Reporting Language
xCBL..XML Common Business Library
XML...eXtensible Markup Language
XPDL..XML Process Description Language
XSD... XML Schema Definition

References

Afuah A (2003) Redefining Firm Boundaries in the Face of the Internet – Are Firms Really Shrinking? *Academy of Management Review* 28 (1):43-53.

Ahmad S, Schroeder RG (2001) The Impact of Electronic Data Interchange on Delivery Performance. *Production and Operations Management* 10 (1):16-30.

Akrich M (1992) The De-Scription of Technical Objects. In *Shaping Technology/Building Society*, edited by Bijker WE, Law J. Cambridge, MA: MIT Press.

Akrich M, Latour B (1992) A Summary of a Convenient Vocabulary for the Semiotics of Human and Nonhuman Assemblies. In *Shaping Technology/Building Society – Studies in Sociotechnical Change*, edited by Bijker WE, Law J. Cambridge: MIT Press.

Albrecht CC, Dean DL, Hansen JV (2003) Market Place and Technology Standards for B2B-E-Commerce: Progress and Challenges. Paper read at *Workshop on Standard Making: A Critical Research Frontier for Information Systems*, at Seattle, WA.

Alt R, Österle H (2003) *Real-Time Business – Lösungen, Bausteine und Potentiale des Business Networking*: Springer.

Amazon (2004) *Amazon Web Services* [cited 2004-10-21]. Available from http://www.amazon.com/gp/browse.html/104-4434613-2363946?%5Fencoding=UTF8&node=3435361.

Anderson P (2001) *Fadi Chehade: 'Deep, clear visibility'*. CNN.com [cited 2004-10-06]. Available from http://www.cnn.com/2001/CAREER/jobenvy/08/20/fadi.chehade.viacore.

Angele J (2003) Einsatz von Ontologien zur intelligenten Verarbeitung von Informationen. *Industrie Management* 19:53-55.

Angeles R, Nath R (2001) Partner Congruence in Electronic Data Interchange (EDI)-Enabled Relationships. *Journal of Business Logistics* 22:109-127.

Antonelli C (1994) Localized Technological Change and the Evolution of Standards as Economic Institutions. *Information Economics & Policy* 6 (3-4):195-216.

Arthur WB (1989) Competing Technologies, Increasing Returns, and Lock-In by Historical Events. *The Economic Journal* 99:116-131.

Ashton AS, Rothenstein B (2003) *SAP NetWeaver Supports RosettaNet and CIDX Data Exchange Standards*. SAP AG [cited. Available from http://xml.coverpages.org/SAPNetWeaver.html.

Atkinson C, Brooks L (2003) StructurANTion: A Theoretical Framework for Integrating Human and IS Research and Development. Paper read at *Americas Conference on Information Systems*.

Avison D, Myers MD (2002) *Qualitative Research in Information Systems: A Reader*. London: Sage.

Bacheldor B, Ewalt DM (2003) Process Oriented. *InformationWeek* (923):20-21.

Bakos JY (1991) A Strategic Analysis of Electronic Marketplaces. *MIS Quarterly* 15 (3):295-311.

Banerjee S, Sriram V (1995) The Impact of Electronic Data Interchange on Purchasing: An Empirical Investigation. *International Journal of Operations & Production Management* 15 (3):29-38.

Barlas D (2003) *Intel*. Line56.com [cited 2004-01-20]. Available from http://www.line56.com/articles/default.asp?articleid=4511.

Barringer BR, Harrison J (2000) Walking a Tightrope: Creating Value Through Interorganizational Relationsships. *Journal of Management* 26 (3):367-403.

Barua A, Lee B (1997) An Economic Analysis of the Introduction of an Electronic Data Interchange System. *Information Systems Research* 8 (4):398-422.

Becker J, König W, Schütte R, Wendt O, Zelewski S, eds (1999) *Wirtschaftsinformatik und Wissenschaftstheorie – Bestandsaufnahme und Perspektiven.* Wiesbaden: Gabler.

Beekun RI, Glick WH (2001) Organization Structure from a Loose Coupling Perspective: A Multidimensional Approach. *Decision Sciences* 32 (2):227-250.

Beimborn D, Mintert S, Weitzel T (2002) Web Services und ebXML. *Wirtschaftsinformatik* 44 (3):277-280.

Benbasat I, Goldstein DK, Mead M (1987) The Case Research Strategy in Studies of Information Systems. *MIS Quarterly* 11 (3):368-387.

Benbasat I, Zmud RW (2003) The Identity Crisis Within the IS Discipline: Defining and Communicating the Discipline's Core Properties. *MIS Quarterly* 27 (2):183-194.

Bensaou M (1997) Interorganizational Cooperation: The Role of Information Technology – An Empirical Comparison of U.S. and Japanese Supplier Relations. *Information Systems Research* 8 (2):107-124.

Benton M, Kim E, Ngugi B (2002) Bridging the Gap: From Traditional Information Retrieval to the Semantic Web. Paper read at *Eighth Americas Conference on Information Systems.*

Bergeron F, Raymond L (1997) Managing EDI for Corporate Advantage: A Longitudinal Study. *Information & Management* 31:319-333.

Berners-Lee T (2003) *Web Services – Semantic Web.* W3C [cited 2004-01-16]. Available from http://www.w3.org/2003/Talks/0521-www-keynote-tbl/.

Berners-Lee T, Hendler J, Lassila O (2001) *The Semantic Web.* Scientific American [cited 2002-10-30].

Besen SM, Saloner G (1989) The Economics of Telecommunications Standards. In *Changing the Rules – Technological Change, International Competition, and Regulation in Communications,* edited by Crandall RW, Flamm K. Washington, D.C.: The Brookings Institution.

Bieberbach F (2001) *Die optimale Größe und Struktur von Unternehmen – Der Einfluss von Informations- und Kommunikationstechnik.* Wiesbaden: Deutscher Universitäts-Verlag.

Bijker W (1995) *Of Bicycles, Bakelites and Bulbs.* Cambridge, MA: MIT Press.

Bitkom (2004) UN/CEFACT Framework Überblick. Working Paper, Berlin.

Blind K, Thumm N, Iversen E, Hossain K, van Reekum R, Rixius B, Bierhals R, Sillwood J (2004) Interaction between Standardisation and Intellectual Property Rights. Technical Report EUR 21074 EN, Institute for Prospective Technological Studies, *European Commission Joint Research Centre.*

Bloor D (1976) *Knowledge and Social Imagery.* London: Routledge and Kegan Paul.

BMEcat (2004) *eBusiness Standardization Committee* [cited 2004-11-13]. Available from http://www.bmecat.org/.

Böhnlein M, vom Ende AU (1999) XML – Extensible Markup Language. *Wirtschaftsinformatik* 41 (3):274-276.

Bosak J (2002) *The Significance of CPPA v2.* XML Cover Pages [cited 2004-10-18]. Available from http://xml.coverpages.org/BosakCPPA-v2.html.

——— (2003) *Re: CSG Answers to Mark Crawford's Questions regarding the UN/CEFACT Position Statement on ebXML* [cited 2004-10-27]. Available from http://lists.ebxml.org/archives/ebxml-dev/200311/msg00005.html.

Bowersox DJ, Closs DJ, Cooper MB (2002) *Supply Chain Logistics Management.* Boston: McGraw Hill.

Bowker GC, Star SL (1996) *How Things (Actor-Net)work: Classification, Magic and the Ubiquity of Standards* [cited 2004-07-19]. Available from http://weber.ucsd.edu/~gbowker/actnet.html.

Boyle T (2002) *The CEFACT Website Horribly Out of Date* [cited 2004-10-25]. Available from http://lists.ebxml.org/archives/ebxml-dev/200210/msg00003.html.

Braun H (2000) Soziologie der Hybriden – Über die Handlungsfähigkeit von technischen Agenten. Working Paper, Institute for Social Sciences, *Technische Universität Berlin*, Berlin.

Brenner W, Neo BS (1997) Informationstechnik als Grundlage wirtschaftlichen Wachstums: Das Beispiel von Singapur. *Wirtschaftsinformatik* 39 (2):155-160.

Brooks L, Atkinson C (2004) Using StructurANTion to Delineate an Actor Network's Information System. Paper read at *Americas Conference on Information Systems*, at New York.

Brown JS, Durchslag S, Hagel J (2002) Loosening up: How Process Networks Unlock the Power of Specialization. *The McKinsey Quarterly* 2002 (Special Edition: Risk and Resilience):59-69.

Broy M, Hegering H-G, Picot A, Alkassar A, Garschhammer M, Gehring F, Keil P, Kelter H, Löwer UM, Pankow M, Schiffers M, Ullmann M, Vogel S (2003) *Kommunikations- und Informationstechnik 2010+3 – Neue Trends und Entwicklungen in Technologie, Anwendungen und Sicherheit*. Ingelheim: Bundesamt für Sicherheit in der Informationstechnik, SecuMedia.

Bruegge B, Dutoit AH (2003) *Object-Oriented Software Engineering Using UML, Patterns, and Java*. Englewood Cliffs, NJ: Prentice Hall.

Brügge B, Harhoff D, Picot A, Creighton O, Fiedler M, Henkel J (2004) *Open-Source-Software – Eine ökonomische und technische Analyse*. Berlin: Springer.

Burns V (2005) *Interorganisational Relationships between British and German Companies – An In-Depth Case Study Using Actor-Network Theory*. Manly: Penfolds.

Burrell G, Morgan G (1979) *Sociological Paradigms and Organisational Analysis*. London: Heinemann.

Bussler C, Fensel D, Maedche A (2002) A Conceptual Architecture for Semantic Web Enabled Web Services. *ACM Special Interest Group on Management of Data* 31 (4):24-29.

Buxmann P (1996) *Standardisierung betrieblicher Informationssysteme*. Wiesbaden: Gabler.

Buxmann P, Ladner F, Weitzel T (2001) Anwendung der Extensible Markup Language (XML): Konzeption und Implementierung einer WebEDI-Lösung. *Wirtschaftsinformatik* 43 (3):257-267.

Calas MB, Smircich L (1999) Past Postmodernism? Reflections and Tentative Directions. *Academy of Management Review* 24 (4):649-672.

Callon M (1986a) The Sociology of an Actor-Network: The Case of the Electric Vehicle. In *Mapping the Dynamics of Science and Technology*, edited by Callon M, Law J, Rip A. Houndmills: The Macmillan Press.

——— (1986b) Some Elements in a Sociology of Translations: Domestication of the Scallops and Fishermen at St. Brieuc Bay. In *Power, Action and Belief*, edited by Law J. London: Routledge.

——— (1991) Techno-Economic Networks and Irreversibility. In *Sociology of Monsters: Essays on Power, Technology and Domination*, edited by Law J. London: Routledge.

——— (1999) Actor-Network Theory – The Market Test. In *Actor Network Theory and After*, edited by Law J, Hassard J. Oxford: Blackwell.

Callon M, Latour B (1981) Unscrewing the Big Leviathan: How Actors Macro-Structure Reality and How Sociologist Help Them To Do So. In *Advances in Social Theory and*

Methodology: Towars an Integration of Micro and Macro-Sociology, edited by Knorr-Cetina K, Cicouvel AV. Boston, MA: Rougledge.

Callon M, Law J, Rip A (1986) How to Study the Forces of Science. In *Mapping the Dynamics of Science and Technology*, edited by Callon M, Law J, Rip A. Houndmills: The Macmillan Press.

Capell S (2003) *UDDI vs ebXML RIM/RSS and Convergence* [cited 2004-10-24]. Available from http://lists.oasis-open.org/archives/uddi-spec-comment/200303/msg00001.html.

Cash JIJ, Konsynski BR (1985) IS Redraws Competitive Boundaries. *Harvard Business Review* 63 (2):134-142.

CEFACT (2000) New Method of Working – UN/CEFACT's Open Development Process for Technical Specifications, CEFACT Steering Committee, *United Nations – Economic and Social Council*, Geneva.

————— (2003a) *UN/CEFACT Announces Successful Completion of ebXML Technical Standards Work Programme with OASIS* [cited 2004-10-23]. Available from http://www.unece.org/cefact/press%20release%20210803.pdf.

————— (2003b) *UN/CEFACT Position Statement on ebXML* [cited 2003-10-29]. Available from http://lists.oasis-open.org/archives/regrep/200310/msg00072.html.

————— (2003c) *UN/CEFACT's Position Re UBL Post Its Announcement of 21 August 2003 Regarding the Successful Conclusion of the ebXML Initiative* [cited 2004-10-25]. Available from http://www.unece.org/cefact/CSGublstst030821.pdf.

————— (2004a) TRADE/R.650/Rev.3: Mandate, Terms of Reference and Procedures for UN/CEFACT, CEFACT Bureau, *United Nations – Economic and Social Council*, Geneva.

————— (2004b) *UN/CEFACT and OASIS cooperate to strengthen work on ebXML*. Press Release 2004-05-10 [cited 2004-10-25]. Available from http://www.unece.org/press/pr2004/04trade_p04e.htm.

————— (2004c) *United Nations Body Moves Global eBusiness Standards Forward*. Press Release 2004-09-24 [cited 2004-10-23]. Available from http://www.unece.org/press/pr2004/04trade_p07e.htm.

Chatfield AT, Yetton P (2000) Strategic Payoff from EDI as a Function of EDI Embeddedness. *Journal of Management Information Systems* 16 (4):195-224.

Chen M (2003) Factors Affecting the Adoption and Diffusion of XML and Web Services Standards for E-Business Systems. *International Journal of Human Computer Studies* 58:259-279.

Choi TY, Dooley KJ, Rungtusanatham M (2000) Supply Networks and Complex Adaptive Systems: Control versus Emergence. *Journal of Operations Management* 19 (3):351-366.

Christopher M (1998) *Logistics and Supply Chain Management – Strategies for Reducing Cost and Improving Service*. London: Financial Times Prentice Hall.

Chwelos P, Benbasat I, Dexter AS (2001) Research Report: Empirical Test of an EDI Adoption Model. *Information Systems Research* 12 (3):304-321.

Clark JB (2002) *Copyrights, Standards and Trash Talk (was) UN/CEFACT: Consultation Process for New Organization* [cited 2004-10-24]. Available from http://lists.ebxml.org/archives/ebxml-dev/200201/msg00060.html.

————— (2003) *OASIS TC Call For Participation: ebXML Business Process* [cited 2004-10-16]. Available from http://lists.oasis-open.org/archives/tc-announce/200309/msg00007.html.

Clemons EK, Reddi SP, Row MC (1993) The Impact of Information Technology on the Organization of Economic Activity: The "Move to the Middle" Hypothesis. *Journal of Management Information Systems* 10 (2):9-35.

Coase RH (1937) The Nature of the Firm. *Economia* 4:386-405.

—— (1960) The Problem of Social Cost. *Journal of Law and Economics* 3:1-44.

Collins H, Yearley S (1992) Epistemological Chicken. In *Sciences as Practice and Culture*, edited by Pickering A. Chicago: Chicago University Press.

Collins HM (1981) Stages in the Empirical Programme of Relativism. *Social Studies of Science* 11:3-10.

Computerwoche (2004) *Microsoft verlässt die UN/Cefact* [cited 2004-20-10]. Available from http://www.computerwoche.de/index.cfm?pageid=254&type=detail&artid=64473&linktype=rss.

Cooper R, Zmud RW (1990) Information Technology Implementation Research: A Technological Diffusion Approach. *Management Science* 36 (2):123-139.

Cooper RG, Kleinschmidt E (1996) Winning Businesses in Product Development: The Critical Success Factors. *Research Technology Management* 39 (4):18-29.

Crawford M (2000) *electronic business XML (ebXML) Requirements Specification Candidate Draft 28 April 2000* [cited 2004-10-12]. Available from http://www.ebxml.org/specdrafts/req428.htm.

Crook CW, Kumar RL (1998) Electronic Data Interchange: A Multi-Industry Investigation Using Grounded Theory. *Information & Management* 34 (2):75-89.

Damsgaard J, Lyytinen K (2001) The Role of Intermediating Institutions in the Diffusion of Electronic Data Interchange (EDI): How Industry Associations Intervened in Denmark, Finland, and Hong Kong. *The Information Society* 17 (3):195-210.

Daugherty PJ, Germain R, Dröge C (1995) Predicting EDI Technology Adoption in Logistics Management: The Influence of Context and Structure. *Logistics and Transportation Review* 31 (4):309-324.

David PA, Greenstein S (1990) The Economics of Compatibility Standards: An Introduction to Recent Research. *Economics of Innovation and New Technology* 1:3-41.

Davies J, Fensel D, Harmelen Fv, eds (2003) *Towards the Semantic Web: Ontology-Driven Knowledge Management*. West Sussex: John Wiley & Sons.

Davis GB (1999) A Research Perspective for Information Systems and Example of Emerging Area of Research. *Information Systems Frontiers* 1 (3):195-203.

Dedrick J, West J (2003) Why Firms Adopt Open Source Platforms: A Grounded Theory of Innovation and Standards Adoption. Paper read at *Workshop on Standard Making: A Critical Research Frontier for Information Systems*, at Seattle, WA.

Degele N (2002) *Einführung in die Techniksoziologie*. München: Fink (UTB).

Denning P, Comer D, Gries D, Mulder M, Tucker A, Turner AJ, Young P (1989) Computing as a Discipline: Final Report of the Task Force on the Core of Computer Science. *Communications of the Association for Information Systems* 32 (1):9-23.

Dietl H (1993) *Institutionen und Zeit*. Tübingen: Mohr.

Downing CE (2002) Performance of Traditional and Web-Based EDI. *Information Systems Management* 19 (1):49-55.

e2open (2003) *The Horizontal Hyper-Competitive Future*. IBM, PWC Consulting [cited 2003-08-19]. Available from http://www.e2open.com.

ebXML (2000) *ebXML Showcases Dynamic Trading Network*. Press Release 2000-08-02 [cited 2004-10-13]. Available from http://www.ebxml.org/news/pr_20000802.htm.

—— (2001a) ebXML Business Process Specification Schema Version 1.01.

———— (2001b) *UN/CEFACT Forms e-Business Transition Ad hoc Working Group.* Press Release 2001-07-30 [cited 2004-10-13]. Available from http://www.ebxml.org/news/pr_20010730.htm.

———— (2003a) *ebXML Adoption Update December 2003* [cited 2004-10-29]. Available from http://www.ebxml.org/documents/ebxml_adopt_update_122203.pdf.

———— (2003b) *UN/CEFACT Plenary Endorses Latest ebXML Specifications.* Press Release 2003-06-03 [cited 2004-10-14]. Available from http://www.ebxml.org/news/pr_20030603.htm.

Economides N (1996) The Economics of Networks. *International Journal of Industrial Organization* 14 (6):673-699.

Egyedi TM (1996) *Shaping Standardisation: A Study of Standards Processes and Standards Policies in the field of Telematic Services.* Delft: Delft University Press.

———— (2003) Consortium Problem Redefined: Negotiating 'Democracy' in the Actor Network on Standardization. *International Journal of IT Standards and Standardization Research* 1 (2):22-38.

Eisenberg B, Nickull D (2001) ebXML Technical Architecture Specification v1.0.4, *OASIS & UN/CEFACT.*

Eisenhardt KM (1989) Building Theories from Case Study Research. *Academy of Management Review* 14 (4):532-550.

Elgarah W, Falaleeva N, Saunders CS, Ilie V, Shim JT, Courtney JF (2005) Data Exchange in Interorganizational Relationships: Review through Multiple Conceptual Lenses. *ACM SIGMIS Database* 36 (1):8-29.

Evan WM (1965) Toward a Theory of Inter-Organizational Relations. *Management Science* 11 (10):217-230.

Eversmann L (2002) Die Wirtschaftsinformatik als Wissenschaft und ihre Erkenntnisziele. *Wirtschaftsinformatik* 44 (1):91-98.

Faisst W (1998) Die Unterstützung Virtuelle Unternehmen durch Informations- und Kommunikationssysteme – Eine lebenszyklusorientierte Analyse. Dissertation, *Friedrich-Alexander-Universität Erlangen-Nürnberg*, Nürnberg.

Farrell J, Saloner G (1985) Standardization, Compatibility, and Innovation. *Journal of Economics* 16 (1):70-84.

———— (1986) Installed Base and Compatibility: Innovation, Product Preannouncements, and Predation. *American Economic Review* 76 (5):940-956.

———— (1988) Coordination through Committees and Markets. *RAND Journal of Economics* 19 (2):235-253.

Fearon C, Philip G (1999) An Empirical Study of the Use of EDI in Supermarket Chains Using a New Conceptual Framework. *Journal of Information Technology* 14:3-21.

Fensel D (2001) *Ontologies – A Silver Bullet for Knowledge Management and Electronic Commerce.* Berlin: Springer.

Fensel D, Patel-Schneider (2002) Layering the Semantic Web: Problems and Directions. Paper read at *International Semantic Web Conference.*

Fiedler M (2004) *Expertise und Offenheit.* Tübingen: Mohr-Siebeck.

Fischer T (2006) Unternehmenskommunikation und Neue Medien – Weblogs als neues emergierendes Medium und dessen Bedeutung für die Public Relations Arbeit, Institute for Information, Organisation and Management, *Ludwig-Maximilians-University of Munich*, Munich.

Fomin V, Keil T (2000) Standardization: Bridging the Gap Between Economic and Social Theory. Paper read at *International Conference on Information Systems*, at Brisbane.

Fomin V, Keil T, Lyytinen K (2003) Theorizing about Standardization: Integrating Fragments of Process Theory in Light of Telecommunication Standardization Wars. *Sprouts: Working Papers on Information Environments, Systems and Organizations* 3.

Fomin V, Lyytinen K (2000) How to Distribute a Cake before Cutting it into Pieces: Alice in Wonderland or Radio Engineers' Gang in the Nordic Countries? In *Information Technology Standards and Standardization: A Global Perspective*, edited by Jakobs K. Hershey, PA: Idea Group.

Fomin VV, Lyytinen K, Keil T (2004) Distributed Cognitive Design and Pro-Tracing of Actor-Networks: The Case of Standards Making. Paper read at *ISOneWorld Conference*, at Las Vegas.

Forrester JW (1958) Industrial Dynamics: A Major Breakthrough for Decision Makers. *Harvard Business Review* 36 (4):37-66.

Franck E (1991) *Künstliche Intelligenz – Eine grundlagentheoretische Diskussion der Einsatzmöglichkeiten und -grenzen*. Tübingen: Mohr.

Frank U (2001) Standardisierungsvorhaben zur Unterstützung des elektronischen Handels: Überblick über anwendungsnahe Ansätze. *Wirtschaftsinformatik* 43 (3):283-293.

——— (2003) Für Sie gelesen: IS Research Relevance Revisited: Subtle Accomplishment, Unfulfilled Promise, or Serial Hypocrisy? *Wirtschaftsinformatik* 45 (3):354-369.

Freudenberg H (1999) *Strategisches Verhalten bei Reoganisationen*. Wiesbaden: Gabler.

Fricke M, Weitzel T, König W, Lampe R (2002) EDI and Business-to-Business Systems: The Status Quo and the Future of Business Relations in the European Automotive Industry. Paper read at *Pacific Asia Conference on Information Systems*.

Fritsch W (2001) Webservices zwischen Vision und Wirklichkeit. *InformationWeek* 2001 (28):32-36.

Fritz F-J (2003) Interview: "Völlig neue Arten der Arbeitsteilung". *look@SAP SI* 2003 (01):17-18.

Fuchs-Kittowski, Heinrich LJ, Rolf A (1999) Information entsteht in Organisationen - in kreativen Unternehmen - wissenschaftstheoretische und methodologische Konsequenzen für die Wirtschaftsinformatik. In *Wirtschaftsinformatik und Wissenschaftstheorie – Bestandaufnahme und Perspektiven*, edited by Becker J, König W, Schütte R, Wendt O, Zelewski S. Wiesbaden: Gabler.

Gaillard J (1934) *Industrial Standardization – Its Principles and Applications*. New York: H. W. Wilson.

Galliers RD (1992a) Choosing Information Systems Research Approaches. In *Information Systems Research: Issues, Methods, and Practical Guidelines*, edited by Galliers RD. Oxford: Blackwell Scientific Publications.

———, ed. (1992b) *Information Systems Research: Issues, Methods, and Practical Guidelines*. Oxford: Blackwell Scientific Publications.

Gannon P (2003) *Achieving Sustainable Business Benefits with XML and Web Services Standards*. Idealliance [cited 2004-01-16]. Available from http://www.idealliance.org/papers/xmle03/slides/gannon/gannon.ppt.

Gaßner W (1999) *Implementierung organisatorischer Veränderungen – Eine mitarbeiterorientierte Perspektive*. Wiesbaden: Gabler.

Gebauer J, Shaw MJ (2002) Introduction to the Special Section: Business-to-Business Electronic Commerce. *International Journal of Electronic Commerce* 6 (4):7-17.

Giddens A (1984) *The Constitution of Society*. Cambridge, UK: Polity Press.

Gilbert A (2004) *Web services patents fetch $15.5 million* [cited 2004-12-17]. Available from http://news.com.com/Web+services+patents+fetch+15.5+million/2100-1038_3-5480341.html.

Glaser B, Strauss A (1967) *The Discovery of Grounded Theory: Strategies for Qualitative Research.* Chicago: Aldine Publishing Company.

Glass G (2002) *Web Services – Building Blocks for Distributed Systems.* Upper Saddle River: Prentice Hall.

Glushko RJ (2000) *The Plug-and-Play Economy* [cited. Available from http://www.manufacturing.net/pur/index.asp?layout=articleWebzine&articleid=C A139717.

Göpfert J (1998) *Modulare Produktentwicklung.* Wiesbaden: Gabler.

Gorry GA, Scott Morton MS (1971) A Framework for Management Information Systems. *Sloan Management Review* 13 (1):55-71.

Gosain S (2003) Realizing the Vision for Web Services: Strategies for Dealing with Imperfect Standards. Paper read at *Workshop on Standard Making: A Critical Research Frontier for Information Systems,* December 12-14, at Seattle, WA.

Graham I, Pollock N, Smart A, Williams R (2003) Institutionalisation of E-Business Standards. Paper read at *Workshop on Standard Making: A Critical Research Frontier for Information Systems,* December 12-14, at Seattle, WA.

Graham I, Spinardi G, Williams R, Webster J (1995) The Dynamics of EDI Standards Development. *Technology Analysis & Strategic Management* 7 (1):3-20.

Grindley P (1995) *Standards Strategy and Policy – Cases and Stories.* Oxford: Oxford University Press.

Grosof B (2004) *Creating and Studying Knowledge-based Web Technologies for E-Commerce.* MIT Sloan School of Management [cited 2004-01-16]. Available from http://ebusiness.mit.edu/bgrosof/.

Grove AS (1996) *Only the Paranoid Survive – How to Exploit the Crisis Points that Challenge Every Company and Career.* 1. publ. ed. London: Harper Collins Business.

Gulati R (1998) Alliances and Networks. *Strategic Management Journal* 19:293-317.

Hagel J (2002) *Out of the Box - Strategies for Achieving Profits Today and Growth Tomorrow through Web Services.* Boston: Harvard Business School Press.

Hagel JI, Singer M (1999) Unbundling the Corporation. *Harvard Business Review* 77 (2):133-141.

Haines MN (2003) Levels of Web Services Adoption: From Technical Solution to Business Opportunity. Paper read at *Ninth Americas Conference on Information Systems,* at Tampa, FL.

Hall RH (1999) *Organizations: Structures, Processes, and Outcomes.* 7 ed. Upper Saddle River: Prentice Hall.

Handfield RB, Nichols ELJ (2002) *Supply Chain Redesign – Transforming Supply Chains into Integrated Value Systems.* Upper Saddle River: Financial Times Prentice Hall.

Hansen JV, Hill NC (1989) Control and Audit of Electronic Data Interchange. *MIS Quarterly* 13 (4):403-413.

Hanseth O (2000) The Economics of Standards. In *From Control to Drift – The Dynamics of Corporate Information Infrastructure,* edited by Ciborra CU. Oxford: Oxford University Press.

Hanseth O, Monteiro E (1997) Inscribing Behavior in Information Infrastructure Standards. *Accounting, Management & Information Technology* 7 (4):183-211.

——— (1998) *Understanding Information Infrastructure* [cited 2004-08-10]. Available from http://heim.ifi.uio.no/~oleha/Publications/bok.pdf.

Hart P, Saunders C (1997) Power and Trust: Critical Factors in the Adoption and Use of Electronic Data Interchange. *Organization Science* 8 (1):23-43.

Hart PJ, Saunders CS (1998) Emerging Electronic Partnerships: Antecedents and Dimensions of EDI Use from the Supplier's Perspective. *Journal of Management Information Systems* 14 (4):87-112.

Hauschildt J (2004) *Innovationsmanagement*. 3. ed. München: Vahlen.

Hauser T, Löwer UM (2004) *Web Services – Die Standards*. Bonn: Galileo Computing.

He J, Wenzel P, Thomasma T (2001) High-Level Conceptual Model for B2B Integration, *Business Internet Consortium*.

Heflin J (2004) *OWL Web Ontology Language Use Cases and Requirements*. World Wide Web Consortium [cited 2004-09-13]. Available from http://www.w3.org/TR/webont-req/#onto-def.

Heinrich LJ (2001) *Wirtschaftsinformatik. Einführung und Grundlegung*. 2. ed. München, Wien.

Heinzl A (2001) Zum Aktivitätsniveau empirischer Forschung in der Wirtschaftsinformatik – Erklärungsansatz und Handlungsoptionen. In *Unternehmensführung und empirische Forschung, Festschrift von R. P. Wossidlo*, edited by Öhler H, Sigloch J. Hummeltal.

Hemenway D (1975) *Industrywide Voluntary Product Standards*. Cambridge, MA: Ballinger.

Hepp M (2003) *Güterklassifikation als semantisches Standardisierungsproblem*. Wiesbaden: Gabler.

Hess T (1996) *Entwurf betrieblicher Prozesse – Grundlagen – Bestehende Methoden – Neue Ansätze*. Wiesbaden: Deutscher Universitäts-Verlag.

———— (2002) *Netzwerkcontrolling – Instrumente und ihre Werkzeugunterstützung*. Wiesbaden.

Hess T, Picot A (2003) Wirtschaftsinformatik und ökonomische Theorie – Ausbau der wechselseitigen Bezüge. *Wirtschaftsinformatik* 45 (5):485-486.

Hill C, Scudder GD (2002) The Use of Electronic Data Interchange for Supply Chain Coordination in the Food Industry. *Journal of Operations Management* 20:375-387.

Hirschheim R, Klein HK, Lyytinen K (1995) *Information Systems Development and Data Modeling – Conceptual and Philosophical Foundations*. Cambridge, UK: Cambridge University Press.

Holmes TL, Srivastava R (1999) Effects of Relationalism and Readiness on EDI Collaboration and Outcomes. *Journal of Business & Industrial Marketing* 14 (5/6):390-402.

Holmström J, Truex D (2003) Social Theory in IS Research: Some Recommendations for Informed Adaptation of Social Theories in IS Research. Paper read at *Ninth Americas Conference on Information Systems*.

Hong IB (2002) A New Framework for Interorganizational Systems Based on the Linkage of Participants' Roles. *Information & Management* 39:261-270.

HP (2003) *Shipment Notification Management Milestone Program Proposal* [cited 2003-12-02]. Available from http://www.edifice.org/87plenary/Poing_HP_ShipmentNotification Management.ppt.

Huemer C (2001) Electronic Business XML. In *XML in der betrieblichen Praxis – Standards, Möglichkeiten, Praxisbeispiele*, edited by Turowski K, Fellner KJ. Heidelberg: dpunkt.

Humphreys PK, Lai MK, Sculli D (2001) An Inter-Organizational Information System for Supply Chain Management. *International Journal of Production Economics* 70 (3):245-255.

Iacovou CL, Benbasat I, Dexter AS (1995) Electronic Data Interchange and Small Organizations: Adoption and Impact of Technology. *MIS Quarterly* 19 (4):465-485.

Intel (2002) Intel Conducts $5 Billion in RosettaNet E-Business, Web Services – E-Business Technology Provides Productivity Gains and Faster Supply Chain Throughput: Intel.

Iskandar B, Kurokawa S, LeBlanc LLJ (2001) Business-to-business Electronic Commerce from First- and Second-tier Automotive Suppliers Perspectives: A Preliminary Analysis for Hypotheses Generation. *Technovation* 21:719-731.

ISO (2004) *The Magical Demystifying Tour of ISO 9000 and ISO 14000* [cited 2004-09-12]. Available from http://www.iso.org/iso/en/iso9000-14000/basics/general/basics_3.html.

ISO/IEC (1996) *ISO/IEC Guide 2: Standardization and Related Activities – General Vocabulary.* Geneva: IOS and IEC.

———— (1997) 14662: Information Technologies – Open-edi Reference Model, ISO/IEC JTC 1/SC 32, Geneva.

Iyer B, Freedman J, Gaynor M, Wyner G (2003) Web Services: Enabling Dynamic Business Networks. *Communications of the Association for Information Systems* 11:525-554.

Jacucci E, Grisot M, Aanestad M, Hanseth O (2003) Reflexive Standardization – Interpreting Side-Effects and Escalation in Standard-Making. Paper read at *Workshop on Standard Making: A Critical Research Frontier for Information Systems*, at Seattle, WA.

Jain H, Zhao H (2003) A Conceptual Model for Comparative Analysis of Standardization of Vertical Industry Languages. Paper read at *Workshop on Standard Making: A Critical Research Frontier for Information Systems*, at Seattle, WA.

Jakobs K (2002) A Proposal for an Alternative Standards Setting Process. *IEEE Communications Magazine* 40 (7):2-7.

Johnston H, Vitale M (1988) Creating Competitive Advantage with Interorganizational Information Systems. *MIS Quarterly* 12 (2):153-165.

Jones A, Ivezic N, Gruninger M (2001) Toward Self-Integrating Software Applications for Supply Chain Management. *Information Systems Frontiers* 3 (4):403-412.

Jones MR (2000) The Moving Finger: The Use of Social Theory in Wg8.2 Conference Papers, 1975-1999. In *Organizational and Social Perspectives on Information Technology*, edited by Baskerville R, Stage J, DeGross JI. Dordrecht: Kluwer.

Jönsson S (1991) Action Research. In *Information Systems Research: Contemporary Approaches and Emergent Traditions*, edited by Nissen H-E, Klein HK, Hirschheim R. Amsterdam: North-Holland.

Kanakamedala K, King J, Ramsdell G (2003) The Truth About XML. *McKinsey Quarterly* 2003 (3):9-12.

Katz M, Shapiro C (1985) Network Externalities, Competition, and Compatibility. *The American Economic Review* 75 (3):424-440.

Kaufman F (1966) Data Systems that Cross Company Boundaries. *Harvard Business Review* 44 (1):141-145.

Kerstetter J (2001) When Machines Chat. *Business Week*, 2001-07-23, 76-77.

Kerstetter J, Hamm S, Ante S, Greene J, Burrows P, Park A (2002) The Web at Your Service. *Business Week*, 2002-03-18, 12-16.

Kettenmann J (2004) Universal Business Language – EDIFACT für Arme. *iX - Magazin für professionelle Informationstechnik* 2004 (Special Issue 1):112-114.

Kieser A (2002) Konstruktivistische Ansätze. In *Organisationstheorien*, edited by Kieser A. Stuttgart: Kohlhammer.

Killian W, Picot A, Neuburger R, Niggl J, Scholtes K-L, Seiler W (1994) *Electronic Data Interchange aus ökonomischer und juristischer Sicht*. Baden-Baden: Nomos.

King JL, Lyytinen K (2003) *Workshop on Standard Making: A Critical Research Frontier for Information Systems*. Seattle: MISQ Special Issue.

Klein B, Crawford RG, Alchian AA (1978) Vertical Integration, Appropriable Rents, and the Competitive Contracting Process. *Journal of Law and Economics* 21 (2):297-326.

Klein HK, Myers MD (1999) A Set of Principles for Conducting and Evaluating Interpretive Field Studies in Information Systems. *MIS Quarterly* 23 (1):67-93.

Kleinaltenkamp M (1993) *Standardisierung und Marktprozess: Entwicklungen und Auswirkungen im CIM-Bereich.* Wiesbaden: Gabler.

Knorr-Cetina K (1998) Spielarten des Konstruktivismus. Einige Notizen und Anmerkungen. *Soziale Welt* 40 (1/2):86-96.

Kolar J, Speicys L, Aleksandrova I (2001) Transformation of EDIFACT message to XML DTD. Working Paper, Department of Computer Science, *Aalborg University,* Aalborg.

Kortmann J, Lessing H (2000) *Marktstudie: Standardsoftware für Supply Chain Management.* Edited by Dangelmaier W, Felser W, *ALB/HNI-Verlagsschriftenreihe.* Paderborn.

Kotinurmi P, Nurmilaakso J-M, Laesvuori H (2003) Standardization of XML-Based E-Business Frameworks. Paper read at *Workshop on Standard Making: A Critical Research Frontier for Information Systems,* at Seattle, WA.

Kotok A, Webber DRR (2002) *ebXML – The New Global Standard for Doing Business Over the Internet.* Boston: New Riders.

Kraege R (1997) *Controlling strategischer Unternehmungskooperationen.* München: Hampp.

Kreger H (2001) Web Services Conceptual Architecture (WSCA 1.0). White Paper, IBM Software Group.

Kuri J (2004) *SCO vs. Linux: Die unendliche Geschichte* [cited 2004-11-12]. Available from http://www.heise.de/ct/aktuell/meldung/44492.

Kuschke M, Wölfel L (2001) Zu Diensten: Web Services als E-Business-Evolution. *iX - Magazin für professionelle Informationstechnik* 2001 (11):149-155.

Lamb R (2003) Alternative Paths Toward a Social Actor Concept. Working Paper, College of Business Administration, *University of Hawaii,* Manoa.

LaMonica M (2004) *You Call That a Standard? – Robert Glushko Has a Problem With Standards* [cited.   Available   from   http://news.com.com/You+call+that+a+standard/2008-1013_3-5200672.html.

Lange U (2005) *Buttons and Wolves – Success Factors of Heterogeneous Relationships.* Karlsruhe: Happypress.

Langlois RN (2003) Cognitive Comparative Advantage and the Organization of Work: Lessons from Herbert Simon's Vision of the Future. *Journal of Economic Psychology* 24 (2):167-187.

Latour B (1987) *Science in Action: How to Follow Scientists and Engineers Through Society.* Milton Keynes: Open University Press.

———— (1991) Technology is Society Made Durable. In *Sociology of Monsters: Essays on Power, Technology and Domination,* edited by Law J. London: Routledge.

———— (1992) The Sociology of a Few Mundane Artifacts. In *Shaping Technology/Building Society,* edited by Bijker W, Law J. Cambridge, MA: MIT Press.

———— (1996) Social Theory and the Study of Computerized Work Sites. In *Information Technology and Changes in Organizational Work,* edited by Orlikowski WJ, Walsham G, Jones MR, DeGross JI. London: Chapman & Hall.

———— (1997) On Actor-Network Theory: A Few Clarifications. *Soziale Welt* 47 (4):369-381.

———— (1999a) On Recalling ANT. In *Actor Network Theory and After,* edited by Law J, Hassard J. Oxford: Blackwell.

———— (1999b) *Pandors's Hope: Essays on the Reality of Science Studies.* Cambridge, MA: Harvard University Press.

———— (2002a) *Die Hoffnung der Pandora.* Frankfurt a.M.: Suhrkamp.

———— (2002b) *Wir sind nie modern gewesen – Versuch einer symmetrischen Anthropologie.* Frankfurt a. M.: Fischer.

Latour B, Porter C (1996) *Aramis or the Love of Technology*. Cambridge: Harvard University Press.

Law J (1986) The Heterogeneity of Texts. In *Mapping the Dynamics of Science and Technology*, edited by Callon M, Law J, Rip A. Houndmills: The Macmillan Press.

——— (1992) *Notes on the Theory of the Actor-Network: Ordering, Strategy, and Heterogeneity*. Centre for Science Studies, Lancaster University [cited 2004-08-06]. Available from http://www.comp.lancs.ac.uk/sociology/papers/Law-Notes-on-ANT.pdf.

——— (1999) After ANT: Complexity, Naming and Topology. In *Actor Network Theory and After*, edited by Law J, Hassard J. Oxford: Blackwell.

——— (2004) *Actor Network Resource – An Annotated Bibliography* (2.13). Lancaster University, Department of Sociology and Centre for Science Studies, UK [cited 2004-07-16]. Available from http://www.comp.lancs.ac.uk/sociology/css/antres.htm.

Law J, Moser I (1999) Managing, Subjectivities and Desires. *Concepts and Transformation* 4 (3):249-279.

Lee AS (1989) A Scientific Methodology for MIS Case Studies. *MIS Quarterly* 14 (1):33-50.

——— (1991) Integrating Positivist and Interpretive Approaches to Organizational Research. *Organizational Science* 2 (4):342-365.

Lee H, Clark T, Tam K (1999) Research Report: Can EDI Benefit Adopters? *Information Systems Research* 10 (2):186-195.

Lee HL (2000) Creating Value through Supply Chain Integration. *Supply Chain Management Review* 4 (September-Oktober):30-36.

Lee HL, Padmanabhan V, Whang S (1997) The Bullwhip Effect in Supply Chains. *Sloan Management Review* 38 (3):93-102.

Levine S, White PE (1951) Exchange as a Conceptual Framework for the Study of Interorganizational Relations. *Administrative Science Quarterly* 5:583-601.

Lim B, Wen HJ (2003) Web Services: An Analysis of the Technology, Its Benefits, and Implementation Difficulties. *Information Systems Management* 20 (2):49-58.

Lim D, Palvia PC (2001) EDI in Strategic Supply Chain: Impact on Customer Service. *International Journal of Information Management* 21 (3):193-211.

Locke J (1690 [1994]) *An Essay Concerning Human Understanding*. Amherst, NY: Prometheus Books.

Löwer UM, Picot A (2002) Web Services - Technologie-Hype oder Strategie-Faktor? *Information Management & Consulting* 17 (3):20-25.

Lutz W-G (1997) *Das objektorientierte Paradigma – Struktur und organisationstheoretische Perspektiven einer Softwaretechnologie*. Wiesbaden: Gabler.

Mabert VA, Venkataramanan MA (1998) Special Research Focus on Supply Chain Linkages: Challenges for Design and Management in the 21st Century. *Decision Sciences* 29 (3):537-552.

Macaulay S (1963) Non-Contractual Relations in Business: A Preliminary Study. *American Sociological Review* 28 (February):55-67.

Mackay D, Rosier M (1996) Measuring Organizational Benefits of EDI diffusion – A Case of the Australian Automotive Industry. *International Journal of Physical Distribution & Logistics* 26 (10):60-78.

Magretta J (1998) The Power of Virtual Integration: An Interview with Dell Computer's Michael Dell. *Harvard Business Review* 76 (2):72-84.

Maingot M, Quon T (2001) A Survey of Electronic Data Interchange (EDI) in the Top Public Companies in Canada. *Information & Management* 39 (3):317-332.

Malone TW, Yates J, Benjamin RI (1987) Electronic Markets and Electronic Hierarchies. *Communications of the ACM* 30:484-497.

Markoff J, Schenker JL (2004) Microsoft Creates a Stir in Its Work With the UN. *New York Times*, February 23, 2004, Section C, p. 1.

Markus L, Steinfield CW, Wigand RT (2003) The Evolution of Vertical IS Standards: Electronic Interchange Standards in the US Home Mortgage Industry. Paper read at *Workshop on Standard Making: A Critical Research Frontier for Information Systems*, at Seattle, WA.

Markus ML, Robey D (1988) Information Technology and Organizational Change – Causal Structure in Theory and Research. *Management Science* 34 (5):583-598.

Martin EW (2000) Actor-Networks and Implementation: Examples From Conservation GIS in Ecuador. *International Journal of Geographical Information Science* 14 (8):715-738.

Massetti B, Zmud RW (1996) Measuring the Extent of EDI Usage in Complex Organizations: Strategies and Illustrative Examples. *MIS Quarterly* 20 (3):331-345.

Medina H (2000) *The Paradox of Rosettanet*. Line56 [cited 2004-10-06]. Available from http://www.line56.com/articles/default.asp?articleid=1257.

Merriam-Webster (2004) Merriam-Webster Collegiate Dictionary. Software Edition.

Mertens P (1966) *Die zwischenbetriebliche Kooperation und Integration bei der automatisierten Datenverarbeitung*. Meisenheim am Glan: Anton Hain.

Mertens P, Bodendorf F, König W, Picot A, Schumann M, Hess T (2004) *Grundzüge der Wirtschaftsinformatik*. 9 ed. Berlin: Springer.

Mertens P, Heinrich LJ (2002) Wirtschaftsinformatik - Ein interdisziplinäres Fach setzt sich durch. In *Entwicklung der Betriebswirtschaftslehre - 100 Jahre Fachdisziplin - zugleich eine Verlagsgeschichte*, edited by Gaugler E, Köhler R. Stuttgart: Schäffer-Poeschel.

Miles MB, Huberman AM (1984) *Qualitative Data Analysis: A Sourcebook of New Methods*. Newbury Park: Sage Publications.

Milling P (1999) Systemtheoretische und kybernetische Empfehlungen für das Supply Chain Management. In *Systemdenken und Virtualisierung*, edited by Scholz C. Berlin: Duncker & Humboldt.

Mingers J (2001) Combining IS Research Methods: Towards a Pluralist Methodology. *Information Systems Research* 12 (3):240-259.

Mintert S (2004) Man sprich XML. *iX - Magazin für professionelle Informationstechnik* Special 1/04:6-10.

Mohr LB (1982) *Explaining Organizational Behavior – The Limits and Possibilities of Theory and Research*. San Francisco: Jossey-Bass.

Monteiro E, Hanseth O (1996) Social Shaping of Information Infrastructure: On Being Specific About the Technology. In *Information Technology and Changes in Organizational Work*, edited by Orlikowski WJ, Walsham G, Jones MR, DeGross JI. London: Chapman & Hall.

Morgan G, Smircich L (1980) The Case for Qualitative Research. *Academy of Management Review* 5 (4):491-500.

Morris CW (1938) *Foundations of the Theory of Signs (International Encyclopedia of Unified Science)*. Chicago: The University of Chicago Press.

Mowshowitz A (1994) Virtual Organization: A Vision of Management in the Information Age. *The Information Society* 10 (4):267-288.

Mozart WA (2001) *The Masterworks Vol. 1-40*. Brilliant Classics.

Mukhopadhyay T, Kekre S, Kalathur S (1995) Business Value of Information Technology – A Study of Electronic Data Interchange. *MIS Quarterly* 19 (2):137-156.

Müller M, Seuring S, Goldbach M (2003) Supply Chain Management – Neues Konzept oder Modetrend? *Die Betriebswirtschaft* 63 (4):419-439.

Mumford E, Hirschheim RA, Fitzgerald G, Wood-Harper T, eds (1985) *Research Methods in Information Systems*. Amsterdam: North-Holland.

Murphy PR, Daley JM (1996) International Freight Forwarder Perspectives on Electronic Data Interchange and Information Management Issues. *Journal of Business Logistics* 17 (1):63-84.

Myers MD (1997) Qualitative Research in Information Systems. *MIS Quarterly* 21 (2):241-242.

Nakayama M (2000) E-Commerce and Firm Bargaining Power Shift in Grocery Marketing Channels: A Case of Wholesalers' Structured Document Exchanges. *Journal of Information Technology* 15:195-210.

Naujok K-D (2000) *The Road to ebXML* [Working Paper] [cited 2004-10-27]. Available from http://lists.ebxml.org/archives/ebxml-dev/200311/doc00001.doc.

――― (2004a) *Standards Talk (Personal Weblog)* [cited 2004-10-19]. Available from http://home.comcast.net/~knaujok/StandardsTalk/.

――― (2004b) *Time to Set the Record Straight! (For the Last Time I Hope)* [cited 2004-10-20]. Available from http://home.comcast.net/~knaujok/StandardsTalk/C1231773887/E721150982/index.html.

Nault BR, Dexter AS, Wolfe R (1998) Electronic Communication Innovations: Overcoming Adoption Resistance. *Wirtschaftsinformatik* 40 (2):114-121.

Nelson KM, Nelson JH (2003) The Need for a Strategic Ontology. Paper read at *Workshop on Standard Making: A Critical Research Frontier for Information Systems*, at Seattle, WA.

Nelson ML (2002) Co-Adoption of XML-Based Interorganizational Systems. Paper read at *Eighth Americas Conference on Information Systems*, at Dallas, TX.

Nelson ML, Shaw MJ (2003) The Adoption and Diffusion of Interorganizational System Standards and Process Innovations. Paper read at *Workshop on Standard Making: A Critical Research Frontier for Information Systems*, December 12-14, at Seattle, WA.

Nelson RR, Winter SG (1977) In Search of Useful Theory of Innovation. *Research Policy* 6:36-76.

Neo BS (1994) Managing New Information Technologies: Lessons from Singapore's Experience with EDI. *Information & Management* 26 (6):317-326.

Neuburger R (1994) *Electronic Data Interchange - Einsatzmöglichkeiten und ökonomische Auswirkungen*. Wiesbaden: Gabler.

Neumeier F, Löwer UM, Picot A (2003) Das Semantic Web – Neue Perspektiven für die verteilte Wertschöpfung? *Information Management & Consulting* 18 (3):77-82.

Nickerson JV, zur Muehlen M (2003) Defending the Spirit of the Web: Conflicts in the Internet Standards Process. Paper read at *Workshop on Standard Making: A Critical Research Frontier for Information Systems*, December 12-14, at Seattle, WA.

Niggl J (1994) *Die Entstehung von Electronic Data Interchange Standards*. Wiesbaden: Gabler.

Nissen HE, Klein HK, Hirschheim RA, eds (1991) *Information Systems Research: Contemporary Approaches and Emergent Traditions*. Amsterdam: North-Holland.

Norberg RW, Banavige JM (1999) Electronics Manufacturing Supply Chain. Minneapolis, MN: U.S. Bancorp Piper Jaffray.

North DC (1990) *Institutions, Institutional Change and Economic Performance*. Cambridge, UK: Cambridge University Press.

OASIS (2001) *OASIS Forms ebXML Technical Committees*. Press Release 2001-06-21 [cited 2004-10-13]. Available from http://www.oasis-open.org/news/oasis_news_06_21_01.php.

――― (2002) *ebXML Messaging Service Specification Approved As OASIS Standard*. Press Release 2002-09-05 [cited 2004-10-14]. Available from http://www.oasis-open.org/news/oasis_news_09_05_02.php.

——— (2003a) *ebXML Adoption Update* [cited 2004-10-21]. Available from http://www.ebxml.org/documents/ebxml_adopt_update_122203.pdf.

——— (2003b) *ebXML Business Process Specification Advances Within OASIS*. Press Release 2003-10-20 [cited 2004-10-24]. Available from http://www.oasis-open.org/news/oasis_news_10_20_03.php.

——— (2003c) OASIS Open Technical Committee Process.

——— (2004a) *Cover Pages: XML Applications and Initiatives* [cited 2004-11-20]. Available from http://xml.coverpages.org/xmlApplications.html.

——— (2004b) *ISO Approves ebXML OASIS Standards*. Press Release 2004-03-29 [cited 2004-10-25]. Available from http://www.oasis-open.org/news/oasis_news_03_29_04.php.

——— (2004c) *OASIS Board of Directors* [cited 2004-10-12]. Available from http://www.oasis-open.org/who/bod.php.

——— (2004d) *OASIS Electronic Business Service Oriented Architecture TC Charter* [cited 2004-10-24]. Available from http://www.oasis-open.org/committees/ebsoa/charter.php.

——— (2004e) *OASIS Homepage – Advancing E-Business Standards Since 1993* [cited 2003-2004]. Available from http://www.oasis-open.org/home/index.php.

——— (2004f) *OASIS Members Marketplace Representation* [cited 2004-10-12]. Available from http://www.oasis-open.org/about/marketplace_rep.php.

——— (2004g) *OASIS Technical Advisory Board* [cited 2004-10-12]. Available from http://www.oasis-open.org/who/tab.php.

——— (2004h) *OASIS Technical Committee Guidelines*. OASIS [cited 2004-10-22]. Available from http://www.oasis-open.org/committees/guidelines.php.

——— (2004i) Universal Business Language 1.0.

Olaisen JL (1991) Pluralism or Positivistics Trivialism: Important Trends in Contemporary Philosophy of Science. In *Information Systems Research: Contemporary Approaches and Emergent Traditions*, edited by Nissen H-E, Klein HK, Hirschheim R. Amsterdam: North-Holland.

Olla P, Atkinson C, Gandceha R (2003) Wireless Systems Development Methodologies: An Analysis of Practice Using Actor Network Theory. *Journal of Computer Information Systems* 2003 (Fall):102-111.

Orlikowski WJ, Baroudi JJ (1991) Studying Information Technology in Organizations: Research Approaches and Assumptions. *Information Systems Research* 2 (1):1-28.

Orlikowski WJ, Robey D (1991) Information Technology and the Structuring of Organizations. *Information Systems Research* 2:143-169.

Österle H (1995) *Business in the Information Age – Heading for New Processes*. Berlin: Springer.

Otto A (2002) *Management und Controlling von Supply Chains – Ein Modell auf Basis der Netzwerktheorie*: Deutscher Universitäts-Verlag.

Paolucci M, Kawamuar T, Payne TR, Sycara K (2002) Importing the Semantic Web in UDDI. In *Web Services, E-Business, and the Semantic Web*, edited by Bussler C, Hull R, McIlraith S, Orlowska ME, Pernici B, Yang J. Berlin: Springer.

Patankar A (2003) Web Services Enabled Architecture for Interorganizational Business Process Management. Paper read at *Ninth Americas Conference on Information Systems*, at Tampas, FL.

Paulen DJ, Yoong P (2001) Relationship Building and the Use of ICT in Boundary-Crossing Virtual Teams: A Facilitator's Perspective. *Journal of Information Technology* 16:205–220.

Peffers K, Dos Santos BL, Thurner PF (1998) Motivation, Implementation, and Impact of Electronic Data Interchange Among US and German Firms. *Information Services & Use* 18 (3):177-190.

Peleg B, Rajwat P (2002) Measuring Benefits of RosettaNet Standards. Stanford: Stanford University, Graduate School of Business.

Pels D (1995) Have We Never Been Modern? Towards a Demontage of Latour's Modern Constitution. *History of Human Sciences* 8 (3):129-141.

Perens B (2004) *Open Standards Principles and Practice* [cited 2004-10-11]. Available from http://perens.com/OpenStandards/Definition.html.

Pfeiffer HKC (1992) *The Diffusion of Electronics Data Interchange*. New York: Springer.

Philip G, Pedersen P (1997) Inter-Organisational Information Systems: Are Organisations in Ireland Deriving Strategic Benefits from EDI? *International Journal of Information Management* 17 (5):337-357.

Picot A (2001) Die Bedeutung von Standards in der Internet-Ökonomie. In *Die Potentiale der Internet-Ökonomie*, edited by Schmidt H. Frankfurt am Main.

Picot A, Breidler J, eds (2002) *Web Services - Bausteine für das e-Business*. Heidelberg: Hüthig.

Picot A, Dietl H, Franck E (2002) *Organisation - Eine ökonomische Perspektive*. 3 ed. Stuttgart: Schäffer-Poeschel.

Picot A, Fiedler M (2002) Institutionen und Wandel. *Die Betriebswirtschaft* 62 (3):240-275.

Picot A, Freudenberg H (1997) Theorie der Unternehmung. In *Wirtschaftslexikon*. Wiesbaden: Gabler.

Picot A, Hess T (2005) Geschäftsprozessmanagement im Echtzeitunternehmen. In *Real-Time Enterprise in der Praxis. Fakten und Ausblick*, edited by Kuhlin B, Thielmann H. Berlin: Springer.

Picot A, Reichwald R, Wigand RT (2003) *Die grenzenlose Unternehmung - Information, Organisation und Management*. 5. ed. Wiesbaden: Gabler.

Picot A, Ripperger T, Wolff B (1996) The Fading Boundaries of the Firm: The Role of Information and Communication Technology. *Journal of Institutional and Theoretical Economics* 152:65-79.

Piller F (2000) *Mass Customization – Ein wettbewerbsstrategisches Konzept im Informationszeitalter*. Wiesbaden: Gabler.

Pinch TJ, Bijker WE (1987) The Social Construction of Facts and Artifacts: Or How the Sociology of Science and the Sociology of Technology Might Benefit Each Other. In *The Social Construction of Technological Systems*, edited by Bijker WE, Hughes TP, Pinch TJ. Cambridge, MA: MIT Press.

Porter ME (2001) Strategy and the Internet. *Harvard Business Review* 79 (3):63-78.

Pouloudi A, Gandecha R, Papazafeiropoulou A, Atkinson C (2004) How Stakeholder Analysis Can Assist Actor-Network Theory to Understand Actors – A Case Study of the Integrated Care Record Service (ICRS) in the UK National Health Service. In *ELTRUN Working Paper Series*. Athens: Athens University of Economics and Business.

Prahalad CK, Hamel G (1990) The Core Competence of the Corporation. *Harvard Business Review* 68 (3):79-91.

Premkumar G, Ramamurthy K (1995) The Role of Interorganizational and Organizational Factors on the Decision Mode for Adoption of Interorganizational Systems. *Decision Sciences* 26 (3):303-336.

Premkumar G, Ramamurthy K, Nilakanta S (1994) Implementation of Electronic Data Interchange: An Innovation Diffusion Perspective. *Journal of Management Information Systems* 11 (2):157-186.

Purao S, Truex D, Cao L (2003) Now the Twain Shall Meet: Combining Social Sciences and Software Engineering to Support Development of Emergent Systems. Paper read at *Ninth Americas Conference on Information Systems*.

Quantz J (2002) *Enterprise Integration Act: Geld für (XML-) Standards* [cited 2004-10-12]. Available from http://www.berlecon.de/presse/spotlights.php?we_objectID=99.

Ramamurthy K, Premkumar G, Crum MR (1999) Organizational and Interorganizational Determinants of EDI Diffusion and Organizational Performance: A Causal Model. *Journal of Organizational Computing and Electronic Commerce* 9 (4):253-285.

Ratnasingam P, Pavlou PA (2002) The Role of Web Services in Business to Business Electronic Commerce. Paper read at *Eighth Americas Conference on Information Systems*.

Rawlins MC (2002) *Will UN/CEFACT torpedo ebXML?* [cited 2004-10-25]. Available from http://www.rawlinsecconsulting.com/contrarian/torpedo_ebxml.html.

Reimers K (1995) *Normungsprozesse – Eine transaktionskostentheoretische Analyse*. Wiesbaden: Gabler.

—— (2001) Standardizing the New E-Business Platform: Learning from EDI Experience. *Electronic Markets* 11 (4):231-237.

Richter R, Furubotn EG (2003) *Neue Institutionenökonomik*. Tübingen: Mohr Siebeck.

Riggins FJ, Mukhopadhyay T (1994) Interdependent Benefits from Interorganizational Systems: Opportunities for Business Partner Reengineering. *Journal of Management Information Systems* 11 (2):37-58.

Robert III HM, Evans WJ, Honemann DH, Balch TJ (2000) *Robert's Rules of Order (Newly Revised)*. 10. ed. Cambridge, MA: Perseus.

Robey D (1996) Research Commentary: Diversity in Information Systems Research: Threat, Promise, and Responsibility. *Information Systems Research* 7 (4):400-409.

Robson C (2003) *General RosettaNet Update* [cited 2003-12-02]. Available from http://www.edifice.org/public/Poing-RN-EuropeOctBoards2003.ppt.

Robson C, Stern-Peltz HF, Tearnen P (2003) RosettaNet Architecture Today and Tomorrow. Paper read at *RosettaNet Architecture Seminar*, at Munich.

Rolf A (1998) *Grundlagen der Organisations- und Wirtschaftsinformatik*. Berlin: Springer.

RosettaNet (1998a) *RosettaNet Announces Early Completion of First Projects for Electronic Commerce Rules*. Press Release 1998-06-14 [cited 2004-06-08]. Available from http://www.rosettanet.org/rosettanetpressreleases.

—— (1998b) *RosettaNet Announces Global Executive-Level Industry Support for Common IT Supply Chain Business Interfaces*. Press Release 1998-06-07 [cited 2004-06-08]. Available from?

—— (1999a) *IT Industry Kicks-Off Implementation Phase Of RosettaNet Initiative To Align Supply Chain*. Press Release 1999-06-09 [cited 2004-06-08]. Available from http://www.rosettanet.org/rosettanetpressreleases.

—— (1999b) *RosettaNet Adopts D&B D-U-N-S Numbering System and UN/SPSC as E-Commerce Standards*. Press Release 1999-10-03 [cited 2004-06-08]. Available from http://www.rosettanet.org/rosettanetpressreleases.

—— (1999c) *RosettaNet Initiative For Developing Collaborative Supply Chain Process Interface Standards Embraces Electronic Components Industry*. Press Release 1999-08-30 [cited 2004-06-08]. Available from http://www.rosettanet.org/rosettanetpressreleases.

—— (1999d) *RosettaNet Opens European Office, Names Director Of European Partner Relations To Extend Global Implementation Of Supply Chain Standards*. Press Release 1999-12-06 [cited 2004-06-08]. Available from http://www.rosettanet.org/rosettanetpressreleases.

—— (2000a) *Formation Of RosettaNet Japan Accelerates Global Deployment Of E-Commerce Business Process Standards*. Press Release 2000-03-31 [cited 2004-06-08]. Available from http://www.rosettanet.org/rosettanetpressreleases.

——— (2000b) *RosettaNet Launches Operations In Singapore And Taiwan To Implement Global E-Business Standards*. Press Release 2000-10-04 [cited 2004-06-08]. Available from http://www.rosettanet.org/rosettanetpressreleases.

——— (2001a) *RosettaNet Consortium Extends Global E-Business Outlook During Visit to China*. Press Release 2001-03-07 [cited 2004-06-08]. Available from http://www.rosettanet.org/rosettanetpressreleases.

——— (2001b) *RosettaNet Launches Operations in Korea*. Press Release 2001-02-08 [cited 2004-06-08]. Available from http://www.rosettanet.org/rosettanetpressreleases.

——— (2001c) *RosettaNet Launches Solution Provider Board To Champion Rapid E-Business Standards Adoption*. Press Release 2001-06-04 [cited 2004-06-08]. Available from http://www.rosettanet.org/rosettanetpressreleases.

——— (2001d) Trading Partner Agreement "Supporting Documentation", *RosettaNet*.

——— (2002a) RosettaNet Intellectual Property Policy.

——— (2002b) *RosettaNet Merges With the Uniform Code Council*. Press Release 2002-08-05 [cited 2004-06-08]. Available from http://www.rosettanet.org/rosettanetpressreleases.

——— (2003a) Annual Summary Report 2002/2003: RosettaNet.

——— (2003b) *BT, Cisco, Deutsche Telekom, Ericsson, Motorola, Nokia and Siemens form RosettaNet Telecommunications Industry Council*. Press Release 2003-06-10 [cited 2004-06-08]. Available from http://www.rosettanet.org/rosettanetpressreleases.

——— (2003c) Intel and Shinko Use RosettaNet Standards to Build Forecast-to-Cash Procurement Process. RosettaNet Case Study.

——— (2003d) *Introduction – RosettaNet Standards Methodology* [cited 2004-10-11]. Available from http://www.rosettanet.org/methodology.

——— (2003e) *Oasis and RosettaNet Form Standards Development-to-Implementation Alliance*. Press Release 2003-06-03 [cited 2004-06-08]. Available from http://www.rosettanet.org/rosettanetpressreleases.

——— (2003f) *Program Organization – RosettaNet Standards Methodology* [cited 2004-10-11]. Available from http://www.rosettanet.org/rsm.

——— (2003g) *RosettaNet – E-Business Standards for the Global Supply Chain*. RosettaNet [cited 2003-2004]. Available from http://www.rosettanet.org/.

——— (2003h) *RosettaNet Announces New Regional Director to Head Consortium Activities in Malaysia*. Press Release 2003-01-29 [cited 2004-06-08]. Available from http://www.rosettanet.org/rosettanetpressreleases.

——— (2003i) *RosettaNet Enters Into Strategic Alliance With China Government*. Press Release 2003-09-17 [cited 2004-06-08]. Available from http://www.rosettanet.org/rosettanetpressreleases.

——— (2003j) *RosettaNet Standards Organization Extends Global Presence With Launch of Consortium's Newest Asia Affiliate*. Press Release 2003-03-12 [cited 2004-06-08]. Available from http://www.rosettanet.org/rosettanetpressreleases.

——— (2004a) Annual Summary Report 2003/2004. Santa Ana, CA: RosettaNet.

——— (2004b) Introduction to Requirements Gathering.

——— (2004c) *Join A Program* [cited 2004-06-12]. Available from http://www.rosettanet.org/joinaprogram.

——— (2004d) PIP3A4: Request Purchase Order V02.03. PIP® Specification.

——— (2004e) RosettaNet 2004 Council Membership Application Form.

——— (2004f) *RosettaNet – E-Business Standards for the Global Supply Chain*. RosettaNet [cited 2003-2004]. Available from http://www.rosettanet.org/.

———— (2004g) *RosettaNet Aligns With EAN Australia to Promote E-Business Standardization For Advancement of Supply Chain Optimization*. Press Release 2004-03-30 [cited 2004-06-08]. Available from http://www.rosettanet.org/rosettanetpressreleases.

———— (2004h) *RosettaNet Consortium Taps Industry Influence and Expertise With Newly Created Architecture Advisory Committee*. Press Release 2004-08-12 [cited 2004-06-08]. Available from http://www.rosettanet.org/rosettanetpressreleases.

———— (2004i) *RosettaNet E-Business Standards Organization Expands Asia Operations With New Penang-Based Engineering Center*. Press Release 2004-02-16 [cited 2004-06-08]. Available from http://www.rosettanet.org/rosettanetpressreleases.

———— (2004j) *RosettaNet Launches Architecture Center of Excellence in Singapore*. Press Release 2004-09-17 [cited 2004-06-08]. Available from http://www.rosettanet.org/rosettanetpressreleases.

———— (2004k) *RosettaNet Launches Global Logistics Council To Promote Collaboration And Leadership Across Multiple Industries*. Press Release 2004-03-30 [cited 2004-06-08]. Available from http://www.rosettanet.org/rosettanetpressreleases.

———— (2004l) *Standards Convergence* [cited 2004-06-12]. Available from http://www.rosettanet.org/standardsconvergence.

———— (2004m) *Trading Partner Directory* [cited 2004-10-03]. Available from http://www.rosettanet.org/RosettaNet/Rooms/Search/TPDSearch.

Rößl D (1993) *Gestaltung komplexer Austauschbeziehungen – Analyse zwischenbetrieblicher Kooperationen*. Wiesbaden: Gabler.

Rowland W (1999) *Spirit of the Web: The Age of Information from Telegraph to Internet*. Toronto: Key Porter Books.

Saunders CS, Clark S (1992) EDI Adoption and Implementation: A Focus on Interorganizational Linkages. *Information Resources Management Journal* 5 (1):9-19.

Schary PB, Skjøtt-Larsen (2001) *Managing the Global Supply Chain*. 2 ed. Copenhagen: Copenhagen Business School Press.

Scheuble S (1998) *Wissen und Wissenssurrogate – Eine Theorie der Unternehmung*. Wiesbaden: Deutscher UniversitätsVerlag.

Schmidt H (2002) Web-Services: Sun und Microsoft konkurrieren um den neuen Megatrend im Internet. *Frankfurter Allgemeine Zeitung*, 2002-02-14, 23.

Schüler H-P (2002) *IBM sabotiert UNO-geförderten freien Standard* [cited 2004-10-14]. Available from http://www.heise.de/newsticker/result.xhtml?url=/newsticker/meldung/26682.

Schulz H (2002) Weltweites Werkeln - Das bringen Web Services für Anwender und Entwickler. *c't - magazin für computertechnik* 2002 (6):236-241.

Schütte R, Siedentopf J, Zelewski S, eds (1999) *Wirtschaftsinformatik und Wissenschaftstheorie – Grundpositionen und Theoriekerne*. Essen: Institut für Produktion und Industrielles Informationsmanagement.

Scott Morton MS, ed. (1991) *The Corporation of the 1990s: Information Technology and Organizational Transformation*. New York, NY: Oxford University Press.

Selen W, Soliman F (2002) Operations in Today's Demand Chain Management Framework. *Journal of Operations Management* 20 (6):667-673.

Selz D (1999) Value Webs – Emerging Forms of Fluid and Flexible Organizations, Institute for Media and Communications Management, *University of St. Gallen*, St. Gallen.

Sengupta A (2003) RosettaNet Software Compliance and Interoperability for the High Technology Industry. White Paper, *RosettaNet*.

Shapiro C, Varian HR (1999) *Information Rules: A Strategic Guide to the Network Economy*. Boston: Harvard Business School Press.

Shepherd WG (1990) *The Economics of Industrial Organization*. London: Prentice Hall.

Shy O (2001) *The Economics of Network Industries*. Cambridge, UK: Cambridge University Press.

Sidorova A, Sarker S (2000) Unearthing Some Causes of BPR Failure: An Actor-Network Theory Perspective. Paper read at *Sixth Americas Conference on Information Systems*, at Long Beach, CA.

Simon HA (1965) *The Shape of Automation for Men and Management*. New York: Harper.

——— (1978) Rationality as Process and as Product of Thought. *American Economic Review* 68 (2):1-16.

Singh R, Iyer L, Salam AF (2003) Web Services for Knowledge Management in E-Marketplaces. Paper read at *Ninth Americas Conference on Information Systems*, at Tampa, FL.

Singh R, Iyer LS, Salam AF (2002) Agents and Web Services in an E-Supply Chain. Paper read at *Eighth Americas Conference on Information Systems*, at Dallas, TX.

Sivan YY (2000) Knowledge Age Standards: A Brief Introduction to Their Dimensions. In *Information Technology Standards and Standardization: A Global Perspective*, edited by Jakobs K. Hershey, PA: Idea Group.

Sliwa C (2004) EDI: Alive and Well After All These Years. *Computerworld* 38 (24):1-2.

Smith A (1776) *An Inquiry into the Nature and Causes of the Wealth of Nations*. London: Strahan and Cadell.

Smith B (2003) Ontology: Philosophical and Computational. Working Paper, *The State University of New York*, New York.

Smith H, Fingar P (2002) *Business Process Management – The Third Wave*. Tampa, FL: Meghan-Kiffer Press.

Soh C, Markus L (1995) How IT Creates Business Value: A Process Theory Synthesis. Paper read at *International Conference on Information Systems*.

Son J-Y, Narasimhan S, Riggins FJ (1999) Factors Affecting the Extent of Electronic Cooperation Between Firms: Economic and Sociological Perspectives. Paper read at *International Conference on Information Systems*, at Charlotte, NC.

Spicker A (2004) Entstehung, Entwicklung und Verbreitung von ebXML. Diploma Thesis, Institute for Information, Organization, and Management, *Ludwig-Maximilians-University of Munich*, Munich.

Sriram RS, Arunachalam V, Ivancevich DM (2000) EDI Adoption and Implementation: An Examination of Perceived Operational and Strategic Benefits, and Controls. *Journal of Information Systems* 14 (1):37-52.

Stalder F (1997) Actor-Network-Theory and Communication Networks: Toward Convergence. Working Paper, Faculty of Information Studies, *University of Toronto*, Toronto.

——— (2001) Making Money: Notes on the Technology as Environment. Dissertation Thesis, Faculty of Information Studies, *University of Toronto*, Toronto.

Stamper R (1991) The Semiotic Framework for Information Systems Research. In *Information Systems Research: Contemporary Approaches and Emergent Traditions*, edited by Nissen H-E, Klein HK, Hirschheim R. Amsterdam: North-Holland.

Starbuck WH (1976) Organizations and their Environment. In *Handbook of Industrial and Organizational Psychology*, edited by Dunnette MD. Chicago: Rand McNally.

Stegwee RA, Rukanova BD (2003) Identification of Different Types of Standards for Domain-Specific Interoperability. Paper read at *Workshop on Standard Making: A Critical Research Frontier for Information Systems*, at Seattle, WA.

Steiner F (2005) *Formation and Early Growth of Business Webs – Modular Product Systems in Network Markets.* Heidelberg: Springer.

Stiemerling O (2002) Web-Services als Basis für evolvierbare Softwaresysteme. *Wirtschaftsinformatik* 44 (5):435–445.

Stix G (2002) *Deep-Sixing the Submarine Patent.* Scientific American [cited 2004-10-12]. Available from http://www.sciam.com/article.cfm?articleID=000C4F59-8093-1D2B-97CA809EC588EEDF.

Sullivan L (2003) RosettaNet Angles for Smaller Catches. *Electronic Buyer News* 2003 (December 15):26.

Supply Chain Council (2004) *The Supply-Chain Council* [cited 2004-09-12]. Available from http://www.supply-chain.org/public/aboutus.asp.

Swaminathan JM, Smith SF, Sadeh NM (1998) Modeling supply chain dynamics: A multiagent approach. *Decision Sciences* 29 (3):607-632.

Tanenbaum AS (2003) *Computernetzwerke.* 4. ed. München: Pearson Studium.

Tatnall A, Gilding A (1999) Actor-Network Theory and Information Systems Research. Paper read at *10th Australasian Conference on Information Systems*, at Wellington.

Techniques and Methodologies Group (2003) *Business Collaboration Framework Tour '03* [cited 2003-09-02]. Available from http://webster.disa.org/cefact-groups/tmg/bcf-tour/.

Teo HH, Tan BCY, Wei KK (1997) Organizational Transformation Using Electronic Data Interchange: The Case of TradeNet in Singapore. *Journal of Management Information Systems* 13 (4):139-166.

Teo HH, Wei KK, Benbasat I (2003) Predicting Intention to Adopt Interorganizational Linkages: An Institutional Perspective. *MIS Quarterly* 27 (1):19-49.

Thomas J (1999) Chain Reaction - Logistics Management and Distribution Report: Cahners Business Information.

Thompson GF (2003) *Between Hierarchies and Markets - The Logic and Limits of Network Forms of Organization.* Oxford: Oxford University Press.

Threlkel MS, Kavan CB (1999) From Traditional EDI to Internet-Based EDI: Managerial Considerations. *Journal of Information Technology* 14: 347-360.

Timmermans S, Berg M (1997) Standardization in Action: Achieving Local Universality through Medical Protocols. *Social Studies of Science* 27 (2):273-305.

Treacy M, Wiersma F (1993) Customer Intimacy and other Value Disciplines. *Harvard Business Review* 71 (1):84-93.

Truman GE (2000) Integration in Electronic Exchange Environments. *Journal of Management Information Systems* 17 (1):209-244.

Turner JA, Bikson TK, Lyytinen K, Mathiassen L, Orlikowski WJ (1991) Relevance Versus Rigor in Information Systems Research: An Issue of Quality. In *Information Systems Research: Contemporary Approaches and Emergent Traditions,* edited by Nissen H-E, Klein HK, Hirschheim R. Amsterdam: North-Holland.

Underwood J (1998) Not Another Methodology – What ANT Tells Us About Systems Development. Paper read at *International Conference on Information Systems Methodologies*, at Salford, UK.

Vakharia AJ (2002) E-Business and Supply Chain Management. *Decision Sciences* 33 (4):495-504.

van der Aalst W, Kumar A (2003) XML-Based Schema Definition for Support of Interorganizational Workflow. *Information Systems Research* 14 (1):23-46.

Veryard R (2001) *The Component-Based Business: Plug and Play.* London: Springer.

Virili F (2003) Design, Sense-Making and Negotiation Activities in the "Web Services" Standardization Process. Paper read at *Workshop on Standard Making: A Critical Research Frontier for Information Systems*, at Seattle, WA.

Vitalari NP (1985) The Need for Longitudinal Designs in the Study of Computing Environment. In *Research Methods in Information Systems*, edited by Mumford E, Hirschheim RA, Fitzgerald G, Wood-Harper T. Amsterdam: North-Holland.

Vlaar PWL (2003) Clarifying the Relation between Formalization and Performance in Interorganizational Relationships: Typologies and Antecedents. Paper read at *Academy of Management Conference*, at Seattle.

Vollmer H (1997) Die Frage nach den Akteuren. *Sociologica Internationalis* 13 (2):168-193.

Walker R (2004) *Some Current Issues Facing UN/CEFACT* [cited 2004-10-12]. Available from http://estrategy.gov/us-tag/documents/CEFACT%20Issues%20-%20Walker0204.doc.

Walker R, Gannon P (2001) *Memorandum of Understanding Between the United Nations Centre for Trade Facilitation and Electronic Business (UN/CEFACT) and the Organisation for the Advancement of Structured Information Standards (OASIS)* [cited 2004-10-13]. Available from http://www.ebxml.org/mou.pdf.

Walsham G (1995) The Emergence of Interpretivism in IS Research. *Information Systems Research* 6 (4):376-394.

—— (1997) Actor-Network Theory and IS Research: Current Status and Future Prospects. In *Information Systems and Qualitative Research*, edited by Lee AS, Liebenau J, DeGross JI. London: Chapman and Hall.

Walsham G, Sahay S (1999) GIS for District-Level Administration in India: Problems and Opportunities. *MIS Quarterly* 23 (1):39-66.

Walton LW, Miller LG (1995) Moving Towards LIS Theory Development: A Framework of Technology Adoption within Channels. *Journal of Business Logistics* 16 (2):117-135.

Web Services lösen Investitionsschub aus. (2002) *Frankfurter Allgemeine Zeitung*, 2002-06-20, 22.

Weick KE (1976) Educational Organizations as Loosely Coupled Systems. *Administrative Science Quarterly* 21 (1):1-19.

Weik E (1996) Postmoderne Ansätze in der Organisationstheorie. *Die Betriebswirtschaft* 56 (3):379-397.

Weitzel T (2004) *Economics of Standards in Information Networks*. New York: Springer Physica.

Weitzel T, Harder T, Buxmann P (2001) *Electronic Business und EDI mit XML*. Heidelberg: dpunkt.

West J (2003) The Role of Standards in the Creation and Use of Information Systems. Paper read at *Workshop on Standard Making: A Critical Research Frontier for Information Systems*, at Seattle, WA.

Wigand RT (1994) Electronic Data Interchange in the United States of America: Selected Issues and Trends. In *Electronic Data Interchange aus ökonomischer und juristischer Sicht*, edited by Killian W, Picot A, Neuburger R, Niggl J, Scholtes K-L, Seiler W. Baden-Baden: Nomos.

Wigand RT, Picot A, Reichwald R (1997) *Information, Organization and Management – Expanding Markets and Corporate Boundaries*. 1 ed. Chichester: Wiley.

Williams LR (1994) Understanding Distribution Channels: An Interorganizational Study of EDI Adopters. *Journal of Business Logistics* 15 (2):173-203.

Williams LR, Magee GD, Suzuki Y (1998) A Multidimensional View of EDI: Testing the Value of EDI Participation to Firms. *Journal of Business Logistics* 19 (2):73-87.

Williamson OE (1975) *Markets and Hierarchies: Analysis and Antitrust Implications*. New York: The Free Press.

——— (1985) *The Economic Institutions of Capitalism*. New York: The Free Press.

——— (1991) Comparative Economic Organization: The Analysis of Discrete Structural Alternatives. *Administrative Science Quarterly* 36 (June 1991):269-296.

Winner L (1993) Upon Opening the Black Box and Finding it Empty: Social Constructivism and the Philosophy of Technology. *Science, Technology & Human Values* 1993 (3):362-378.

Winograd T, Flores F (1987) *Understanding Computers and Cognition: A New Foundation for Design*. New York: Addison-Wesley.

World Wide Web Consortium (2003) *Web Services Glossary* [cited 2003-07-13]. Available from http://www.w3.org/TR/ws-gloss/#general.

——— (2004) *Semantic Web* [cited 2004-09-12]. Available from http://www.w3.org/2001/sw/.

Wurche S (1994) *Strategische Kooperationen*. Wiesbaden.

Xia M, Zhao K, Shaw MJ (2003) Open E-Business Standard Development and Adoption: An Integrated Perspective. Paper read at *Workshop on Standard Making: A Critical Research Frontier for Information Systems*, December 12-14, at Seattle, WA.

Yendluri P (2000) RosettaNet Implementation Framework (RNIF) 2.0. White Paper, WebMethods.

Yin RK (1984) *Case Study Research: Design and Methods*. Beverly Hills, CA: Sage.

——— (2003) *Case Study Research: Design and Methods*. Beverly Hills, CA: Sage.

Young D, Carr HH, Rainer RK, Jr. (1999) Strategic Implications of Electronic Linkages. *Information Systems Management* 16 (1):32-40.

Zerdick A, Picot A, Schrape K, Artopé A, Goldhammer K, Lange UT, Vierkant E, Lopez-Escobar E, Silverstone R (2000) *E-Conomics – Strategies for the Digital Marketplace*. Berlin: Springer.

Zerdick A, Picot A, Schrape K, Burgelman J-C, Silverstone R, Feldmann V, Wernick C, Wolff C, eds (2004) *E-Merging Media – Communication and the Media Economy of the Future*. Berlin: Springer.

Zollo M, Reuer JJ, Singh H (2002) Interorganizational Routines and Performance in Strategic Alliances. *Organization Science* 13 (6):701-713.

Index